From Cheechakos to Sourdoughs

Two Ivy Leaguers' Quest for Yukon Gold

Steve Lundin

With John Willard Lundin, III

FROM CHEECHAKOS TO SOURDOUGHS © 2024 by Steve Lundin. All rights reserved. No part of this book may be transmitted in any manner or by any means without the prior written permission from the publisher, except in the case of brief quotations embodied in critical articles and.

ISBN-13: 978-1-944234-61-4
First Edition 2025
0 9 8 7 6 5 4 3 2 41

Last Word Press
Olympia, Washington 98501
www.lastwordpress.com

Front cover: Ellis Aldrich (left), their trusty buckskin horse they named "Buck," and Mark Odell (right). Off prospecting on the trail from Fort Selkirk to their cabin and mining site at the headwaters of Wolverine Creek. July 1898. Odell Collection.

Contents

List of Illustrations   *vi*

Acknowledgements   *ix*

Introduction   1
  Odell's Gold Rush Records; Odell's Goldrush Experiences "Commonplace;" Major Events

Chapter 1 – Background   19
  Early Years; Cornell University Undergraduate Years; Attending Cornell Law School and the Decision to Leave for the Yukon

Chapter 2 – The Preliminaries   30
  Initial Activities; Different Routes into the Yukon; Taking the Train to Seattle; Purchasing Outfits and Supplies; Hoglen/Wood Party

Chapter 3 – Sailing to Alaska   46
  Major Fiasco; S.S. Al-Ki Departure; Sailing up the Inside Passage; Arrival at Skagway

Chapter 4 – From Skagway to the Summit of Chilkoot Pass   62
  Skagway; Dyea; Chilkoot Trail; Golden Stairs to the Summit; Coming Back

Down the Golden Stairs; North-West Mounted Police; Storms

Chapter 5 -- *Sledding Goods to Lindeman and Bennett*   **96**
    The Two Lakes; Hauling Goods to Lake Lindeman; Move to Lake Bennett; Breakup of Thompson Party

Chapter 6 -- *Constructing Their Boat From Scratch*   **113**
    Whipsawing Logs; Breakup of Ice and Immediate Surge of Boats; Constructing Their Boat

Chapter 7 -- *Voyage from Lake Bennett to Fort Selkirk*   **125**
    Sailing from Lake Bennett to Lake Tagish; Registering Their Boat; Joining with Walt Hoglen & Tom Wood; Miles Canyon; Lake Laberge; Initial Mining Activity; Pushing Ahead to Fort Selkirk

Chapter 8 – *Initial Efforts to Prospect at Wolverine Creek*   **153**
    Despair; Getting to Wolverine Creek Headwaters; Gold and Drift Mining Techniques; Initial Mining Efforts

Chapter 9 – *Mining at Wolverine Creek Headwaters*   **166**
    Building a Cabin at Wolverine Creek Headwaters; Return to Mining Efforts; Frequent Snowshoeing to Fort Selkirk;

Odell's Descriptions of First Nation Peoples; Cabin Life at Wolverine Creek; Decision to Get Aldrich Out of the Yukon

Chapter 10 -- Grueling Trek Out of the Yukon Over the Winter River Trail   *189*
Preparing for the Trek to the Outside; 400 Mile Trek to Outside Over the Winter River Trail; Skagway; Did Odell and Aldrich Return with Gold?

Afterwards   *219*
Ellis Aldrich; Walt Hoglen; Harry Granger; Tom Wood; Mark Odell

Appendices   *239*
Appendix A – Fort Selkirk; Appendix B – Postal Service (First Letters from Odell, Cost and Postal Locations, Later Letters, Tale of a Missing Letter, North-West Mounted Police); Appendix C – Dalton Trail; Appendix D – White Pass and Yukon Route; Appendix E – Winter River Trail (Use and Development of the Winter River Trail, Table and Details about the Winter River Trail)

Bibliography   *286*

Endnotes   *297*

Index   *317*

List of Illustrations

Item	Page
Photo, Odell & Aldrich off prospecting	Cover
Photo, Odell Diary	4
Photo, Hoglen list of photos	9
Photo, Odell's Cornell Pennant	14
Table, Major Events	17
Photo, Odell & brother on farm	20
Photo, Odell farm	20
Photo, 1897 Cornell crew	24
Photos, Odell & Aldrich Cornell graduation	25
Photo, Seattle Outfitters	37
Photo, Seattle Outfitters	37
Photo, Seattle PI news article	42
Table, Typical gear list	43
Photo, Dogs loading on ship	45
Photo, S.S. Al-Ki advertisement	50
Photo, S.S. Al-Ki	51
Photo, Bella Bella	54
Photo, Wrangell Meat Market & Chop House	57
Photo, Wrangell YMCA	57
Photo, Wrangell totem pole	58
Photo, Skagway harbor	63
Photo, Skagway harbor	64
Photo, Skagway laying RR tracks	64
Photo, Skagway River	65
Photo, Dyea from distance	67
Photo, Dyea Main Street	67
Photo, Dyea Trail Street	68
Photo, Dyea warehouse	68
Photo, Dyea street cars	70
Photo, Dyea dog train Taiya River	71
Photo, Dyea dog train	71
Photo, Dyea burro train loading	72
Photo, Hoglen/Wood camp at Sheep Camp	76
Photo, Below Scales	79
Photo, Below Scales	81
Photo, Chilkoot Pass from Scales	82
Photo, Chilkoot Pass, aerial tramway bucket	82
Photo, Chilkoot Pass in 1987	83

Photo, Chilkoot Pass climb up	83
Photo, Debris at Scales	83
Photo, Golden Stairs	88
Photo, Looking down from false summit 1987	89
Photo, Looking towards summit of Chilkoot Pass 1987	90
Photo, Klondikers at the Scales	91
Photo, Summit Chilkoot Pass	93
Photo, Klondikers waiting in line for customs	93
Photo, Hoglen & Wood camp at summit	95
Photo, Hoglen & Wood cache & dinner	95
Photo, Awaiting turn to coast down from summit	96
Photo, Wood & Hoglen caravan to haul goods	97
Photo, First view of Lindeman	98
Photo, Bluff across Lake Lindeman	98
Photo, View looking up Lindeman	99
Photo, Boat at Barto & Walters camp	99
Photo, Boat at Morgan & Williams camp	99
Photo, Hoglen/Wood boat clearing Lake	100
Photo, Rapids between the two lakes	101
Photo, Looking northward down Lake Bennett	102
Photo, View at Lake Bennett	102
Photo, View of Bennett City	108
Photo, Salvation Army meeting	109
Photo, Whipsawing logs	115
Photo, Bennett City in 1987	119
Photo, Enticing view down Lake Bennett 1987	119
Photo, View of Hoglen/Wood boatyard	120
Photo, View from Hoglen/Wood camp	121
Photo, View from Hoglen/Wood camp	121
Photo, Walt Hoglen at Lake Lindeman	122
Photo, Boats built on Lake Bennett	123
Photo, Boat building at Bennett	123
Photo, Thomas J. Wood	129
Copy, NWMP boat registration records Tagish Post	130
Photo, Walter J. Hoglen	133
Photo, Tagish NWMP station	133
Photo, One night's troll, Lake Tagish	135
Photo, Waiting for Pilot to shoot Miles Canyon	136
Photo, View of head of Miles Canyon	136
Photo, Miles Canyon	137
Photo, Macaulay's Tramway	138
Photo, Boat going through Miles Canyon	141

Photo, Boat going through Squaw Rapids	141
Photo, Shooting Whitehorse Rapids	142
Photo, End White Horse Rapids	143
Photo, Indian village, Lake Laberge	145
Photo, Sluice work, Cassiar Bar	146
Photo, Notes posted at Little Salmon River Post	147
Photo, Later photo of Harry Granger	148
Photo, Boat navigating Rink Rapids	149
Photo, Arrival at Fort Selkirk	151
Photo, Fort Selkirk in distance	153
Sketch, Mining site on Wolverine Creek	159
Sketch, Placer mining technique	161
Photo, Odell & Aldrich off prospecting	167
Photo, Rear of cabin on Wolverine Creek	171
Photo, Work area behind Wolverine Creek cabin	172
Photo, Trail from Ft. Selkirk to cabin	172
Photo, Another photo of trail	173
Photo, Wolverine Creek as it bends	173
Images, Odell's wallet and shopping list	174
Photo, Odell's last pair of moccasins	176
Photo, Placer mining shaft and windlass	177
Photo, Hotel Selkirk	179
Photo, "Lonely supper" at Wolverine Creek cabin	190
Photo, '97 comes back	191
Photo, Sled ready to leave	191
Photo, Walt Hoglen near Wolverine Creek cabin	192
Photo, Harry Granger near cabin	193
Image, Mark Odell's pass to leave Yukon	194
Image, Records leaving Yukon, Mar. 2, 1899	207
Photo, Hotel Klondike, Bennett City	208
Image, Ad for Dewey Hotel	210
Image, Headline article on gold	212
Photo, Ellis Aldrich in later life	223
Photo, Odell and Hoglen at work in Seattle	224
Photos, Odell in later life	236
Photo, Odell circa. 1958	237
Photo, Fort Selkirk	241
Photo, Harper's Post, Fort Selkirk	242
Photo, Canadian Army Field Force	242
Photo, WP&YR stationary masthead	257
Table, Stops on Winter River Trail	274

Acknowledgments

Several people provided invaluable help with this book.

Karl Gurcke, a retired historian from the Klondike Gold Rush National Historical Park, U.S. National Park Service, in Skagway, Alaska, provided information about the gold rush, Skagway, Dyea, and Chilkoot Pass. Karl also reviewed the entire book and provided many insightful comments and direction.

Frank Norris, also a retired historian from the Klondike Gold Rush National Historical Park, U.S. National Park Service, in Skagway, Alaska, reviewed the draft and provided insightful comments and direction.

Gord Allison, creator of the Yukon History Trails blog, has been great help. He provided information about Fort Selkirk and nearby historical sites, including bunkhouses or stopovers along the Winter River Trail. Gord also provided an invaluable critique of the text and Odell/Aldrich adventure, especially the location on the headwaters of Wolverine Creek (south of Fort Selkirk) where Odell and Aldrich prospected, mined, and built their cabin. His blog is found at https://yukonhistorytrails.com.

Linda Bondurant, wife of Steve Lundin, spent hours reviewing the draft and making many helpful comments.

Introduction

Nearly fifty years had passed since the once inseparable Ivy League college chums and Yukon prospecting partners had seen each other. Letters had been exchanged, but there had been no in-person contact. All was to change during the sunny days of June 1947 in Ithaca, New York, at the Fifty-Year reunion of the Cornell University class of 1897. Mark Odell lived in Seattle and flew back east to the event. Ellis Leeds Aldrich lived in Maine and traveled by train to the event.

The men had last seen each other in April of 1899, when Odell bade Aldrich farewell on a train steaming eastward out of Seattle after the men had returned from the Yukon gold rush. At the reunion, the men reminisced about college and the years afterward. But mostly, they revisited their trying ordeal seeking their fortunes in the wilds of the Yukon during the fabled Klondike, or Yukon, gold rush in the late 1890s. They discussed the recent passing of Walt Hoglen, one of their partners in the Yukon, who had died in the Yukon Territory a month before the Cornell Class of 1897 reunion. Odell was featured at a dinner where he gave an oration about the famous 1897 varsity crew of which he was a member.[1]

This book describes the two Ivy Leaguer adventurers who sought their fortunes in the Yukon. The lure of the Yukon, and especially the Klondike, was a dominant driving force throughout the United States in the late 1890s. It is said that the gold rush brought the United States out of a deep economic depression known as the Panic of 1893. American mythology and culture still venerate the Klondike gold rush and its resulting flurry of economic activity.

Odell and Aldrich were part of the many thousands of eager argonauts traveling by train to Puget Sound port cities and then sailing to the north in quest for riches in the Yukon gold fields. Seattle was a primary port of embarkation for the hordes seeking their fortunes in the north, in part due to its central location on the eastern shores of Puget Sound, recent development, and an aggressive nationwide scheme of promotional activities. Odell and Aldrich witnessed a white-hot fever pitch of economic activity when they arrived in Seattle.

They would soon enter the Yukon in late spring of 1898 as eager Cheechakos.* Most prospectors who made it into the Yukon sought their fortunes outside of the newly founded Dawson City on the Yukon River and its nearby tributary, the Klondike River.

---

* Chinook jargon for a newcomer who has not spent a winter in the Yukon. The Chinook jargon was a trade language used in the Pacific Northwest, Alaska, and western Canada, comprised of words from local indigenous languages and later a few English and French words.

Some prospected and mined other Yukon rivers and creeks, including the Stewart River and White River, major Yukon River tributaries south of Dawson City. Odell and Aldrich prospected and mined over the 1898/99 winter outside of Fort Selkirk on the little-known Wolverine Creek, south of these other sites.* In February of 1899, Odell and Aldrich trekked to the "Outside" over the little-discussed Winter River Trail† -- the frozen Yukon River -- as exhausted and sore Sourdoughs,‡ with many memories and at least some gold. The extent of the gold is shrouded in mystery.

Odell's Gold Rush Records

Mark Odell, the authors' maternal grandfather, left many records of his Yukon experience.§ Ellis Aldrich or Ellie, Odell's best college chum, left almost no records of his Yukon experience.

---

* A discussion of Fort Selkirk is found in Appendix A.

† A discussion of the Winter River Trail is found in Chapter 10, and Appendix E.

‡ A Sourdough was an old-time Alaskan or Yukon prospector, or a prospector who had spent at least one winter in the Yukon and experienced the rigors of that effort. The term was derived from sourdough bread that was a mainstay of prospectors' diets in the Yukon.

§ Odell's records are part of the Odell Collection in the possession of the authors.

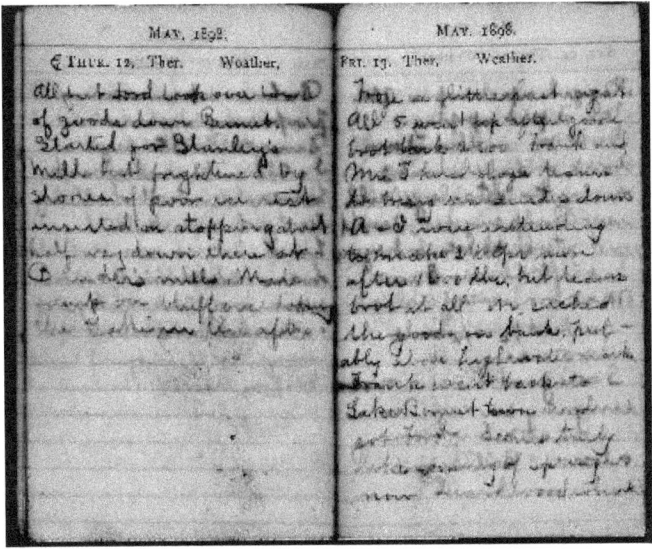

Page from Odell's 1898 diary. Odell Collection.

Odell wrote daily entries in a small pocket diary book that he brought to the Yukon.* The writing is cryptic, given the small size of the diary. A single page for each separate daily entry measures three and 5/8s inches by two inches. Odell wrote in pencil, mostly with a purple hue, but sometimes in a dark grey hue. The writing is still quite legible. Some of the entries include spelling errors and shortcuts in spelling and punctuation.

---

* To avoid the use of many footnotes citing Odell's Yukon diary, this book describes the events mentioned in his Yukon diary but does not cite the date of the diary entry from which the information was obtained.

An example of an abbreviated diary entry is from November 11, 1898, when Odell wrote

> D & B good thaw quite clayey with rock crushed fined. Washed pan pair nut Cold again and finer snow during day. Clear and colder at night 40 degrees at noon 51 last night.

This entry, in part, describes one day of the mining efforts of Mark Odell and his partners. More completely, the entry would be

> Dug and burned logs at the bottom of our mine shaft. Good thaw in the soil at the bottom of the mine shaft. Quite clayey with crushed rock found. Washed a pan of gravel in their cabin and found a pair of nuggets. Cold again and finer snow during the day. Clear and colder at night. 40 degrees below zero at noon. 51 below zero last night.

Odell also wrote letters to his father that were published in his hometown newspaper, the *Gazette & Farmers' Journal* in Baldwinsville, New York. Most of the letters were of medium length. Two were quite long, providing greater details about his adventures.

These letters and the other written material reveal Odell as an accomplished writer. His dry sense of self-deprecating humor is evident in the longer writings. Initially, his writing reflected an upbeat state of mind as the men neared the fabled Chilkoot Pass. Growing frustration and a sense of despair are evident in his later writings when the men faced adversities as they proceeded into the Yukon. As with most diaries and letters of that era, Odell wrote little of a personal nature and rarely expressed his feelings in a straightforward manner. Often, his feelings must be intuited from the brief text.

Odell's last published letter was mailed on July 2, 1898, after he and Aldrich had successfully passed through the dangerous Miles Canyon and White Horse Rapids on the Yukon River. The cost of mailing long letters out of the Yukon was exorbitant. Odell continued writing daily diary entries throughout the adventure.

Aldrich wrote a lengthy letter on October 6, 1898, to D. Maujer McLaughlin, a fellow graduate of Cornell and a Brooklyn resident, describing his and Odell's Yukon adventures up to that date. Major portions of this letter were printed in the December 25, 1898, edition of the *Brooklyn Daily Eagle*, and are quoted in this book.[2]

This letter also reflects Aldrich's accomplished writing style. Unfortunately, this is the only written record of the Yukon that Aldrich left. In a telephone conversation one of the authors had with Ellis Aldrich's daughter-in-law decades ago, she related how she and her deceased husband had often asked Ellis to write about his Yukon experiences, but he never did. However, as discussed below, the Cornell University archives lists a several page-long article about their Yukon experiences that Aldrich wrote for their 50th year reunion entitled "'97 Comes Back." Unfortunately, the essay has been misplaced.

Later in life, Odell wrote several letters to an old friend, Leslie Voorhees, the historian of Van Buren Township, Onondaga County, New York, from where Odell hailed, discussing both his family and adventures in the Yukon. These letters are part of the Voorhees records held by the Onondaga County Library in Syracuse, New York. Drafts of some of these letters, and other letters, describing Odell's life and Yukon adventure were part of Odell's personal records. Descriptions from these letters are included in this book.

On occasion, the Odell records mention both women and Native peoples that he and Aldrich encountered during their adventure.* At their initial encounters with women traveling to the Yukon, Odell and Aldrich shaved to look more presentable. Soon this

---

* The genesis of Odell's deep interest in Native peoples may have arisen from a small swale on his father's farm a few miles west of Baldwinsville, N.Y. Salt was found in the swale, along with arrowheads and other artifacts. Family stories hold that this site was a major source of salt for Native peoples in upstate New York. Presumably the young Odell played at this site as a youth and found treasures. A newspaper article in the local area newspaper reported that the young Odell had found "three tommy-hawks and two skinning stones" at this swale located "near dark rolling waters of the Seneca [River]." ("Correspondence," *Gazette and Farmers' Journal*, Baldwinsville, N.Y., May 27, 1886, 165.)

gentlemanly behavior was abandoned. Although the descriptions of Native peoples Odell encountered were quite brief, they did not include stereotypically racist views found in many writings by others from those times.[3]

An old shoebox in a bookcase on the second story of Odell's Seattle home held photos from 12 rolls of film. Each roll included 12 exposures of a trip into the Yukon seeking gold.* The photographs were taken by Walt Hoglen, who joined Odell and Aldrich on their quest for gold as they sailed down the Yukon River.

Descriptions of the photos are found in three places. First, very brief descriptions of some of the photographs were etched onto their borders by Walt Hoglen. Second, the first six of the twelve rolls of film had a more detailed handwritten list of the exposures for each frame attached to the applicable set of twelve exposures written by Walter Hoglen on old envelopes. Third, descriptions of the photos in the remaining rolls are found in Walt Hoglen's Yukon diary that is included in Odell's Records. The latter descriptions have more limited utility. Many of the descriptions do not reflect the actual exposures in the collection. Others are descriptive of photos in the

---

* These photos probably were taken using a newly introduced Eastman Kodak Folding Pocket KODAK camera, first sold in 1897. The camera is known as the first modern "roll-film" camera using film with twelve images per roll and 2 1/4-inch by 3 1/4-inch negatives.

collection. None of these photographs from the Odell collection have been published. Many are included in this book.

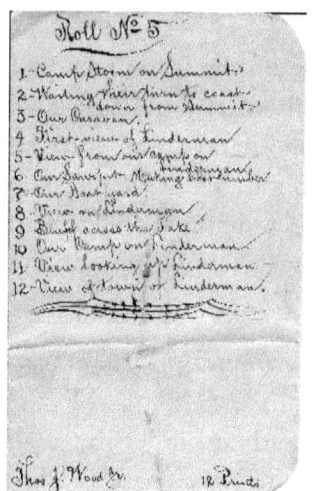 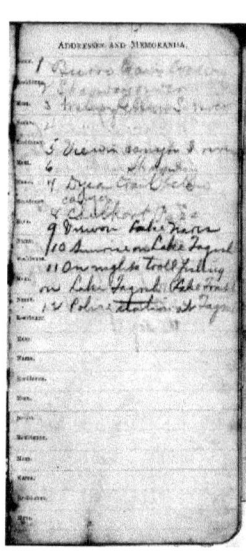

At left, example of Hoglen listing photos on the back of an envelope. At right, example of Hoglen listing photos in his hardly used diary.

Photos of sites from one roll of film overlap with photos of sites that appeared in earlier rolls of film. Perhaps this film roll came from someone else's collection. More probably, Hoglen returned to Skagway after he and his then partners had begun constructing their boat on Lake Lindeman and Hoglen took pictures of that return trip. Photos in that roll of film include many of the sites found in several earlier rolls of film.

In his later years, Odell would talk about his Yukon adventures, but only if asked. His reserve may be like the hesitancy of later generations reticence discussing their experiences in World War II, although the Yukon experiences were far less traumatic than experiences of fighting a war.

When young boys, the authors had visions of their grandfather's adventures in the Yukon. These visions were reinforced by looking at his photos and last pair of moccasins he used in the Yukon, listening to his responses to our questions about his experiences, and being captivated by radio broadcasts of the "Challenge of the Yukon" (later "Sergeant Preston of the Yukon"). We also read comic books and viewed television programs about Sergeant Preston of the Yukon. Along with thousands of other youths, the authors proudly held "title" to several square inches of the Yukon obtained from the "Klondike Big Inch Land Promotion" appearing on the back of Quaker Oats breakfast cereal boxes. The authors' experiences were quite common in Seattle, as thousands of descendants of Klondike and Yukon gold rushers lived and still live in Seattle.

Odell Goldrush Experiences "Common place"

Odell described his Yukon experiences as being "common place." Many others had similar experiences, including old-timers who had settled in Seattle after the gold rush. In 1960, Odell summarized his Yukon gold rush experiences in terse prose.

March, 1898, left with my college chum Ellis L. Aldrich for the Klondike via Chilkoot Pass, Miles Canyon, Windy Arm, White Horse Rapids, Five Fingers Rapids, Squaw Rapids, and the like, building our boat with raw lumber built from green trees on Lake Bennett near the source of the Yukon River, loading it with a year's supplies bought in Seattle, brought over the [Chilkoot] pass in many, many pack loads and then sled loads to our camp on Lake Bennett. All we would need to eat, wear, and use for a year, a requirement of the Canadian Police stationed at the Alaska-Canada border line. In our case about a ton and a half. A year of wonderful adventure and experiences. But remember – there were thousands upon many thousands of people who did this in 1897 and 1898. *In Seattle above tale is common place.*[4] [Emphasis added.]

This is a succinct and typical description, listing many of the major geographic areas passed *en route* into the Yukon gold fields. Missing from his description is the grueling nature of the effort to enter the Yukon, frequent illness, homesickness, the lack of news from home, the tedious life in a cabin and mining during the long dark Yukon winter, physical and emotional exhaustion, and Odell's and Aldrich's 400-mile trek to the Outside, returning from the Yukon over the Winter River Trail.

Although Odell's and Aldrich's route into the Yukon was shared by many, readers will find Odell's descriptions uncommon and witty. Their exhaustion, sickness, anguish, difficulties and bouts of despair and indecision are noted as the men faced many crossroads in their adventure in the north. Several factors led to Odell and Aldrich being one month behind most stampeders racing down the Yukon River* to the fabled goldfields. As a result, they prospected and mined outside of Fort Selkirk, many miles south of the fabled Klondike River.

Along with two new partners (Walt Hoglen and Harry Granger), Odell and Aldrich constructed a cabin and prospected over the winter of 1898-99 near the headwaters of Wolverine Creek, a creek entering the Yukon River south of Fort Selkirk. Almost nothing has been written about gold mining near Fort Selkirk. Their one month-long trek out of the Yukon over the Winter River Trail in the late winter of 1899

---

* The Yukon River ran generally in a northerly direction through British Columbia and the Yukon Territory, beginning with a series of lakes that were connected by short channels, and then what was called the Lewes or Upper Yukon River, that became the Yukon River at the confluence of the Pelly and Lewes Rivers near Fort Selkirk. The waterway continued in a general northward direction past Dawson City and then turned to a westerly direction running across Alaska and emptying into the Bering Sea. In the early 1950s, the name of the Lewes River was dropped and became the "Upper" Yukon River. As used in this book, the term "Yukon River" includes the lower and upper Yukon Rivers.

was uncommon. Although Odell failed to mention the name of this trail in his records, he provided many details about the trail that rarely have been published. These descriptions and details are unique and are not found in most other books about the Klondike or Yukon gold rush.

Odell was a strong and eager 29-year-old when he reached the Yukon. His strength was honed from working on his father's upstate New York farm and rowing on Cornell University's famous varsity crew. He was slightly under six feet tall and weighed 184 pounds. Ellis Aldrich a short and slight of stature 22-year-old, when he reached the Yukon. He played baseball at Cornell for three years. The extreme and debilitating conditions they would soon face would tax their strength and health.

Odell and Aldrich considered themselves to be part of an Ivy League-educated elite, and proper, Victorian gentlemen. They took pride in their higher educations. Although likely most stampeders were not college graduates, Odell and Aldrich met and socialized with many other highly educated men seeking their fortunes in the Yukon. Odell, as a self-described "man of letters," noted in his diary fellow collegians they met, including their schools and graduation years.

Phil Rice, a fraternity brother, gave Odell a red and white Cornell pennant when he left Ithaca, New York, *en route* to the Yukon. Odell and Aldrich proudly displayed the pennant as they floated down the Yukon River, announcing their self-felt elitism and educated status. They met several Cornell classmates in the Yukon and were told about Cornell's victory in the 1898 Intercollegiate Rowing Association's national championship.

Odell's slightly moth-eaten Cornell pennant he took to the Yukon.

Odell's writings reflect a degree of disdain and contempt for the British and Canadians, feelings that were common among the Americans who arrived in the Yukon seeking gold. They perceived Canadian authorities as interfering with their freedom to seek gold. Odell was critical of the postal systems in British Columbia and the Yukon.* Many of the American stampeders seemed to consider the Yukon Territory, and Canada for that matter, as mere vassals of the United States. Evidence of Odell's earlier disdain for Canada is found in an essay entitled "The Annexation

---

* A discussion of the postal service is found in Appendix B.

of Canada" that he wrote and presented as an oration at his graduation from the Baldwinsville Free Academy in 1889.*

Odell seemed to be oblivious of the system of government in the Yukon. A careful reader will note that the shopping list reproduced in Chapter 9, for purchases to be made at Fort Selkirk on August 20, 1898, identifies Fort Selkirk as part of the North West Territories ("N.W.T.") rather than Yukon Territory ("Y.T."). This was an error.

In 1870, Canada acquired the area that eventually became Yukon Territory from the Hudson's Bay Company and included this area as part of its North West Territories. The first recognition of the "Yukon" as a distinct political entity occurred on October 2, 1895, when Canada divided the North

---

* Since the independence of what became the United States from Britain after the Revolutionary War, strong sentiment existed for the new nation to annex or join with Canada. Article XI of the Articles of Confederation provided "Canada acceding to this confederation, and adjoining in the measures of the United States, shall be admitted into, and entitled to all the advantages of this Union; but no other colony shall be admitted into the same, unless such admission be agreed to by nine States." In 1810, the young Henry Clay spoke on the Senate floor in favor of seizing Canada – "the last of the immense North American possessions" of Britain and "acquire the entire fur trade connected with that country." (Beschloss, Michael. *Presidents of War.* New York, Crown Publishing Groups, a division of Penguin Random House, 2018, 45.) Later, Clay was elected to the United States House of Representatives and became Speaker of the House.

West Territories into four provincial districts (Ungava, Franklin, Mackenzie, and Yukon) for "the convenience of settlers ... and for postal purposes."[5] Canada created a Yukon Judicial District in response to the needs of the Klondike gold rush on August 16, 1897. However, no form of local government existed in the Yukon at that time, other than Canadian and Britain laws being enforced from time to time. After the arrival of a few officers and men, the North-West Mounted Police (NWMP) became the *de facto* government in the Yukon, controlling the postal service, law enforcement and criminal prosecutions. Their first presence in the Yukon began in the summer of 1895, when the NWMP erected a post at Fort Cudahy on Fortymile Creek near the yet to be founded Dawson City.[6] Before the arrival of the NWMPs, a minimal form of government was provided for prospectors on an *ad hoc* basis by informal "miners' committees" composed of the miners in the local vicinity who would meet and vote on matters.[7]

On June 13, 1898, Canada formally created the Yukon Territory out of the western portion of the North West Territories and appointed members of the new Yukon Territorial government.* At that

---

* The Colony of British Columbia was created by Great Britain in 1858 under somewhat similar circumstances during the Fraser River gold rush. Prior to the creation of the new colony, British government in what became British Columbia was exercised by employees of the Hudson's Bay Company on

time, Odell and Aldrich were frantically constructing their boat on the shores of Lake Bennett, British Columbia. They set sail from Lake Bennett on June 23, 1898, soon passing out of British Columbia and into the newly created Yukon Territory.

The two Ivy Leaguers may not have known of the existence of the Yukon Territorial government. Ironically, Fort Selkirk,* out of which Odell and Aldrich would soon prospect and live, was under strong consideration for the first capital of the newly created Yukon Territory. However, the far more appropriate Dawson City received that honor.

Major Events

Major events on Odell's and Aldrich's one-year effort seeking gold in the Yukon included the following

> March 2, 1898 – A friend proposed going to Klondike gold rush.
>
> March 16 to 21, 1898 – Odell and Aldrich left Ithaca, N.Y., by train to Seattle.

Vancouver Island. Britain created the new Colony of British Columbia to govern Vancouver Island and the mainland during the gold rush. Americans rushed into British Columbia searching for gold as they would almost forty years later in the Yukon. (Fricken, Robert E. *Unsettled Boundaries, Fraser Gold and the British-American Northwest.* Pullman, WA, Washington State University Press, 2003, 97-100.)

* Fort Selkirk is discussed in Appendix A.

March 22 to 25, 1898 – Joined the Thompson party and purchased outfits in Seattle.

March 26 - April 3, 1898 – Sailed from Seattle to Skagway, Alaska, via Inside Passage.

April 4 to 14, 1898 – Moved supplies from Dyea to Chilkoot Pass.

April 15 to May 14, 1898 – Moved supplies from Chilkoot summit to Lake Bennett.

May 15 to 19, 1898 – Breakup of partnership with Thompson party.

May 20 to June 22, 1898 – Odell and Aldrich constructed their boat

June 23 to July 26, 1898 – Sailed & rowed down Yukon River to Ft. Selkirk, meeting Tom Wood and Walt Hoglen.

July 27 to August 19, 1898 – Initial prospecting at Wolverine Creek.

August 20, 1898, to February 14, 1899 – Built cabin & mined at Wolverine Creek with Walt Hoglen and Harry Granger.

February 15 to March 8, 1899 – Odell and Aldrich trekked out of Yukon over the Winter River Trail to Skagway.

Mid-March 1899 – Returned to Seattle, Aldrich leaves for NY.

March - to at least May 1899 – Odell works in Seattle for White Pass & Yukon Route (WP&YR) railway.

Chapter 1
Background

Mark Odell grew up in a rural area on his parent's farm in upstate New York. Ellis Aldrich grew up in urbanized Brooklyn. Although Odell was five years older than Aldrich, and they were raised in different environments, the two men became fast friends after meeting during their freshman years at Cornell University in 1893.

Early Years

Mark Odell was born on January 13, 1869. He grew up on his family's 100-acre farm partially abutting the south side of the Seneca River, a few miles west of Baldwinsville, New York. Baldwinsville is a suburb of Syracuse. The Odell family raised a wide variety of crops, along with tobacco and dairy products that served as cash commodities. In his late 80s, Odell retained his crisp writing style when he described the family farm as located

> in New York State, Onondaga County, Van Buren Township, School District No. 1 –

named Pleasant Valley, alias Dingle Hole – last farm at the dead end of Gunbarrel Road, so named in the muzzle loading gun days because one had to get out at the same end one went in.[8]

Mark Odell, right, brother Burr Odell, left, Odell farm. Odell Collection

Odell farmhouse, outside of Baldwinsville, NY. Odell Collection

The third of four children of Benjamin Bradford Odell and Mary Augusta Betts Odell, Mark's youth reflected the family's strong focus on education. His mother taught in local public schools before her marriage. It is thought that she attended, and may have graduated from, the nearby Baldwinsville Free Academy, described both as a teaching preparatory school and a high school. All four of the Odell children graduated from the local public school and the Baldwinsville Free Academy.

Mark completed his studies at the local Pleasant Valley public school in 1884, when he was fifteen years old. The schools had two terms in those days – winter and summer.[9] Younger pupils attended both terms. Older pupils, especially boys, only attended the winter term and worked on their parents' farms during summer term. He graduated from the Baldwinsville Free Academy in 1888. Curricula included Greek, Latin, and astronomy, as well as other subjects leading Odell to a short career as a teacher and then a principal at the local public schools.

Odell was an ardent opponent of alcohol. His uncle, Harvey Odell, lost his farm due to alcoholism in the early 1890s. This left an indelible mark on his young nephew. Odell once ran unsuccessfully for the local Pleasant Valley School District board of directors, on the Prohibitionist Party ticket. More than sixty years later, he described this failed attempt stating that he "ran, say crept if you want to," for the school board, receiving only 26 votes.[10]

Ellis Leeds Aldrich was born in Upper Montclair, Montclair Township, Essex, New Jersey, on June 12, 1874. He was the son of Charles H. and Josephine M. Aldrich. The family lived in the Bedford Stuyvesant neighborhood of Brooklyn, where his father worked as a carpenter. Ellis graduated from the Brooklyn Boys High School in 1893 as the class valedictorian at age eighteen. He was a noted high school baseball star.

Cornell University Undergraduate Years

In 1893, the 24-year-old Odell won a competitive examination for a New York State scholarship to attend Cornell University.* Aldrich won the same competitive state examination, also receiving a state

---

* Cornell University is unusual as it is both a privately endowed university and public land-grant university. The New York State Legislature enacted legislation in 1865 establishing Cornell University and designating Cornell as the State's land-grant college under the federal Morrill Act of 1862, 7 U.S.C. § 301 et seq., which provided federal funding for the teaching of agriculture and technical education in general science, military science, and engineering. Unlike most other Ivy League schools, Cornell was founded as a non-sectarian school. New York State's public funding of Cornell expanded in 1887 with the creation of state-funded scholarships for students regardless of their major studies. A scholarship was provided to one student from each of the then 128 state Assembly districts, awarded using a competitive examination. Testing was conducted in June of each year. (New York State Laws, Chapter 291, Laws of 1887.)

scholarship to study at Cornell. The scholarships paid tuition at Cornell for four years.

The two men met during their early days at Cornell. They formed an immediate and strong friendship focusing on their studies, oratory, debate, and class politics which they dominated. Aldrich was elected to the freshman class presidency.

Odell kept meticulous financial records while at Cornell, noting in a ledger that that included purchasing items such as shirt collars, writing paper, postage, notebooks, shirts, coats, trousers, and shoes. He paid as little as one dollar for monthly lodgings and borrowed money from his father and two older sisters to help cover his living expenses.

Odell noted that he entered Cornell University with $75 cash. He described his next four years of undergraduate study, and his efforts to provide for his living expenses at Cornell.

> Waited on table. Solicited roomers for rooming house. With a fellow classman operated a boarding table [providing food for other students]. Local correspondent for Buffalo, Syracuse, and New York papers. Studied some. Graduated Bachelor of Letters, June 1897.[11]

More than sixty years later, Odell described this Bachelor of Letters major as what then would be called Liberal Arts.[12] A person graduating with a Bachelor of Letters degree required only one year to complete Law School at Cornell. The last two years of undergraduate studies included all the classwork from the first year of a two-year course of studies in law, plus regular undergraduate courses. Aldrich also graduated in 1897 with the same undergraduate major.

Odell was a member of Cornell's still-famous 1897 crew that established Cornell's rowing reputation. To the surprise of almost everyone, Cornell's Big Red crew won the Intercollegiate Rowing Association (IRA) race in 1897 at Poughkeepsie, New York, defeating Harvard and Yale to become the "champions of America."[13]

1897 Cornell Varsity Crew. Mark Odell back row, second from right. Odell Collection.

Odell's home town of Baldwinsville celebrated the victory and its local hero with a parade when he returned. More than sixty years later, he described his rowing experiences.

> Contrary to the enthusiastic imaginings of many of my home Baldwinsville friends,

> I was not the only one in the crew. There were seven other oarsmen and a coxswain in the crew which won the races.[14]

Cornell crew coach Charles Courtney, known as both "Pop" and the "Old Man," was a strict coach believing in moral character and bodily fitness, along with a belief in absolute abstinence from any form of alcohol. "Let a man take a glass of whiskey or a glass of beer and the next day Mr. Courtney knows about it, and he will tell him his presence is no longer desired at the boat house."[15]

These traits were attractive to Odell, who was described in the 1897 Cornell annual as the biggest reformer in their midst. He was a very focused individual with an iron will power.

Odell presented an oration in his sophomore year at Cornell entitled "An Argument for Inter-collegiate Athletics," in which he extolled the virtues of scholarship, moral rectitude, and strong physical training that is part of the life of a university athlete.[16]

Mark Odell, left, Ellis Aldrich, right, Cornell graduation photos, 1897. Odell Collection.

Aldrich played baseball at Cornell during his first three years, but for some reason was not on the team during his senior year.

Both Odell and Aldrich were very attuned to self-promotion as part of their political efforts. News articles about the two, and their various campus activities, appeared regularly in the *Cornell Sun*, the daily student newspaper, as well as other newspapers in New York state.

As part of an educated elite, Odell and Aldrich kept abreast of news and current events. They possibly were aware of Klondike gold strikes in 1896, but surely were aware of the widespread publicity beginning in July 1897 when the "Klondike Fever" began in earnest. Civic boosters in Seattle and Tacoma took every opportunity to promote gold discoveries in Alaska and the Yukon, competing to be the gateway to the north.[17]

On April 5, 1896, The New York Times reprinted a newspaper article from Tacoma, Washington, describing how an unprecedented number of men had rushed to Alaska and the Yukon in search of gold.[18] The four steamers serving southeast Alaska were not adequate to transport all those wishing to prospect, especially in the Yukon Basin where most were headed. Nine more schooners were expected to join the run later in the year. Ambitious prospectors flocked to the north, filling all available berths and deck space on ships leaving Seattle, Tacoma, and Port Townsend for Alaska.[19]

In August of 1896, Keish (Skookum Jim Mason), Ka Goox (Dawson Charlie or Tagish Charlie), and Lying George (George Washington Carmack) discovered gold on a tributary of the Thron-dieck or Klondike River near what is now Dawson City. Hundreds of prospectors from the nearby Yukon and Alaska flocked to the goldfields. The discovery led to the famous Klondike gold rush.

Most books about the Klondike gold rush claim that, due to the inaccessibility of the Klondike, news of the gold strike in the continental United States was delayed until July of 1897, when two steamships returned with Klondike gold to the continental United States.[20] On July 14, 1897, the Steamship *Excelsior* docked near Market Street in San Francisco with returning Klondike prospectors, gold and tales of wealth from the Klondike.[21] Three days later, on July 17, 1897, the Steamship *Portland* docked at Schwabacher's wharf in Seattle with sixty-eight returning Klondike prospectors, more than two tons of gold nuggets and gold dust, and tales of abundant riches in the Klondike.[22]

News of the gold strike began trickling out of the Yukon in the fall of 1896, months before the arrival of these two steamers. However, the later news reports of the *Excelsior* and *Portland* returning with Klondike gold in July of 1897, had the effect of pouring gasoline onto glowing coals, igniting an even greater intensity of interest than the earlier reports. Gold fever swept across the United States, like a prairie wild fire generating a flurry of economic activity ending the severe economic depression known as the Panic of 1893. Banner headlines accompanied these July 1897 news articles announcing the Klondike gold strike, unlike the much smaller and less prominent headlines that had accompanied earlier news articles about the Klondike gold strike.

Attending Cornell Law School and the Decision to Leave for the Yukon

After graduating with bachelor's degrees, Odell and Aldrich entered Cornell Law School in the fall term of 1897. They toiled at their studies while rooming at the McCallister boarding house near the Cornell campus. Odell was contemplating the start of another rowing season at Cornell.

Initially, the early news about a large gold strike on the Klondike River in what became the Yukon Territory, and the resulting mania sweeping the nation, were probably of little interest to Odell and Aldrich. However, as excitement over the gold rush intensified after the arrival of the *Excelsior* and *Portland* with Klondike gold, they discussed dropping their law studies and joining the frantic rush to the Yukon.

In March of 1898, more than six months after the docking of the *Portland* and *Excelsior*, Odell and Aldrich decided to drop out of law school and join the madness seeking their fortunes in the Yukon.

They had only one quarter term of their law studies remaining to complete before graduation. These decisions would change their lives and lead to a year of hard labor, mental anguish, many adventures, and some gold.

Pierre Berton described the impact of the Klondike on Yukon stampeders – in their later years they looked back on the adventures.

> ... for the rest of their days with insistent pangs of nostalgia. In all the written memoirs of the gold rush there is scarcely one note of regret, except for the general regret that it ended so soon. Though few of the writers found any gold, it turned out in retrospect to have been a golden period for them. And the times that were remembered with zest and affection were not the easy times in the dance halls, but the hardest times: the chilling days on the passes, the thrilling moments in the rapids.[23]
>
> They returned from the Klondike, as young men return from war, wise beyond their years. In the brief span of the gold rush they learned more about life, more about their fellows, and more about themselves than many mortals absorb in threescore years and ten.[24]

Chapter 2

The Preliminaries

Aldrich and Odell were very focused individuals and made detailed plans for their journey to the Yukon. Odell believed they could overcome any adversity with superior intelligence and planning. He had disdain for the many "reckless, crazy idiots" sailing down the Yukon River who endangered themselves at Miles Canyon and White Horse Rapids.[25] They were members of the educated elite and would not act rashly. Their hubris was evident.

Initial Activities

Once they made their decisions to join the mad rush into the Yukon, the men acted with dispatch getting ready for their adventure. Odell purchased a pocket diary and began making entries in early March of 1898.

Articles in the *Cornell Sun* described Odell as still practicing with the crew team on March 4, but he was absent on March 6. It is clear from his initial diary entries that their preparations for the adventure had begun by at least March 12, the date of his third diary entry, when Odell traveled home to Baldwinsville with Aldrich, presumably to say goodbye to his parents before leaving for the Yukon. Press reports describe how Odell's decision to leave school and seek his fortune in the Yukon was a total surprise and the difficulty in replacing him on the Cornell crew.[26]

Neither man had much money, although Aldrich hailed from a prominent family of early settlers on Long Island and his family probably was well to do.[27] Odell owed money to his father and sisters who had loaned him money for his college living expenses.

Using his fame gained from rowing on the championship Cornell crew, Odell sought support from backers of the sports team. He secured funding from wealthy backers who created a corporation to finance Odell's and Aldrich's prospecting efforts.[28] Details about this corporation are sparse. Newspaper accounts refer to the corporation without revealing the corporate name or the individuals who had created the corporation. The backers would pay for the men's expenses, as well as provide them with "liberal" compensation whether they found any gold. They supplied $750 in cash to each of the men who stowed the cash in money belts.[29] An article written after their return from the Yukon stated that they would share one-half of the profits that were made.[30] Aldrich later described the company as a stock corporation.[31]

The S*yracuse Herald* identified the primary backer as a local industrialist. It is clear from Odell's diary entries that their primary financial backer and head of the corporation was a "Mr. Smith." Odell mentioned in several entries that he wrote or wired "Mr. Smith" to obtain permission for making changes in their prospecting plans. It is probable that this Mr. Smith was the industrialist Lyman Cornelius (L.C.) Smith who manufactured famous breech-loading shotguns and typewriters. L.C. Smith lived in Syracuse.

It was quite common for backers to finance or "grubstake" prospecting activities in the Yukon.[32]

Different Routes into the Yukon

Although the Yukon could be entered using different routes, most stampeders followed one of two very similar routes.

The two most common routes into the Yukon were over saltwater from the American west coast, then over a short stretch of land, and then over fresh water from the headwaters of the Yukon River into the Yukon gold fields. Prospectors sailed in steamships from west coast ports up the Inside Passage to the Lynn Canal at the north end of the Alaskan panhandle. Although Seattle was the primary embarkation point, ships also left for Alaska from San Francisco, Tacoma, Vancouver, BC, and Victoria, BC. It is estimated that about 70% of the 100,000 people who left for the Yukon came through Seattle.[33]

After reaching two boom towns on the Alaskan panhandle (Skagway or Dyea), stampeders trekked over Coast Range into Canada, to either Lake Lindeman or Lake Bennett, where they built boats and sailed northward down Lake Bennett crossing from British Columbia into Yukon Territory, and followed a string of lakes and rivers that eventually became the Yukon River and into the Yukon gold fields.

The only difference between the two most common routes was the pass taken over the Coast Range into Canada. After arriving in Skagway, most prospectors took boats a short distance to Dyea and trekked over the Chilkoot Trail into Canada, following an ancient trail used by Native peoples. Others trekked directly from Skagway on a new trail over White Pass into Canada. The two trails over the Coast Range met in the northwest corner of British Columbia at the southern end of Lake Bennett. The boundary between British Columbia and Yukon Territory is part way up Lake Bennett.

The route over Chilkoot Pass was more rugged and with a greater elevation gain than the route over White Pass. It was known as the "poor man's pass" as during the winter stampeders could haul their own outfits over the pass with their own labor.[34]

The White Pass route was less rugged. It was known as the Dead Horse Trail from the number of horses that died hauling goods on the route.

Other routes were less commonly used. Some took steamers from west coast ports to Valdez and trekked into the Yukon. A few took an all-Canadian overland route from Edmonton, Alberta, into the Yukon. A few took an all-water route, sailing from west coast ports north to St. Michael, then transferred to paddle wheel boats and steamed up the Yukon River through Alaska into Yukon Territory, once the ice broke on the Yukon River in the late spring. Some prospectors took the Dalton Trail out of Pyramid Harbor, near what became Haines, Alaska, into the Yukon interior and then by boat down the Yukon River to Dawson City.[35]

Odell and Aldrich opted for the most common Chilkoot Trail route into the Yukon. They would confront two major physical barriers using this route – the formidable Golden Stairs on the Chilkoot Trail and the treacherous Miles Canyon and White Horse Rapids. The other most common route – the White Pass Trail – avoided the steep climb up a mountain pass but included passing through the treacherous Miles Canyon and White Horse Rapids.

It is estimated that about 100,000 people from different nations attempted to reach the Yukon and Klondike gold fields, many of whom traveled through Seattle. About 30,000 to 40,000 made it to the Yukon interior, but only 4,000 struck gold, and only a few hundred became rich.[36] It is estimated that $2.5 million in gold was taken from the Klondike in 1897, $10 million in 1898, $16 million in 1899, and $22.3

million in 1900.³⁷ However, it was the merchants, especially in Seattle, who prospered in the long run, selling prospectors their supplies and outfits.

Taking the Train to Seattle

On March 13, 1898, Odell and Aldrich departed from the Ithaca rail station for Seattle. Odell made two observations in his diary about what they observed on the train – two other stampeders whom they took as "sharks" and "two suspicious girls in our lower berth." Although Odell did not note similar conditions they found in Seattle, the city was rife with swindlers and prostitutes.

On board the train, Odell and Aldrich met four men in the Thompson Party, a company formed to prospect and mine on the Stewart River, a tributary of the Yukon River south of Dawson City. The four-member Thompson Party included J.A. Thompson and George F. Trowbridge, both from Poughkeepsie, New York; and Frank Reed and D.B. Cole*, both from nearby Sharon, Connecticut.³⁸ Odell and

---

* Michael Gates mentions D.B. Cole, or David Bradford Cole, in a recent article. Cole appeared in an undated photo of members of the Yukon Order of Pioneers, and was described as a druggist by profession who had mined for years, and then became a painter and decorator. He was described as "a true and loyal friend, but quiet, retiring and humorously philosophical." Cole died on May 17, 1947. (Michael Gates, "History Hunter: Every photo has a story to tell, sometimes more than one," *Yukon News*, Whitehorse, YT, Oct. 20, 2023.)

Aldrich would join forces with the Thompson Party after receiving authorization from Mr. Smith.

Odell described their train ride from the Cascade Mountains into the Puget Sound region of Washington State on the Northern Pacific Railroad.

> Monday morning, March 21st, we rolled down the slope of the mountains to Tacoma, where for half hour the clouds were raised high above the peaks to give us a view of the beautiful Mount Rainier, or Tacoma (usually spelled Tahoma), to call it by its old Indian name. From the snowy plains of Montana and the wintry wilds of Idaho we passed down into the green fields of western Washington, where cows were out at pasture, lawns had been clipped, and early shrubs had already put forth blossoms.... And still the damp, raw air from the ocean made us wear more clothes than we do here in Alaska at Sheep Camp, or than we did in Dyea.[39]

Once in Seattle, they secured rooms at 318 Marion Street, a house with a yard full of blooming hyacinths in what now is the middle of Seattle's central business district. In 1898, this area at the northern end of Seattle's downtown included an array of shops, small office buildings, expensive houses, and smaller houses that were converted into rooming houses to accommodate incoming Yukon gold rushers. The boarding house where they secured lodging was located several blocks north of the wild open area of Skid Row in the southern portion of downtown Seattle.

Seattle was a young city when Odell and Aldrich arrived in 1898. The Euro-American settlement in Seattle was only 46 years old. Seattle had grown into a thriving dynamo bustling with energy and economic activity, ready and able to be the Gateway to the North into the Yukon and Alaska.

Cooper & Levy Outfitters. Asahel Curtis Collection. CUR1008, University of Washington Libraries, Special Collections.

Supplies piled on the sidewalk in front of the John B Agen store. SEA1335, University of Washington Libraries, Special Collections.

Much of Seattle's early success arose from its prime location in the geographic center of the eastern side of Puget Sound due west of the lowest pass over the Cascades Mountains.[40] The settlement had a deep, natural harbor. However, Seattle's greatest asset was the nature and drive of its early settlers and residents.[41] Early settlers aggressively recruited entrepreneurs to locate in the new community.

From the onset, Seattle had the most diversified and sophisticated economy among Euro-American communities on Puget Sound.[42] It was the major shopping location on Puget Sound. Settlers from other communities often would travel to Seattle and make purchases or order goods that were shipped to their homes from Seattle. Lumbermills and the shipping of coal mined from nearby mines were major factors in Seattle's early development.[43] Logs were slid down a ramp on what became known as Skid Road – today's Yesler Avenue – from a nearby hill down to Yesler's Mill. A fleet of boats operated out of Seattle, transporting people and goods throughout Puget Sound.[44] The fleet eventually was called the Mosquito Fleet. Early Seattle was said to have prospered during a "coal rush" beginning in the 1860s, foreshadowing the prosperity it would garner from the later Klondike gold rush.

However, Seattle had other attractions -- bars, gambling, and prostitution.[45] These attractions provided an economic spark for Seattle and was a major reason for Seattle's emerging dominance over other Puget Sound communities. These attractions continued throughout much of Seattle's history.

Economic troubles throughout the nation began in 1888 when the price of silver fell. By the early 1890s, the national economy had taken a nose-dive in what has been called the Silver Depression or the Panic of 1893. Economic activity throughout the nation and world slowed. Many argue that the gold fever arising from the discovery of gold on the Klondike River, with the arrival of the *Portland* in Seattle with Klondike gold in July of 1897, led to the end of this Depression, at least in the Puget Sound area.[46]

A torrent of activity gripped Seattle as prospectors readied to leave for the Yukon and locals were in business supplying their needs. Stores were jammed with equipment and supplies ready to be purchased, often overflowing into sidewalks. Hotels were overbooked.[47] Cots were added to hotel rooms and up and down hallways to accommodate the new arrivals. Sleeping space was rented in livery stables. Residences became boarding houses. Restaurants and cafes were filled. Ships lined the docks readying for the sail northward. Seattle's historic seamy side flourished, south of Yesler Avenue or Skid Road, where gambling joints, saloons, and both high-end and lower-end houses of prostitution were filled.[48]

Innovation was the name of the day, as schemes of all kinds were hatched. Congress funded an audacious relief mission to feed hungry prospectors in Dawson City. Rumors abounded of starvation in Dawson City during the prior winter of 1897-1898, so Congress appropriated money to import reindeer from Norway that would be used to feed hungry prospectors. The project was known as the Klondike Relief Expedition or the Yukon Relief Expedition. Lapp herders and 538 reindeer arrived in Seattle in early 1898. The herd was kept at Woodland Park waiting for shipment north to what was then called the Haines Mission (modern day Haines), Alaska. The plan was to bring a herd of reindeer over the Coast Range into the Yukon using the Dalton Trail out of Pyramid Harbor, located on the Chilkat Inlet, near the old Haines Mission. At first, too much snow was on the trail to make the passage, so reindeer were taken to hills to forage. However, lichen is the primary food for reindeer and most of the reindeer starved as there was no lichen for them to eat. Only 114 reindeer made it to Dawson City by January of 1899, long after any need for emergency food stuffs.[49]

Horses, oxen, and dogs were transported to the Yukon. Sleds were pulled by goats, as well as the more common dogs. Dogs of all breeds and horses were purchased all over the United States and shipped to Alaska and the Yukon. Pet dogs were not safe on the streets of Seattle, as budding entrepreneurs grabbed dogs and sold them for shipment to the north. Gold Rush photos show a stampeder using an elk to drag his outfit over Chilkoot Pass. Donkeys and burros were also used to transport goods.

Purchasing Outfits and Supplies

As with many other stampeders, the Thompson Party purchased their outfits and supplies in Seattle.

After it was thought that some people nearly starved to death in Dawson City during the winter of 1897-1898, the NWMP instituted several requirements for supplies to be taken into the Yukon. The initial requirement was for a full year's supply of provisions. A later requirement was that each person crossing the border into Canada in search of Yukon gold have an outfit with either "assorted provisions" for six months or "assorted provisions" for two months and at least $500 in money. Confusion exists over this requirement and its enforcement. First, the NWMP requirement did not specify the weight of provisions that were required to be brought into the Yukon. Second, the Mounties did not weigh outfits at the bottom of the Golden Stairs of Chilkoot Pass at a place called the Scales. The Scales was a location where porters weighed outfits and goods that they hauled up Chilkoot Pass.

Although the official requirement for stampeders to bring in adequate outfits did not specify the weight of supplies and equipment, various NWMP reports refer to a required weight.

> At the foot of Lake LaBarge the only police duties were the carrying out of the regulations requiring (1,000) one thousand pounds of provisions to be

taken in by the miners coming into the country.[50]

But taking the stormy days into consideration, when it is impossible to work, very few can pack their 1,000 pounds of provisions, camp outfit, hardware, etc., in less than a month.[51]

Odell and Aldrich made varying comments about the weight of their outfits. Some sixty years after his Yukon adventure, Odell wrote that he and his chum Ellis Aldrich brought about a ton and a half, or 3,000 pounds, of goods, equipment, food, a stove, a sled, and a tent into the Yukon.[52] In October of 1898, Aldrich described their outfit as weighing 2,500 pounds.[53]

THEY GO NORTH WELL SATISFIED

Big Party of Easterners Who Outfitted in This City and Pay Sound Merchants a Fine Tribute.

The Alaska and Northwest Co-operative Mining Company's Stewart river expedition will leave this morning on the Al-Ki for Dyea. They have just purchased an outfit from Seattle merchants weighing six and one-half tons. They expect it to last for a year and a half. The six men in the party are James A. Thompson, of Poughkeepsie, N. Y., president; F. K. Reed, of Sharron, Conn., treasurer; George F. Trobridge, secretary, of Poughkeepsie, N. Y.; Ellis L. Aldrich, M. M. Odell, of Cornell university, and D. B. Cole, of Sharron, Conn.

President Thompson said to a Post-Intelligencer reporter last night: "We are more than pleased with the treatment we have received at the hands of Seattle merchants. We can say without hesitation that any one makes a great mistake who purchases any part of his outfit in the East, or at any other point on the Coast. Prices here are never higher, and in many instances much cheaper. The merchants know what you need and are able to supply any demand. The stories sent out through the East that board in Seattle cost $10 per day, we have found to be entirely without foundation. We boarded here as cheaply as we could at home."

Seattle Post Intelligencer, Seattle WA, March 26, 1898, p. 11.

A news article in the *Gazette & Farmers' Journal* quoted Odell that the Thompson Party's outfit

> weighed over seven tons, including a ton of flour, 1,200 pounds of pork, bacon and beef, and 'other stuff in proportion.' They will stop at Stewart river, about seventy miles above Dawson City, for their first prospecting. The letter concludes 'Remember me to all friends, and think of me in about two weeks lugging my share, and perhaps a little more, of that seven tons on my back over the Chilkoot.[54]

Guide books had lists of suggested supplies. The table below[55] describes a typical supply list costing about $500 in Seattle.

Food		Cooking utensils, etc.	
Flour	400 lbs.	2-qt galvanized coffee pot	1
Bacon	150 lbs.	Fry pan	1
Split peas	150 lbs.	Knife & fork	1 each
Evaporated apples	25 lbs.	Granite saucepan	1
Evaporated peaches	25 lbs.	Sheet iron stove	1
Butter	25 lbs.	Granite cup	1
Pepper	1 lb.	Pie plate	1
Evaporated potatoes	25 lbs.	Wash basin	1
Condensed milk	1 ½ doz. cans		
Rice	25 lbs.	**Tools and hardware**	
Rolled oats	40 lbs.	Pick	1
Apricots	25 lbs.	Handle	1
Sugar	100 lbs.	Shovel	1
Salt	10 lbs.	Gold pan	1
Baking powder	8 lbs.	Whip saw	1
Coffee	15 lbs.	Hand saw	1
Tea	10 lbs.	Jack plane	1
Yeast cakes	2 doz.	Brace	1
Vinegar	1 gallon	Bits, assorted	4
Beef extract	¼ doz.	Tape measure	1
		Compass	1
Miscellaneous items		Rivets	1 package
Soap, Castile	5 bars	20d nails	5 lbs.
Matches	1 tin	10d nails	5 lbs.
Candles	1 box	6d nails	6 lbs.
Canvas sacks	25	8" mill file	1
Medicine chest	1	6" mill file	1
Pack straps	1 set	Broad hatchet	1
Soap, tar	6 bars	Chisel 1 ½"	1
Candlewick	3 lbs.	Axe handle	1
Miner's candlestick	1	Axe stone	1
Rubber sheet	1	Emery stone	1
Towels	6	Covered pails	3
Sled for winter travel	1	14 qt. galvanized pail	1
Personal clothes, extra boots		Single block	1
		5/8" rope	200 ft.
		Solder outfit	1
		Oakum	10 lbs.
		Pitch	10 lbs.

Other lists suggested a pair of rubber waders, a wash basin, a tent, a sleeping bag, and blankets. Most stampeders bought three suits of heavy underwear, a wool mackinaw coat, a rubber coat, two pairs of work pants, two pairs of overalls, a dozen pair of wool socks, six pairs of mittens, two pairs of work boots, two pairs of shoes, blankets, and mosquito netting.[56]

Odell complained of only being able to purchase poor fitting clothes in Seattle.

> We spent the remainder of the week in outfitting in Seattle, which is no easy task anywhere. One of the greatest difficulties I encountered was in getting clothing of the proper size. If I were to outfit again, I should select suits very large and a very loose fit, then pass those by and choose suits about three sizes larger and no fit at all. My coats are already too small; I wonder what I shall do in six months. I selected suits very large and a very loose fit.[57]

Hoglen/Wood Party

Three other men (Walter Hoglen, Thomas Wood, Jr., and Bill Owens), all from Dayton, Ohio, were a few weeks ahead of Odell and Aldrich and the Thompson Party, having sailed north from Seattle and Tacoma in early March of 1898. As discussed below, Hoglen and Wood would join forces with Odell and Aldrich in the Yukon.

Loading dogs on steamer in Seattle, Odell Collection.

Chapter 3
Sailing to Alaska

A major fiasco soon struck the Thompson Party.

The *Gazette & Farmers' Journal* included a short tickler notice promoting Odell's long letter about the men's early experiences in Seattle and on the trail to Chilkoot Pass. An "exciting experience at Seattle" and Odell's first cooking efforts that "will please the ladies."[58]

Major Fiasco

Odell and Aldrich completed buying their outfits in Seattle. Matching the status and position of their new partners, they upgraded their tickets from 2nd Class to 1st Class from Seattle to Skagway on board the *S.S. Al-Ki* – a $10 increase from $15 to $25 per person. Odell's long letter described loading their gear on the ship.

> The steamer on which we had engaged passage was scheduled to leave Seattle Saturday morning at nine o'clock. It finally left about nine in the evening with thirty-two passengers for Wrangell, twenty-two for Juneau, and sixty-two for

Skagway and Dyea. Meanwhile we had something of an experience. I was standing on the wharf watching the loading about 6:30 in the evening. This loading is done with a derrick on the boat. There was a space of about eight feet between the steamboat and the wharf.

The hands were then using a sling instead of a net on the crane and were putting on bags of baggage. Something apparently went wrong. They stopped the load directly over the water, and the crew on the boat yelled at the wharf hands, the wharf hands yelled at the crew, while the mate swore at each gang alternately and volubly. Finally two bags dropped into the water, then they swung the rest of the load over upon the vessel. The mate swore a few minutes longer until a sailor clambered down the side and tried to fish the bags out with a rope. He finally got one and came up quite satisfied, saying resignedly that the other was out of his reach.

About that time my pity for the owner of the other bag changed to an uncomfortable feeling that I was interested in the accident deeply. I asked a man standing on deck how the bag was marked, and my hair stood up when he told me "Thompson Party" with a big O encircling an A. I then rushed up to the mate and begged him to do something. He was very busy loading the other freight, but sent off a hand to hunt up a boat, who by the way returned fifteen minutes later, saying he couldn't find one. I entreated the hands to get a pike and hunt for the bag and haul it in. Everybody was very busy and everything was confused and bustle. Meanwhile the tide was setting in strong and floating the bag off somewhere up under the wharf, which covered probably about one quarter of an acre. The situation was getting desperate.

There is only one man in our party who is at all good at swearing and I couldn't see or find him anywhere around, so I returned to the spot convinced that everything depended upon me, and in two or three minutes time I developed quite a respectable vocabulary. I cursed the wharf hands and damned the mate, I went into the steamship office, berated everyone inside from the superintendent to the entry clerk, and came out again and swore at everybody in sight. I repeated this with variations *ad libitum*, until the further loading was practically suspended and all hands were under and around the wharf searching in the gathering darkness for the bag which I pictured sunk long before.

Finally, after fully three quarters of an hour, the bag was hauled up from where it had stuck between two posts. It was soaked through, yet a sailor took it and started aboard to dump it in the hold. Aldrich collared him and I seized the bag, and in spite of rules, regulations, orders, and the articles of incorporation of the company, we forced our way down into the engine room, aiding our passage there by fragments of my vocabulary. It was Aldrich's bag and contained his whole outfit of clothes, every article soaking wet. We worked down in that oven until one o'clock in the morning, wringing out the goods, rigging up lines and watching the clothes dry. During the rest of the trip I spent a part of each day in sackcloth and ashes, doing penance, but we had the bag.[59]

S.S. Al-Ki Departure

The *S.S. Al-Ki* departed Elliott Bay, Seattle, on March 26, 1898, with 116 passengers, steaming southward to Tacoma where more passengers and freight were loaded before heading northward to Alaska.[60]

Odell noted in his diary entry for the day the *S.S. Al-Ki* left Seattle, that "Cole took a good bye." Cole was an original member of the Thompson Party.

Finally, the *S.S. Al-Ki* steamed northward up Puget Sound, stopping at Port Townsend where they heard bells ringing for evening service. Odell was upbeat.

> The night was clear and quiet and we stood leaning over the rail listening to their sweet tones gradually growing fainter and fainter, and watching the twinkling lights disappear one by one, silently wondering how many long months would pass before we should once more listen to the calling of church bells.
>
> At [Port] Townsend a party for Wrangell, containing three ladies, came on our boat, whereupon we promptly took a shave, although we had promised ourselves that after leaving Seattle shears would be the only barber tools we would torture ourselves with.[61]

This was Odell's and Aldrich's last attempt to be cultured gentlemen. As they traveled northward, no more shaving pretenses were taken when they saw women heading to the Yukon gold fields.

Steamer *Al-Ki,* Eric A. Hegg Photographs, PH Coll. 248, University of Washington Libraries, Special Collections.

Sailing up the Inside Passage

The steamer passed into Canadian waters and stopped at Nanaimo on Vancouver Island, Canada. Odell and Aldrich purchased their miner's licenses at the customs office.* A mining license or certificate granted the holder all the rights and privileges of a "Free Miner" for one year with permission to engage in general mining activities, as well as authority to fish and shoot, and the right to cut timber for purposes of

---

* A mining license for the Yukon gold rush cost $10 for one year. (Adney, 435-436.) The Hudson's Bay Company instituted a similar license for miners during the Fraser River gold rush in 1857 and 1858, when a mining license cost $5. (Ficken, 90–92.)

building a cabin, a boat, and engaging in mining activities.

The *S.S. Al-Ki* steamed northward through the treacherous Seymour Narrows between Vancouver Island and Quadra Island, north of the mouth of the Campbell River. Many ships grounded and sank on the Seymour Narrows until rocks at the Narrows were dynamited in 1958. Seattle's KING-TV station promoted its upcoming live coverage of this event that ended up being quite anticlimactic and only a few seconds long with a geyser of water shooting upwards out of the sea when the dynamite blew.

The shipmates played cards and sang in the evenings. Optimism was in the air. Dreams of Yukon gold beckoned the men and others onboard the steamer.

Odell continued his colorful description of sailing northward through the Inside Passage.

> The trip up the coast I will not try to describe. It is not an ocean voyage at all. The route is a winding one where a vessel threads its way up through the long group of mountainous islands which line the coast from Puget Sound north. It reminds one at times of the Hudson River, at another of the St. Lawrence at the Islands. At times it seems as though the ship were passing through a succession of inland lakes. At some places the course is so narrow that a stone could be thrown from the deck to the shore. Then the tide must

be at the proper ebb or flood or the ship lies to, awaiting its opportunity to pass.

As Seattle is left farther and farther behind, the scenery grows grander and more wildly beautiful. The mountainous island and the coast of the mainland rise sheer from the water many hundred feet in height, with snow capped peaks always in sight. Glaciers large and small came into view each day. At Sumdum Bay [more commonly called Holkham Bay] many small icebergs were floating about or left stranded by the tide. I have read much of the beauty and grandeur of these and had imagined them beautiful, very grand, but chill and forbidding. At nothing else have I been so delightfully surprised as I was over these wonders of the sea. Such delicate changing azure tints they showed that from the little grottos in their sides it seems as though the mermaids had but just slipped off into the dark green waters and were watching us from the waves to see us lured into those attractive waters, fascinated by the warm looking, delightful little sheltered nooks they had left. And those in a huge mass of ice off which a chill wind was blowing in our faces.[62]

The *S.S. Al-Ki* steamed across Queen Charlotte Sound, the only major open water portion of the Inside Passage, exposing ships to rough Pacific Ocean waters between the northern end of Vancouver Island

and the sheltered waters east of smaller coastal islands that lay to the north of Vancouver Island. Odell noted in his diary that nearly everyone was green to the gills and seasick as they experienced rough water.

Old town of Bella Bella. Odell Collection.

The ship steamed past the old Bella Bella Indian village. This is the first of eleven diary entries Odell made about Native peoples and their villages.

The *S.S. Al-Ki* re-entered American waters and stopped at Wrangell, where the steamship fouled on buoy lines and beached during low tide. Odell walked through the small village and saw totem poles and gambling houses.

Odell described their stopover at Wrangell.

> Occasionally we would pass a little Indian village with its curious and grotesquely carved Totem poles. At Wrangell we had an excellent chance to study these poles carefully and to get a few snap shots with a camera one of the party is carrying.

Wrangell! My first experience in a boom mushroom town. A man who has been there three months is an old resident. A man who attempts to go through it without wearing hip rubber boots is an idiot. I wore leather shoes myself.

This town they hope to make the metropolis of Alaska, the gates of the Yukon Valley when the Sitkeen [now spelled Stikine] route is fully opened. Here in this combination of Indian huts, Klondikers' tents, high front saloons, hotels, mud, fish, tin cans and Siwash dogs, I met a man from Leland Stanford [Stanford University], two graduates of the University of Illinois, and a C.E. [civil engineer] from the University of Virginia, who took post graduate work at Cornell. Here were gambling houses run by sharks, others by respected citizens who operate them "on the square." I was introduced to the proprietor of the leading place by one of the better business men of the town. We shook hands and he was "pleased to meet me" in quite a genteel manner.

On the street one jostles against respectable men from the states, notorious gamblers, Siwash Indians, miners, "butchers, bakers and candle stick makers," children, women lacking both these and other qualities; he steps into the mud and pulls himself out by clinging to a Totem pole, or by hanging onto a barber's sign; he runs against a vicious looking, sneaking little Siwash dog, treads on an empty tomato can, and steps over a dead halibut with a form like a good Christian fish but both eyes on one side so he can swim on the other. Before he has been in the place two hours he catches this boom town spirit and wants to buy a few square feet of mud and speculate in it for a building lot.[63]

In another letter, Odell described the trip to Wrangell and what he saw in that village.

> We are to stop at Wrangell some time tonight, so I will write another bulletin. I wrote you at Nanaimo Monday morning and have been sailing steadily since through beautiful and grand scenery, with little rough water to disturb our stomachs. Twice or three times the boat has pitched some, enough to send about three-quarters of the crowd to their bunks, but I have not been disturbed any. Yesterday we saw whales, seals, porpoises and Indians. Today we saw rain drizzling all day. I expect the rain will continue all the way to Dyea unless it turns to snow. It is getting colder now each day as we go farther north, and snowcapped mountains are in sight most of the time. This town, Wrangell, we get to about one o'clock in the morning and leave about six. I don't know whether I will get up to see it or

not, probably not, but I will give this letter to a man who gets off here, and he will post it. I reckon it will be about fifteen days before you get it. I suppose you have begun plowing by now. I haven't seen anything to plow for four days except rock and water.[64]

Meat Market & Chop House in Wrangell, Odell Collection.

YMCA, Wrangell, Odell Collection.

Totem Pole, Wrangell, Odell Collection.

The steamer soon departed but in the fog and grounded again.⁶⁵ Once re-floated by the high tide, the *S.S. Al-Ki* steamed past the Patterson and Powers Glaciers and stopped at Sumdum Bay. Odell continued his ebullient description of the scenery.

> The scenery was grand. The route was the same as before through a channel between mountainous islands, with a glacier appearing occasionally in a valley between two lofty peaks. Thousands, yes thousands of wild ducks floated about on the water scarcely disturbed by the appearance of our ship. Occasionally whales would spout, off near the shore, then roll up their big brown backs to

view, and disappear only to spout and roll again farther on. A school of porpoises at times came along the ship and gamboled about, disporting themselves for our entertainment.[66]

The steamer docked at Juneau where Odell mentioned the large stamping mill at the Treadwell mines on Douglas Island

> roared greeting to us, grinding out a hoarse cry, "gold, gold, gold," which echoed up and down the valley, while the mountains re-echoed back a fainter cry, "gold, gold," to lure the daring prospector up those dangerous slopes and ravines. Juneau is like the picture of a Swiss village, built on the shore of a niche between two high mountains, one of them 3,326 feet in height, seeming ready to topple over upon the village at any moment. Here we passed a day waiting for a storm in Lynn canal to abate, and I felt as though that moment was coming continuously.[67]

Coal was unloaded all day at Juneau, so Odell and Aldrich went ashore during a big storm. Odell noted in his diary that they explored three miles up a valley and went to the theater at night.

Arrival at Skagway

The *S.S. Al-Ki* steamed northward and finally docked in Skagway at 4 p.m. on April 3, 1898. Odell was struck by the beauty of the voyage north from Seattle to Alaska.

> This is the eighth day we have been on our water trip, a trip worth going many miles to take and enduring many inconveniences to enjoy. I had a long letter planned to write for the paper, yesterday and today, describing the wonders of the trip, but have been attacked by some trouble of the eyes which prevents my writing much. We are within a couple of hours of Skaguay [an old spelling of Skagway], where we leave the ship and lighter up to Dyea. I can probably write again after we land.[68]

They arrived at Skagway on Palm Sunday and soon learned of a horrible snowslide on Chilkoot Trail earlier that day where many died – "I have witnessed many a sad sight here, the result of that terrible affair."[69] Concerns were raised about their chosen route over Chilkoot Pass after the deaths at the snow slide. The avalanches between Sheep Camp and the Scales at the bottom of Chilkoot Pass were the deadliest event of the Yukon gold rush and were widely reported. This was the first sense of foreboding Odell and Aldrich experienced on their journey into the Yukon.

The option of using the White Pass Trail, which passed directly out of Skagway over the Coast Range into Canada, was quickly rejected. They remained committed to the Chilkoot Pass route. A major argument against the White Pass route was potential entanglements with the infamous Soapy Smith and his gang of cutthroats in Skagway and along the White Pass route. Gang members were also in Dyea and the Chilkoot Trail, but Skagway was the headquarters of the gang. Smith was a long-time con artist and gangster who moved his criminal operations to Skagway in August 1897. He was shot and killed by Frank Reid on the evening of July 8, 1898.

Odell wrote home.

> Should I return from the Yukon Valley without an ounce of dust which has quite the balance of probabilities, I cannot regret the time spent after passing this part of the route.[70]

Chapter 4

From Skagway to the Summit of Chilkoot Pass

The Thompson Party had reached Skagway and its access over the Coast Range into Canada.

Skagway

Skagway was a new settlement that mushroomed out of the wilderness. The NWMP Annual Report for 1898 noted that in 1897 Skagway grew out of nothing within a couple of weeks.[71] However, in 1887, Captain William Moore and his son had staked land in Skagway, opened a sawmill, and built a home and a wharf at Skagway.

The new community was a bustling site when the Thompson Party arrived in April of 1898. New docks extended out into the harbor. Stampeders were greeted by saloons, hotels, restaurants, shipping companies, money lenders, journalists, real estate salespeople, longshoremen unloading boats, and con artists. More colorfully – Skagway "was conceived in lawlessness and nurtured in anarchy" and "little better than a hell on earth."[72]

Odell noted it was dark when the *Al-Ki* arrived at 5 p.m. They stayed overnight paying 50¢ apiece for bunks. Odell failed to note the name of the hotel or bunkhouse where the men stayed. He described the weather as rainy and the town as muddy.

Skagway Harbor. Odell Collection. Karl Gurcke identifies this photo as being taken from Skagway Beach looking down the harbor.

Skagway Harbor, Eric A. Hegg Photographs, PH Coll. 274, University of Washington Libraries, Special Collections.

A photograph from the Odell collection includes an image of railroad tracks laid on Broadway Street in Skagway. This image is of the first track laid for the White Pass and Yukon Route (WP&YR) railroad.

View in Skagway – laying the railroad on Broadway. Odell Collection.

Construction of the railway tracks down Skagway's Broadway Street commenced on June 15, 1898.

Skagway River. Odell Collection

Dyea

The Thompson Party took a lighter (a small boat with a shallow draft) from Skagway to nearby Dyea. Unlike the new settlement of Skagway, Dyea was a traditional hunting and fishing camp for Tlingits and their starting point for trading trips into the interior. (*Dayéi* means "to pack" in Tlingit.) The Healy and Wilson trading post at Dyea opened in the mid-1880's.*

---

* Karl Gurcke notes a photograph with a date of 1884 shows the trading post. (Email from Karl Gurcke to Steve Lundin, April 23, 2014.) Neufeld and Norris put the date as 1886. (Neufeld, David and Frank Norris. *Chilkoot Trail, Heritage Route to the Klondike.* Whitehorse, Yukon Territory, Canada, Lost Moose Publishers, 1996, 55.)

Odell described the scene at Dyea.

> Lynn Canal is a narrow arm of the sea, reaching up into the land through a narrow valley to receive the waters of the little Dyea [more commonly known as the Taiya] river. At the head of this canal is the village of Dyea, another mushroom town, built on old beach sand, river mud and gravel.[73]

By at least January of 1898, a dock known as the Dyea dock or DKT dock had been constructed in Dyea where ships could be unloaded.[74] A longer dock, known as the Long Wharf, reaching deeper water, began three months later.[75] In many instances, barges and lighters were run aground on the mud flats when the tide was out, goods unloaded onto the mud, and a mad rush was made to haul goods by hand and wagon above the high water mark into the town proper to avoid the incoming tide.

The population of Dyea varied each day, its maximum was estimated at between 5,000 and 8,000, but tens of thousands of prospectors passed through the town on their way over Chilkoot Pass. Two new trading posts opened in 1895, one operated by the Koehler and James partnership, and other operated by Joseph Fields.[76] By 1898, Dyea resembled Skagway with "a jumble of frame saloons, false-fronted hotels, log cafes, gambling houses, stores, and real estate offices bound together by a stiff mortar of flapping tents."[77]

Scores of new buildings were erected in a few weeks. Ground was broken for many more, including new hotels that were started every day.[78]

"Time picture" of Dyea, meaning that the camera aperture held open. Odell Collection.

"Main Street, Dyea" Eric A. Hegg Photographs, HEG116, University of Washington Library, Special Collections.

Trail Street, Dyea, Alaska, Eric A. Hegg Photographs, HEG114, University of Washington Library, Special Collections.

Dyea – unloading at Chilkoot Railroad & Transport Co.'s warehouse, Odell Collection.

The boomtown mostly disappeared within two years. Access into the Canadian interior was easier with the construction of the WP&YR, running from neighboring Skagway over White Pass to Lake Bennett, and eventually reaching Whitehorse in 1900.* Dyea had lost its reason to exist as a city. The WP&YR purchased the then three existing tramways operating over Chilkoot Pass, eliminating competition with its soon to be finished railroad over White Pass.[79] The Dyea Post Office closed in June 1902. Fire took some buildings in Dyea, but others were carefully disassembled, and the valuable lumber was shipped to Skagway and elsewhere and used to erect new buildings. Other buildings were reused by homesteaders but later were abandoned and are now in ruins.

Dyea now is an archaeological site. The National Park Service provides amenities and is making archeological excavations. Tourists flock to Dyea in the summers. In the early 1960s, the State of Alaska built a recreational train along the route of the old Chilkoot Trail. The portion of the trail in the United States was designated a National Historic Landmark in 1978. The portion of the trail in Canada was designated a National Historic Site of Canada in 1987.

---

* A discussion of the White Pass and Yukon Route railway is found in Appendix E.

Odell and Aldrich stayed at the Hall and Coleman Hotel during their first night in Dyea. The official name of this facility was the Hall and Coleman Chop House, Meals and Beds.[80]

"Dyea street cars" – Central RR Co., Odell Collection.

The street car photo is a rare photo. It appears that the street cars were surplus carriages from the San Francisco transit system's old fleet of horse drawn street cars. The wheels and the platform where drivers would stand with reins leading to a horse were removed. For a brief time, the Chilkoot Railroad & Transport Company operated a wooden track street car system for a short distance in Dyea. The street cars were possibly used on that system.[81]

Dyea – dog train in frozen Taiya River, Odell Collection.

Dog train in Dyea. Odell Collection.

Burro Train Loading, Dyea, Odell Collection.

Odell's diary does not indicate whether their backer, Mr. Smith, had approved of Odell and Aldrich joining the Thompson Party, but it is clear Odell and Aldrich had joined the Thompson Party. Odell noted mailing letters to Mr. Smith from Juneau, Skagway, Dyea, and along the Chilkoot trail at Sheep Camp, presumably providing Mr. Smith with more details about the Thompson Party.

Chilkoot Trail

The Chilkoot Trail (also called the Taiya Trail or Dyea Trail) lay ahead.* This was the traditional trade

---

* Canadian surveyor William Ogilvie used "Taiya Trail" to describe what was later better known as the Dyea Trail or Chilkoot Trail. (Ogilvie, William, Dominion [Canadian] Land Surveyor, Department of Interior. *Information Respecting the* route that the Tlingit Raven clan of the Chilkoot village near Haines, Alaska, took over the Coast Range into the interior.[82] In earlier years, the Tlingits defended the trail from use by others. The U.S. Navy negotiated an agreement with Tlingits in 1880 enabling prospectors to use the trail to transit into the interior without interference, although they were obligated to hire Tlingits to haul their goods over the pass.

By 1897, many prospectors hauled their goods by themselves up the Chilkoot Trail and over the Pass. Some hired shipping companies, using native and non-native packers or freighters to haul their goods. Others hauled some of their goods themselves and hired shipping companies to pack the rest of their goods. The Thompson Party would follow the latter course, hauling some of its own supplies and paying others to pack the remainder of its supplies.

Lines of men, wagons, and pack trains left Dyea for Chilkoot Pass. An expensive and fast way to haul goods involved aerial tramways. Eventually, five aerial tramways were constructed, one which started part way to Chilkoot Pass at Canyon City, a few miles outside of Dyea.* Other tramways started closer to the

---

Yukon District. Ottawa, CA, Government Printing Bureau, 1897, 12-13.)

* Shape, 35. More accurately, historians for the National Park Service describe these transport systems as consisting of three aerial tramways and several surface hoists. (Norris, Frank and

base or foot of Chilkoot Pass. The Chilkoot Railroad and Transport Company operated the most significant tramway, running from Canyon City over Chilkoot Pass to Crater Lake, part of the way to Lake Lindeman. An old boiler which powered the Dyea-Klondike Transportation Company's aerial tramway is still found in Canyon City. Tramway cables are still visible, lying on the rocks leading up what had been the Golden Stairs of Chilkoot Pass.

The Chilkoot Trail left Dyea, following the Taiya River to the foot of Chilkoot Pass. Along the route, prospectors traveled on a "passable" road about five miles to Finnigan's Point, another two miles up the frozen river bed on a "go-as-you-please zig zag" trail to Canyon City.[83] Eventually, a wagon road was built from Dyea to Canyon City, described as an "unpretentious city" with hotels, restaurants, saloons, and other businesses.[84]

This Canyon City, on the Alaskan side of Chilkoot Pass, should not be confused with another Canyon City located in Canada on the Yukon River immediately upstream of Miles Canyon. Odell described the American Canyon City as consisting of several tents, a few log huts, and a house or two constructed with milled wood.

Karl Gurcke. "The Chilkoot Trail Tramways." Klondike Gold Rush National Historical Park, United States National Park Service, Skagway, Alaska.)

The Thompson Party contracted with the Yukon Navigation Company to transport five tons of their goods from Dyea to Sheep Camp at a cost of 1¾¢ per pound. This left about two tons of the party's outfit that the partners planned on hauling themselves. Odell described the "road" from Dyea to Canyon City as the worst wagon trail he had ever seen. At Canyon City, they slept in the Yukon Navigation Company's tent where they rolled their blankets on bales of hay that "were piled with a great lack of care, precision or evenness."[85]

From Canyon City, the trail led about five miles to Sheep Camp. Two stories exist about the derivation of the name Sheep Camp. Most claim that the camp was named after mountain sheep seen in the area. Another source claims the name referred to a flock of sheep that a few years before had been penned there for several weeks before being herded to Dawson City.[86] All available space in the one-street town was covered with tents that provided shelter for stampeders, as well as hotels, restaurants, saloons, coffee stands, two drug stores, a hospital, lodging houses, two laundries, a bathhouse, and other stores.

On April 6, Odell hiked from Canyon City to Sheep Camp, describing the trail.

> Here the valley closes up to a narrow, deep canon, about four miles long, above which the valley widens out again. A mile above the head of the canon is Sheep Camp, a city of tents, and a few log and

board houses. The population is, I reckon, somewhere between three and five thousand,* constantly changing. The elevation here is, I believe, about 1,800 feet, although I may be wrong. It is a comparatively gradual ascent from Dyea here, but the trail is up knolls, and down gullies, over logs, boulders, and brush, full of pitch-holes and very dirty. All my description, remember, applies only to today. A month ago it was different; a month hence it will be greatly changed.[87]

Hoglen's and Wood's camp at Sheep Camp, Odell Collection, Wood at right, Hoglen either in background or sitting next to man with a stick.

He chose a camp site under some hemlocks at the lower end of Sheep Camp. The snow was about six

---

* At its peak, Sheep Camp had a population of about 8,000.

feet deep. Sawdust from a nearby sawmill was strewn over the snow and boughs were used for their beds. The men slept rolled up in blankets.[88]

Odell noted in his diary that he saw three bodies brought down from the snow slide on April 6 and then attending a funeral at the Odd Fellows on April 7. He took over the cooking chores for the Thompson Party.

> We have a little Yukon sheet iron stove about twenty-six inches long, fourteen wide by twelve high, which is a marvel. I was unwise enough to admit that I had cooked a little. You can imagine the rest if you can imagine what six men will eat in this country. We got a cook book [*Klondike Edition of Scientific Cooking*] in Seattle made especially for miners by one Miss Suzy Tracy.
>
> I tackled her recipe for baking powder bread. She talks glibly about quarts, pints, gills, and ounces of this, and teaspoons, tablespoons, cups and pinches of that; but by the use of a two-quart pail and a big iron spoon and some guessing. I followed her until she directed the miner to mix his dough to about the consistency of pound cake batter, when I was in some doubt. This particular bread was to be baked in a very hot oven, accent on very. I got what I took to be quite a warm oven and stuck in the bread, being careful to cover the loaf with a paper according to directions

to keep the crust from baking too hard. This paper went up in flame before I got the door shut so I judged the oven must be hot. When I took out the bread a few minutes later and cut off about a half inch of burnt crust from both top and bottom I found some quite palatable bread inside and had learned something about hot ovens, Yukon stoves, and several little things, though I am still in a state of ignorance concerning pound cake.

Since then I have turned one bread pan over another when I bake and produced something quite presentable in the way of bread and Johnnycake* from the oven, besides several choice concoctions from the top of the stove of the fried, boiled, stewed and baked kinds.[89]

Suzy Tracy's *Klondike Edition of Scientific Cooking* cost 25 cents in 1898.

Odell and Aldrich hauled four loads of their goods from Canyon City to Sheep Camp – a 5¼ mile distance. They arranged for the rest of their goods to be hauled from Sheep Camp to the summit of Chilkoot Pass at a cost of 3¢ per pound.

From Sheep Camp, the trail led about three miles to the Scales at the bottom of the famous Golden Stairs

---

* A Johnnycake was an unleavened cornbread resembling a pancake, made from cornmeal, salt and water. Johnnycakes were popular in northeast United States and in the Yukon.

leading up Chilkoot Pass. The base of Chilkoot Pass was called the "Scales" as the location where freighting companies reweighed supplies before company employees hauled goods over the Pass. The formidable Golden Stairs loomed ahead, with its 1,500 steps cut into ice on a "trail" rising to the summit of Chilkoot Pass with a 35% slope.

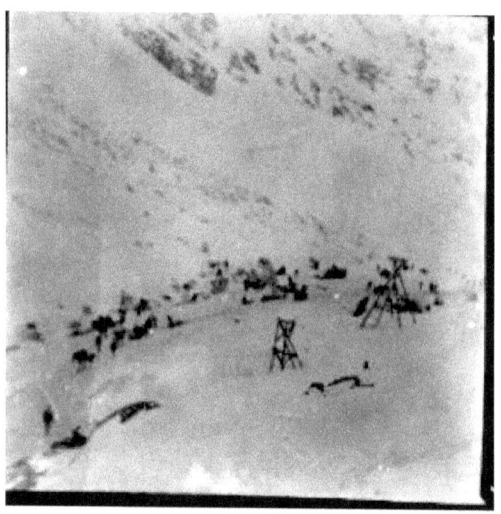

Below Scales. Odell Collection.

Odell described the trail from Sheep Camp towards Chilkoot Pass.

> After leaving Sheep Camp the climbing begins. The first objective point is the Stone House, which, as far as I can see, is the name of a spot. I could see nothing there except tents, piles of goods, a shanty restaurant, and the inevitable shell-game table. No stone structure was visible, but

a man can find plenty of material there for such a house. The incline from Sheep Camp to the Stone House is just to break a man in. These two points are about a mile apart.

From Sheep Camp to the Stone House, which is at the foot of two very steep hills leading to the Scales, which are at the foot of the summit proper, all sorts of beasts of burden are used to haul the sleds. Horses, large and small; oxen, mules, goats, asses, cows, dogs, all lugging at sleds over the trail, now is in fearful condition.

Above Stone House the traveler climbs a very steep hill and thinks he has got somewhere until he looks up and sees another which he must climb up to the Scales. This is another name given to the place, because their goods are weighed out to the packers to carry up the summit proper. Do not picture to yourself, however, scales like those on which Jack Munroe weighs out his coal to you, on which one could drive with a team and wagon. [Clearly, Odell is referencing a shop in Baldwinsville where coal was sold.] If such a set of scales were there you couldn't get a wagon from Sheep Camp up to them, nor would there be any place to set the scales unless you piled them up on twenty feet of snow. All the weighing affairs you will see by little steelyards on a stick or a small set of grocer's scales. Our five tons of freight and baggage is all out at our tent here on a little set of counter scales.⁹⁰

Below Scales, right. Odell Collection.

Golden Stairs to the Summit

Climbing the grueling one-half mile "Golden Stairs" from the Scales at the foot of Chilkoot Pass up to the summit was the most difficult part of the passage to Lake Bennett. This was the first major physical barrier that the Odell and Aldrich, and the Thompson Party encountered. Men carried up to one hundred pounds of gear or supplies on their backs each trip. Dozens of trips were required to transport their supplies. A fee was required for each climb up to the summit.⁹¹

Photographs show an unending line of stampeders carrying their gear up Chilkoot Pass.

Chilkoot Pass from Scales. Odell Collection.

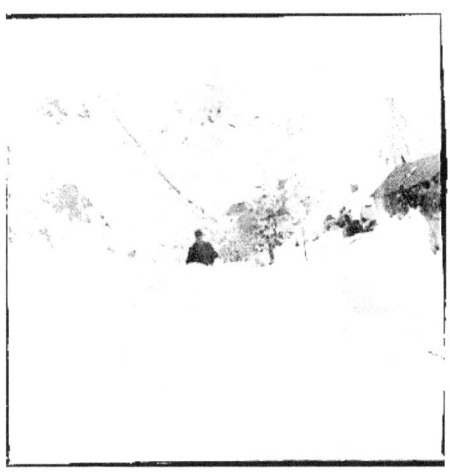

Aerial Tramway bucket or car visible in upper center of photo, Chilkoot Pass. Odell Collection.

View of Chilkoot Pass in 1987. Lundin Collection.

Climb up Chilkoot Pass, Hegg Collection,
University of Washington Libraries Collection
HEG408

View of debris in 1987 at Scales, looking towards Stone House. Lundin Collection.

Odell described his first climb up the Golden Stairs.

> I stopped at the foot of summit to give my dissertations on names and scales. Now let me take you to the top if you have rested sufficiently after climbing the mile and a half from the stone house to the scales. You have only about three-quarters of a mile farther to go, but it is three-quarters of a mile of slippery stairs. This is the summit proper, very proper indeed. It is divided in two parts; a long hill, and a shorter hill, with a narrow level ledge [False Summit] between. Up these hills are stretched ropes. The climber seizes the rope in his right hand, a climbing pike in his left, and moves on with the slowly moving line. I packed up two sacks of flour, fifty pounds each, my first trip up. Going up the last hill the one thing in my mind was that last mile at Poughkeepsie [the IRA rowing finals] when I was straining my ear to hear the coxswain shout 'give her twenty-five boys.'
>
> When I finally reached the top I was quite ready to fall against a snow bank and rest. There on the summit is the customs officer's tent, and piles of freight on top of the snow, and buried deep under the snow. The Chilkoot Pass is not such a formidable place to cross light. The great difficulty comes in getting one's freight and outfit over. Beyond the summit all is unknown to me except what I hear. We

> expect to break camp here about Wednesday and go over to Lake Linderman [Odell used a spelling for this lake that was somewhat common in his day, but the lake now is known as Lindeman] for a camp, then haul our goods from the summit down, about nine miles. I think we can haul our goods from there on to Lake Bennett where we expect to build boats for the trip down the river.[92]

A day later, he further described his first climb up the Golden Stairs.

> The weather is remarkable here. It is difficult to believe oneself in Alaska. Yesterday I went up the pass over the Scales, and to the top of the summit in my shirt sleeves, my coat on my arm. The snow is getting very soft, and the trail is getting in worse condition day by day. Goods are hauled from here to the Scales on small sleds, then packed up the summit by men or taken up on one of the two steam tramways.[*] "There is a stream of men passing up the summit all the time

---

[*] Only one big steam powered aerial tramway operated on Chilkoot Pass, the Chilkoot Railroad & Transport Company. The Dyea-Klondike Transportation Company powered its aerial tramway with electricity generated by a steam boiler at Canyon City. The Alaska Railroad & Transportation Company operated an aerial tramway powered by a gasoline engine. (Karl Gurcke, email to Steve Lundin, April 23, 2014.)

one stepping in the tracks of another, very much like a line of men going up stairs – the incline seems about the same. Every fifteen or twenty feet are resting places where the weary packer steps out of the line to rest his shoulders and catch his breath.

From a distance away it looks much like a string of tolling ants creeping up a small mound. Such scenes I never saw nor imagined, nor can I attempt to describe them. At some of the steeper places on the pass below the summit men have rigged up pulleys. Several men haul an empty sled down the hill, which sled is attached to a rope running through a pulley at the top of the hill. At the other end of the rope is a loaded sled which is hauled down [probably up].[93]

This system of pulleys rigged to haul sleds of goods up the steeper parts of the Golden Stairs may be a description of Archie Burns' surface hoist system.

Climbers were hesitant to step off the trail and stop at one of the many resting places. A climber who stepped out of the line to rest sometimes had to wait hours to get back into the line climbing up the Golden Stairs.[94] Stampeders were deadly serious about their efforts to get into the Yukon and were not about to let anyone step from these resting places back into the line of men climbing up to the summit. Each man for himself, and in some instances each woman for herself. It took from three to six hours to climb the

Golden Stairs, depending on the pace set by slower climbers.[95]

Photographs showing hundreds of men "forming a human chain" on their climb up to the summit of Chilkoot Pass are the most recognized images of the Yukon Gold Rush.[96]

An alternative trail from the Scales up to the top of Chilkoot Pass, known as the Peterson Trail, was located to the right of the Golden Stairs as one looks from the Scales northward. Some pack animals could make it up this less steep Peterson Trail, but this route was plagued with snow slides. This alternative trail was named after Peter Peterson who constructed and operated a hoist system to carry goods from the Scales to the summit. Although the exact location of the hoist system is not known, it is possible that the loaded sleds hauling goods that Odell described was the upper part of the Peterson Trail.[97] Several photographs of Chilkoot Pass show a few men and animals ascending the slope on this little used trail. Modern day hikers are directed to use the main Golden Stairs route to the left and are warned not to use the Peterson Trail, due to avalanche dangers. Karl Gurcke (a Skagway historian who works at the National Park Service in Skagway) hiked up the Peterson Trail during the summer of 1998 and noted many artifacts, including shovels, picks, and horse skeletons.[98]

Golden Stairs, Chilkoot Pass, Odell Collection.

The above photo shows the Golden Stairs up Chilkoot Pass. Note, in the foreground of the photo what appears to be a canvas collapsible boat near stacks of supplies at the bottom of the Golden Stairs in the Scales area. This may be a rare photograph of a collapsible boat at the Scales, but does not appear to be one of the hundreds of "nonpareil canvas compartment boats" found at Chilkoot Pass itself.[99] An archeologist working for the National Park Service discovered an advertising flier from the Flowers, Smith & Company describing 232 "nonpareil canvas compartment boats" and forty-nine "Chicago Sectional Metal boats."[100] Another source described these crafts as being "knockdown" boats.[101]

The Thompson Party contracted to have some of their goods taken to the summit for 3¢ a pound, although when they were ready to leave on April 9, the contractor failed to appear. On April 10, Odell hauled fifty pounds to the Scales and one hundred pounds to the summit. The partners hauled the remainder of their goods to the Scales and then up the Golden Stairs to the summit of Chilkoot Pass.

They contracted with J.J. Evans to take most of their goods to the summit for 3½¢ per pound.

Near the top of Chilkoot Pass, wood frames and canvas debris from old collapsible boats are still seen.

Looking down from the false summit, Chilkoot Pass, 1987. Lundin Collection.

Looking towards summit of Chilkoot Pass, tramway cable on right side, 1987. Lundin Collection.

Aldrich noted in an interview after returning to Ithaca, New York, in April of 1899, that because of the difficult efforts hauling goods up the Golden Stairs, many men died from over-exertion and spinal meningitis.[102] This disease rampaged throughout Skagway and along the trails to the Klondike during the spring of 1898.[103] Meningitis had hit people in Skagway and Dyea before this outbreak Aldrich described.

Coming Back Down the Golden Stairs

Odell described the trip back down the Golden Stairs.

> The funniest sight is the return trip of the packers down [from] the summit. It is too steep to walk. They sit down and slide in long grooves in the snow worn by many slides in many days. I tried it yesterday and came down like a whirlwind. It gives one a very exhilarating sensation coming

down, and quite a moist sensation after he gets down. The regular packers reinforce their garments with a piece of canvas or sealskin.[104]

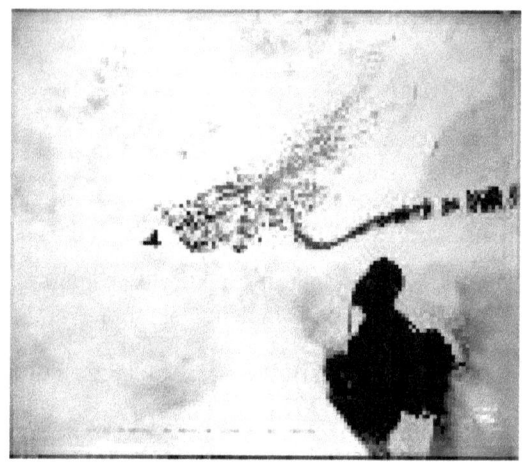

Klondikers at The Scales, descending the Chilkoot Pass, Eric A. Hegg Photographs, HEG135, University of Washington Library, Special Collections.

North-West Mounted Police

With the aid of professional packers, as well as hauling some of their own goods, it took a little more than one week to haul the Thompson Party's goods from Dyea to the summit of Chilkoot Pass.

Odell mentioned seeing "a custom officer's tent" at the summit but did not mention seeing Mounties. This was probably the Custom Brokers tent. However, the summit would have been the first location that the men encountered the NWMP.

Inspections of gear and supplies by the NWMP at the summit were perfunctory. More thorough inspections would have resulted in much crowding and suffering.[105] Duties imposed on goods purchased outside of Canada were high and ran as follows: hardware at 30-35%, provisions at 15 - 20%, tobacco at 50¢ per pound, with the average duty at 25%.[106] Another source refers to these customs duties as ranging from 25% to 30%.[107] Odell did not mention paying duties on their gear, but they must have made these payments.

Goods were cached at the summit after each trip up the Golden Stairs, later to be transported by sleds the sixteen or so miles to the southern head of Lake Bennett, passing by Crater Lake and Lake Lindeman. Poles with identifying flags were stuck into the snow at the site of each cache allowing a stampeder to find his goods once they became buried by snow. Odell's diary and letters failed to note whether the men took any precautions to guard their gear and supplies at the bottom or top of the Golden Stairs. Presumably, they relied on an unwritten honor code to keep their gear and supplies from being stolen.

Note in the photo below a goat pulling a sled. E.A. Hegg, a famous gold rush photographer, was known to have had a goat powered sled during the gold rush. No name was provided for the man with the goat-powered sled.

Summit Chilkoot Pass. Odell Collection.

Klondikers waiting in line for customs, Chilkoot Pass, Alaska, Eric A. Hegg Photographs, HEG629, University of Washington Library, Special Collections.

The NWMP, in their red serge jackets, provided general police protection throughout Canada. This law enforcement was, by far, more effective and of a much higher caliber than law enforcement provided by American authorities in the panhandle of Alaska.

Early action by the NWMP to occupy the summit of Chilkoot Pass, and the summit of White Pass out of Skagway, established the boundary between Canada and the United States along the crest of the Coast Range, rather than farther inland.

Records maintained by the Mounties reveal about 22,000 stampeders crossing Chilkoot Pass in 1898.[108]

The North-West Mounted Police force was created in 1873 to police all the North West Territories (including what became known as the Yukon Territory) and merged with the Dominion Police in 1920 creating the Royal Canadian Mounted Police (RCMP).* Commissioner Samuel Benfield Steele headed the Yukon detachment of the NWMP during the Yukon gold rush.

Storms

There were snow slides at the Scales on the night of April 12, but no one was killed. The Thompson Party's supplies were stored at the top of Chilkoot Pass while the storm blew past.

---

* "Royal Canadian Mounted Police." Wikipedia. The NWMP force was modeled after aspects of the Royal Irish Constabulary and the Northern Army during the Civil War. (Dobrowolsky, Helene. *Law of the Yukon, A History of the Mounted Police in the Yukon*. Madeira, BC, Lost Moose, 2013, revised edition, 18.)

Odell included diary entries describing the bad weather experienced by the party on some of the days they worked to haul their goods over Chilkoot Pass.

Hoglen & Wood camp at summit in storm. Odell Collection.

Hoglen & Wood Cache & Dinner of Bread & Biscuit. Odell Collection.

Chapter 5
Sledding Goods to Lindeman and Bennett

After reaching the Chilkoot Trail summit, stampeders hauled their supplies on sleds northward to either Lake Lindeman or, past Lake Lindeman, to Lake Bennett. The prospectors set up camps on the shoreline of either lake and constructed boats that they would use to sail northward down the Yukon River to the fabled Yukon gold fields.

"Awaiting turn to coast down from summit." Odell Collection.

Hoglen & Wood Caravan to haul goods to Lake Lindeman. Odell Collection.

The Two Lakes

The most populated communities on the two lakes were located at the southern ends of the lakes. Campsites spread northward along both shorelines of the lakes. Encampments were described as "tent cities" as well as cities or towns. Bennett City was somewhat more populated with an estimated maximum population varying between 10,000 and 30,000.[109] Poor sanitary conditions were a major problem.

Stampeders camped in tents, but more formal hotels, restaurants, commercial shipping yards, and other businesses also massed along the shores of Lake Lindeman and Lake Bennett. Budding entrepreneurs sought to serve the needs of the stampeders. Once the boats were built, the crews waited for the ice to melt before launching their boats.

First view of Lindeman. Odell Collection.

Bluff across Lake Lindeman. Odell Collection.

View looking up Lindeman. Odell Collection.

Boat at "Barto & Walters camp, Lake Lindeman." Odell Collection.

Boat at "Morgan & Williams camp, Lake Lindeman." Odell Collection.

Hoglen/Wood boat clearing Lake Lindeman. Odell Collection.

Most prospectors opted to camp and construct their boats on the southern end of Lake Bennett. As a result, they avoided the task of lowering their boats down a short and treacherous set of rapids connecting the two lakes. Some boats were destroyed while being lowered or floated down this passageway. The high water from the spring runoff lessened the danger of these rapids.[110]

The short rapids between the two lakes were known by different names – One Mile Rapids, King Rapids, and the Bell River.[111] Frederick Augusta Schwatka, a United States military officer who made several expeditions into the Yukon, built his raft on Lake Lindeman during his first expedition in 1883 and lowered the raft down the passageway to Lake

Bennett before sailing down the Yukon River to its mouth.¹¹²

Rapids between the two lakes. Odell Collection.

The large tent-city at Lake Bennett

encircled the lake in a white cloud: the bell tents and the pup tents, the square tents and the round tents, the dog tents and the Army tents, the tiny canvas lean-tos and the huge circus marquees, some of them brand-new, and some soiled, patched, and tattered by the winter storms. There were tents for hot baths and tents for haircuts, tents for mining agents and tents for real-estate men; there were tent hotels, tent saloons, tent cafes, tent bakeries, tent post-offices, tent casinos, and tent chapels. In between the tents was heaped the familiar paraphernalia of the stampede: sleds stacked vertically against mounds of supplies; crates of food and tinned goods; furniture, sheet-iron stoves, mining equipment, and tethered animals – oxen, pigs, goats and chickens. And everywhere, occupying every flat place along the beach, sandwiched between the tents and the shacks and the supplies, were half-built boats and mounting piles of logs and lumber.[113]

Looking northward down Lake Bennett. Odell Collection.

View at Lake Bennett. Odell Collection.

Although the hike from the summit to Lake Bennett was about the same distance and much less strenuous than the trek from Dyea to the summit, the Thompson Party took more than one month to drag sled loads of their outfits to Lake Bennett. The men were exhausted and sick the whole time. Welcome to the travails of reaching the Yukon goldfields. Hoglen and Wood, who would later join Odell and Aldrich in prospecting for gold out of Fort Selkirk, located their main camp and boatyard on the shores of Lake Lindeman and had to lower their boat down the rapids into Lake Bennett.

Hauling Goods to Lake Lindeman

The first task for the Thompson Party was to transport their supplies by sled from the summit of Chilkoot Pass to Lake Lindeman once the supplies had been hauled up the Golden Stairs and stored at the summit. Odell made no reference of passing through Canadian Customs on the summit, although the Party clearly passed through Customs on its way down the Yukon River. On April 16, the Thompson Party pitched their tents on the eastern shore of Lake Lindeman, two miles north of the town of Lindeman, and remained there until May 10. Initially, the men slept on balsam fir boughs brought down from the mountains, but they later "made bunks by stretching sled canvasses on frames."

Each day, the men rose very early, from 1:00 to 3:45 a.m., and started sledding their supplies from the summit to Lake Lindeman. They pulled their sleds over land as well as over frozen creeks and small lakes. At times, due to bad weather, they had to leave their supplies at Crater Lake, located between the Chilkoot Pass and Lake Lindeman, and hike back to their camp.

Odell described their efforts.

> Sheep Camp, you remember is about five miles on the other side of the summit, i.e. the ocean side. When we got our goods on the summit we broke camp and came over to Linderman, twelve miles, there being no place to camp between, no timber, nothing but mountains and snow. Then we came two miles down the lake to find a suitable camping spot. The timber is very sparse in this country, growing only in patches.
>
> It was an awful job to get our goods from the summit here [their camp at Lake Lindeman]. You see we had to walk fourteen miles back there, then load up our sleds and haul them back the fourteen miles, which were mighty long and hard ones before we got there. Some days when it would be pleasant here at the Lake we would find a nasty, bad storm after we traveled five miles and gotten up on the plateau among the clouds, storms that no one had any business to be out in. Other days the sun shone so hot that we had to work in our shirt sleeves and nearly swelter. On one of these hot days, the thermometer was only six degrees above

zero when we started at four o'clock in the morning. The morning before it was down to zero when we got up. You see the sun is up a long time here now – it gets dark about 9:30 and daylight at 3:30. A month later there will be no night at all to speak of.

We have all been having a run of the meanest, nastiest, darndest, most disagreeable, most weakening colds that ever was struck. It attacks a man in every vulnerable spot. I weighed 184 pounds when I was over in Sheep Camp. Last Sunday I weighed 170 and would tire out after a nine-mile walk, with no sled. We are all getting around now so we can work again.[114]

Often the weather was horrible. Some days it rained all day. Snow slides occurred at the Scales. The men stayed one night at the Hotel Lindeman at a cost of $1 per meal and 50¢ per bed, which included blankets.

Odell described very hard work sledding their five tons of supplies from the summit down to their camp at Lake Lindeman. He noted that he had a cold making him "as weak as a rag" and felt more like "a pack horse or drought mule than a man of letters."[115]

The other men in the party also got sick, but they continued moving their supplies from the summit to their temporary camp on Lindeman.

Odell wrote home.

> I suppose that there at home flowers are in blossom and leaves are out, and everything is lovely. Here it froze last night quite hard. The ice is between two and three feet thick on the lakes yet, and the snow is still all over the ground, although for the last week or more it has been going rapidly. But there was lots to go. We put up our tent on four feet of snow when we came, and are on about two feet of it yet. When we went back on the mountain for wood we would drop in up to the waist every little while.[116]

He complained about the Canadian postal service and not receiving any letters from home.[*]

Odell and Aldrich kept abreast of outside news from reading newspapers and listening to the constant gossip and tales. They bought newspapers with stories about the war with Spain that had started on April 21, 1898. Odell wrote to his father about the war with Spain.

> I suppose the seat of war is not yet located at Baldwinsville. We do know that war is declared. We pay 25¢ for a two weeks old Seattle paper and devour the *news* with avidity. It seems very strange to think of the United States being at war. I suppose it drives everything else out of people's

---

[*] The postal service is discussed in Appendix B.

> minds. I would give a good deal for a morning paper myself to know the state of affairs, but would give more for a letter from Baldwinsville.[117]

Although this is difficult to believe, it is claimed that newspapers sold for as much as $50 a copy when they finally reached Dawson City on June 8.[118]

Odell noted meeting fellow collegians from the University of Michigan and Columbia.

Move to Lake Bennett

As the next step, the men began to move their goods from Lake Lindeman to Lake Bennett where they would construct their boats.

Odell hired freighters to haul the Thompson Party's goods down to the foot of the canyon separating Lake Lindeman from Lake Bennett, paying 1½¢ per pound. On May 6, three of the men took 1,500 pounds of their supplies from the head of the lake down to their new camp at Lake Bennett. Odell wrote to his father on May 6 that they will move their goods over the ice to the foot of Lake Lindeman, pack their goods on their backs about one mile to Lake Bennett, and then sled their gear down Lake Bennett to a suitable campsite with timber near the shore for building boats.[119]

They hauled 3,200 pounds to Bennett on May 7. On May 10, 1898, the men broke their camp at Lake Lindeman, intending to move to their new campsite at Lake Bennett, but they only could make it to the northern end of Lake Lindeman where they pitched their tent and hired a freighter to haul some of their supplies to the new campsite at Lake Bennett. They hauled over a ton of supplies to their camp on May 12 and an additional 2,500 pounds on May 13.

View of Bennett City, May 30, 1898, Yukon Archives, Print No. 2455, E.A. Hegg Collection

A main issue facing stampeders was finding suitable campsites to construct their boats. Prime sites had been taken by early arriving stampeders. Chilkoot Pass, and areas immediately north of the summit, are barren with few or no trees. Gradually, more and more trees are found as one approaches Lake Lindeman. Trees become sparser at the north end of both Lake Lindeman and around Lake Bennett. Spruce, hemlock, and balsam fir predominated.[120]

Stampeders sought campsites with flat ground near the shoreline where logs would be whipsawed into timber, and a boat could be built and launched. Close access to timber stands was also considered.

On May 14, the men set up their new camp on Lake Bennett. Mr. Thompson raised an American flag. Odell heard some good male singing voices in a nearby tent. He wrote to his father describing his increasing cooking skills: "I wish you had been here this noon to eat some of my warm Johnny cake with a little bacon gravy on it. If you were here I would make up a batch of biscuits for supper."[121]

They socialized in the evenings, singing with others. Spring was coming. The men were upbeat.

"Salvation Army meeting at Lake Bennett, 9 p.m." Odell Collection.

Odell mentioned more serious duties when he helped bury Harry Bluth from Victoria, who was found dead on his sled on the lake. He did not mention who Bluth was.

He noted seeing quite a display of *Aurora Borealis* in the evening and bluebirds during the day. Seemingly, all was going well for the five men of the Thompson Party.

Breakup of Thompson Party

It was like a horse-kick to the gut. At their campsite on Lake Bennett, Odell experienced the ultimate insult. It struck like a tsunami – **Ford got drunk**. Presumably, "Ford" in George F. Trowbridge and Odell referred to him by his middle name. Odell was faced with a troubling decision whether to stay with the Thompson Party. Drunkenness in a partner was the last straw for Odell.*

Five days after the incident, Odell and Aldrich decided to "cut loose" from the Thompson Party, but it took three days of tense negotiations before an agreement was made on a fair distribution of the goods between the two groups. A contract was signed

---

* The breakup of partnerships and destruction of friendships along the route into the Yukon gold fields were quite common, although normally the splits arose over frustration from the hard work experienced by the stampeders including most commonly over disputes arising in the sawpits where green lumber was cut to make planks for the home-made boats that would be sailed down the Yukon River. (Berton, 271.)

by each of the men agreeing to the distribution. On June 3, Aldrich hiked up to Thompson's camp and finished the work of dividing up their supplies. Then, on June 12, Odell paddled a canvas petrel up to the Thompson camp and paid $9.15 for some food.

In a later letter written to his father, Odell merely wrote that "Aldrich and I separated from the other party about a month ago."[122] In another letter, Aldrich described the breakup in a little more detail.

> I am tempted to write you in full of the experiences of this summer, but I know that I could not hope to finish the letter inside of a month, so I shall relate only the more striking and interesting portions and give but a brief description of them. Before ice left the lakes we succeeded in getting our outfits to a point about three miles below the head of Lake Bennett. While camping there, Odell and I decided that it would be to our interest and ultimate happiness to cut loose from the party which we had joined, so we started to paddle our own canoes.[123]

No reason to grouse. Odell and Aldrich had to focus on getting to the Yukon goldfields. Apart from receiving a letter from Mr. Thompson several months later, this was the last contact between Odell and what remained of the Thompson Party.

Odell and Aldrich were at a loss what to do. This was the first major bout of indecision. Perhaps they would buy a boat for themselves or build a boat for the sail northward down the Yukon River?

Chapter 6

Constructing Their Boat from Scratch

Odell and Aldrich purchased plans to construct a boat. The men would build their boat from scratch and sail northward down the waterway leading to the Yukon River.

Like most other stampeders, Odell and Aldrich had little experience with boating other than Odell rowing on the Cornell crew team. His rowing experience in a shell would not prepare the men for passing through the turbulent whitewater rapids they would encounter on the Yukon River leading northward into the Yukon gold fields.

Whipsawing Logs

Odell and Aldrich worked as "tail end men" or "chopping blocks" whipsawing green trees into lumber for their boat at Stanley's Mill on Lake Bennett. They had met Stanley on board the steamer *Al-Ki* sailing up the Inside Passage. The mill was four miles from their camp, so they arose at 4 a.m., and cooked and ate breakfast before walking on a path along the lake shore over immense rocks and boulders.

Aldrich described their efforts.

> ... [W]e were confronted with the task of getting lumber for our boat. The timber on the lakes has been pretty well culled out, and we had serious doubts as to our ability to get enough for our craft. However, we made an arrangement with a sawmill man [Stanley], whom we had met on our trip up the coast, whereby we were to work in his mill for lumber. Lumber, by the way, sold from 15 to 25 cents a foot, and some 300 odd [square] feet were necessary for our craft.
>
> "The mill was located about four miles from our camp. The hours were from 7 [a.m.] until 6 [p.m.] and you may imagine that it was an awful case of hustle for us to cook breakfast, eat and walk four miles by 7 o'clock each morning. We used to rise at 4, thereby managing to get to work about ten minutes before the whistle blew. During that time we used to do some tall resting. The four mile walk was the hardest trip I ever had. Our path lay along the shore of the lake, over immense rocks and bowlders. I used to feel that I had done a day's work before our labor began. I had the pleasure of receiving the lumber as it came from the saw and of pitching it across the carriage. Each night

I would find me covered with sawdust. My, but those days seemed long. I felt that I could not stand the walk back to camp, but we grinned and bare[d] it [and] walked home each evening, cooked our supper, smoked and went to bed.

This lasted for a week, at the end of which time Stanley, the mill man, offered to give us as much lumber as we might need.[124]

Odell echoed these sentiments in his diary.

Sawing planks was horrible, distasteful work. Odell described these labors with his typical understatement - "Considerable difficulty and some profanity." Tales of partners breaking up while whipsawing timber were common. Woe be it to the man in the sawpit pulling a whipsaw downward.

Whipsawing logs, Hoglen/Wood boatyard. Walt Hoglen is probably at the top. Odell Collection.

Before sawing could begin, trees were felled, branches were removed and bark was peeled, logs were cut into proper lengths, and the logs were dragged or rolled up to a whipsaw platform. Skids leaned from the ground up against the top of the platform, functioning as a ramp for logs to be rolled or pulled up by ropes to the top of the assembly for sawing. Frequently, a sawpit was dug under the sawing platform, shortening the distance a log had to be rolled or pulled up to the top of the platform. Once on top of the platform, the log was secured or wedged into place before the sawing process began.

Two men would whipsaw the green timber into lumber using a six-foot long, coarse-toothed whipsaw with a handle at each end. A plumb bob and chalk line were used to mark a vertical saw line on the end of the log to guide the cutting one-inch-thick boards that were nine to ten-inches-wide.[125]

The man standing on the top of the platform held the upper handle and guided the saw as the man on the bottom in the saw pit grabbed the lower handle and pulled the saw downward. Cuts were only made on the downward stroke. Sawdust showered down on the man in the pit with each downward stroke of the whipsaw. Then, the man on the top pulled the saw upward, while the man in the pit pushed the saw upward. The process was repeated over and over. Wedges were inserted in the cut end as a log was whipsawed. The green timber was normally cut in varying lengths, depending on the length of the boat that was to be constructed.

Mills to whipsaw logs "were called 'arm-strong' mills and worked efficiently if tempers did not grow too short."[126]

As an alternative, a stampeder could purchase a boat constructed at a mill on Lake Bennett at prices ranging from $250 to $600.[127]

Breakup of Ice and Immediate Surge of Boats

Ice on the lake was breaking up and many stampeders sailed northward on their boats into the Yukon gold fields.* On May 23, Odell mentioned that wind from the prior day removed the ice from just above Stanley's mill. He noted on May 28 that heavy winds finally blew the ice off Lake Bennett. A flotilla of boats left on the first day the ice cleared. Eager prospectors launched their boats by the hundreds on

---

* Although the annual spring breakup of ice on the Yukon River was a riveting spectacle that had been witnessed by First Nation peoples for centuries, the first recorded breakup of ice on the Yukon River occurred in 1896 at Forty Mile, below what became Dawson City. Michael Gates, "History Hunter: When was the first recorded river break-up?," *Yukon News*. Whitehorse, YT, Canada. April 11, 2019. See, also "The Dawson City ice guessing pool goes back to Gold Rush days, Breakup also used to be how Dawson got rid of its sewage and trash, which is gross." *Yukon News*. Whitehorse, YT, Canada. May 3, 2018. The word "Tagish" in the Tagish language refers to the spring breakup of river ice.

Lake Lindeman and Lake Bennett sailing northward down the Yukon waterway to the goldfields.

A total of 7,124 boats set sail within the first two days of the ice breaking up. At first, the boats bunched up together. Gradually the boats spread out racing towards the northern gold fields. Within a week, boats holding about 30,000 stampeders were strung out along the sixty miles from Lake Lindeman to Lake Tagish. A small contingent of about 150 boats led the way immediately behind the mass of melting ice as it floated northward.

Ice jammed up the Yukon River at the mouth of the Pelly River, slightly upstream from Fort Selkirk. The lead boats had to wait for the ice to break up. Once the ice began moving again, the lead boats followed racing towards Dawson City. Boats began arriving at Dawson City on June 8.[128]

The Mounties calculated that more than 28,000 people passed the Tagish Post in 1898, with 23,000 arriving at Dawson City and the remaining 5,000 stopping to prospect on tributaries of the Yukon south of Dawson City.[129]

Odell and Aldrich were frantic – they had not started constructing their boat while most of the argonauts had already set sail northward.

Neither man wrote about the haunting sound of the ice breaking up on Lake Bennett. This is surprising, given the loud and eerie ice cracking sounds that were heard for weeks. However, these sounds were familiar to Odell, as he was raised on his father's farm in upstate New York near the Seneca River and had heard these sounds every spring.

Since at least 1900, Dawson City residents have celebrated the annual spring breakup of the ice on the Yukon River.[130]

Bennett City in 1987, remnants of wharf pilings visible at lower end of photo. Lundin Collection.

Enticing view down Lake Bennett in 1987. Lundin Collection.

Odell also failed to describe the enticing view looking northward down Lake Bennett. Modern photos reveal this enchanting view which, when added to the lure of gold and fortune for the stampeders, must have resembled the Sirens beckoning Odysseus. The stampeders were enticed to go farther and farther northward into the Yukon gold fields. Perhaps feelings of despair over not even having started to construct their boat, and thoughts of the backbreaking efforts involved in this task, had dulled Odell's senses. His normal upbeat nature had begun to change.

Constructing Their Boat

The Thompson Party had hoped to complete constructing their boats by June 1, but these hopes no longer applied to Odell and Aldrich.

View of Hoglen/Wood camp & boatyard, Lake Lindeman. Odell Collection.

View from Hoglen/Wood camp, Lake Lindeman. Odell Collection.

View from Hoglen/Wood boat yard on Lake Lindeman, Odell Collection.

On May 30, Odell and Aldrich built their new camp site using a log foundation left by others. They constructed bunks, shelves, and a floor. Their camp was located some three miles north of the head of Lake Bennett.¹³¹ They started building their boat on May 31. Although the prior and following photos from the Odell Collection were from Lake Lindeman, they are representative of the scene on Lake Bennett.

Walt Hoglen at Lake Lindeman Camp. Odell Collection.

Aldrich wrote that "[a]fter considerable difficulty and labor, we succeeded in building a craft that would float, but whose sailing qualities did not warrant us in entering her in any prize contests."¹³² Odell noted that "[w]e worked a week in a saw mill to buy our boat lumber. Then built our boat ourselves, which carries our ton and a half of goods in good shape."¹³³

They purchased tools for their boat building endeavor. Odell noted, prices in his diary without using dollar or cent signs – "saw 2.50, hammer 1.25, chisel .25, knives & forks & wire .60, pails 1.75, pan .50, brace 1.25, bits 1.00 - .25, shears 1.00, mirror 1.00, thread."

Boats being built on Lake Bennett, Asahel Curtis Collection, CUR1720, University of Washington Library, Special Collections.

Boat building at Bennett. Eric Hegg Photographs, HEG159, University of Washington Library, Special Collections.

Day by day, Odell noted the methodical steps taken to construct their boat and sailing equipment. They hewed out the prow, made a stem, beveled out ribs, framed the boat's ribs, re-braced the frame to give the boat more slant, made a stern frame, and installed the bottom boards and side boards "with considerable difficulty and some profanity." They rolled oakum and caulked between the boards with tree pitch. They cut small trees and fashioned the poles into oars and push poles. They applied pitch over the oakum and installed a false bottom, oar locks and guard strips on the outside of the boat. They made a mast, sewed sails, made a steering oar, and built a pump. On June 22, they had finished constructing their boat, almost one month after boats left Bennett for the Klondike.

Two people were necessary to operate a boat like theirs, one steering and the other managing the sail.[134] When the current was swift, they let the boat drift. Other times one would row while the other steered. Sufficient freeboard was necessary to accommodate the weight of the men with their outfits to avoid swamping the boat in the rough water that lay ahead.

Chapter 7

Voyage from Lake Bennett to Fort Selkirk

At long last, Odell and Aldrich were on their way down the Yukon River to the fabled goldfields. The men were upbeat.

> We do not know just to what point we are going, perhaps to Dawson, perhaps closer on down to American Territory in far Alaska. We shall stop along at different places along Yukon river, see what we can see, hear what we can hear and get what we can get. We may try to go up the Stewart river, as we planned when with the other [Thompson] party.[135]

Neither Odell nor Aldrich noted a dominant feature along the inland water route.

> From the time that the rush of boats to Dawson commenced from Bennett, through the carelessness and willful neglect of individuals, nearly every mile

of timber on the Yukon River was in flames.[136]

Perhaps smoldering ashes were all that remained when Odell and Aldrich journeyed down the Yukon River system. They were too focused sailing to mention the remains of wildfires. In his account traveling down the Yukon water way in 1883, Fredrick Schwatka mentioned seeing evidence of wildfires along the shoreline.[137] As with other aquanauts, the men had little concern about the environment they were passing through. They were here to find gold, with little or no care about anything else.

Sailing from Lake Bennett to Lake Tagish

After leaving the southern end of Lake Bennett, Odell and Aldrich encountered a string of lakes closely connected by short channels -- Lake Bennett, Lake Nares, Lake Tagish, and finally Lake Marsh. They would pass from British Columbia into Yukon Territory midway down Lake Bennett.

Dangerous rapids were found on the Yukon River between Lake Marsh and the confluence of the Pelly and Yukon Rivers near Fort Selkirk. After the last of these rapids (Rink Rapids) the Yukon River is relatively free of dangerous areas as it flows to Dawson City.

Odell proudly hung his Cornell pennant from the top of the mast. The Big Red (as Cornell is known) pennant was "fluttering gaily in the Northern winds."[138] The proud Ivy Leaguers were announcing their status as they sailed northward. Their spirits were on the rise.

The men left their campsite at the southern end of Lake Bennett on the afternoon of June 23. They sailed and rowed northward, nearly reaching the foot or northern end of the lake where they were becalmed, tied up to the shore, and slept in their boat. Then they sailed across Cariboo Crossing (now called Carcross) and Lake Nares. The wind failed again, so they tied up to the shore and slept, and ran into a fellow named Stevens, and his two partners, whom they had met onboard the *S.S. Al-Ki*. They learned that a man named McFadden and his partner, who had also sailed with them on board the *S.S. Al-Ki*, had died at Sheep Camp.

A severe thunderstorm and dangerous conditions greeted them at the aptly named Windy Arm on Lake Tagish. They beached their boat on the left shore, unloaded, and waited for calm weather. Aldrich described the situation.

> Where the wind sweeps down with terrific velocity. With the wind sweeping out of that arm and the clouds hanging low over the mountains, one could easily imagine the Valley of Death. We started across at a great clip, hoping to 'make the ripple,' but the waves soon bounced us about like a cork and we saw that we would have to make for the shore directly opposite. The wind drove us on strongly

and much to our horror we struck on rocks, where we had hoped to find a sandy beach and before we could do anything, the boat was half full of water from the waves, which washed over the stern and wet our outfit. We completed the misfortune by getting soaked, while taking our 2,500 pounds of stuff ashore. All this occurred about 4 a.m.

After getting into dry clothes, which we donned in the bushes, the warmest place we could find, we started around the cove in which we found ourselves until we came upon a fellow reading in a little boat by a sheltered spot. He proved to be a Yale '96 man and was then occupied in reading Cicero, while he sat out his watch from 12 to 1. His name was Wood, a son of General T.J. Wood of Ohio. Wood and his partner had been waiting three days for the gale to abate.[139]

The man standing watch was Thomas J. Wood, Jr., of Dayton, Ohio. His father, Thomas J. Wood, Sr., was a retired United States Major General who served in the Civil War.* Odell noted in his diary that Tom

---

* Wood commanded a division in the Army of the Ohio and then another division in the Army of the Cumberland. He fought in the Battle of Shiloh, was wounded in the Battle of Murfreesboro, fought in the Battle of Chickamauga, fought at the Mission Ridge assault, fought at the Battle of Lovejoy's Station where he was badly wounded, and fought at the Battle of Nashville. He was promoted to the rank of major general.

Wood Jr. was a member of Yale College, Class of 1896. However, Wood only attended a few terms at Yale.[140] He would have graduated as a member of the class of 1896, had he matriculated following a normal four-year schedule. Tom Wood would soon become an important part of Odell and Aldrich's quest for gold.

Thomas J. Wood, Jr. Odell Collection.

After a wait, Odell and Aldrich set sail again. The weather was still blustery after they rowed down to Taku Arm, so they camped. After resting, they crossed Taku Arm, but were stopped by a head wind

---

Wood retired from the service after the Civil War but did not pursue another career. Either Wood or his wife apparently had sufficient wealth to support the family. This included paying the expenses of his son Tom Wood, Jr. attending Yale College for at least one year. ("Thomas J. Wood," Wikipedia; & "Thomas John Wood, American History Central.)

and thunder storm, so they camped to wait out the foul weather.

Registering Their Boat

Odell and Aldrich continued sailing down the Yukon River and stopped at the Tagish NWMP Post where their boat was registered as boat No. 14,039.

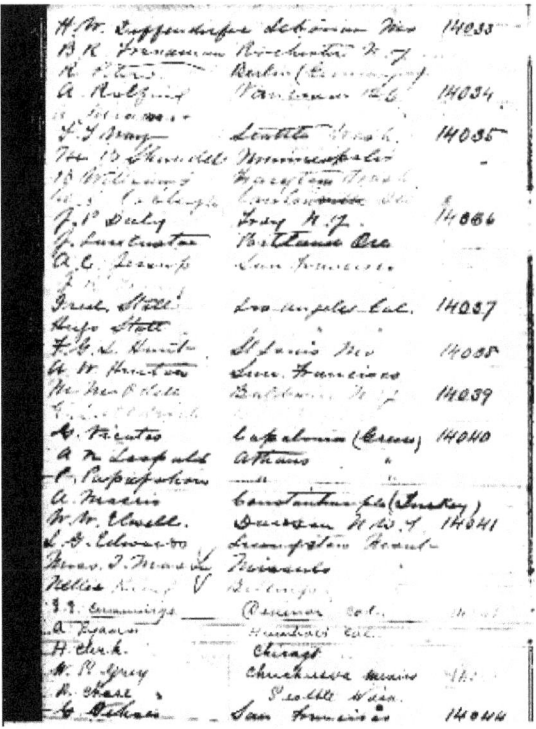

Boat registration records, June 28, 1898, Tagish NWMP post, Yukon Archives. M.M. Odell and E. Aldrich boat No. 14,039 in middle of page.

The men failed to make note of it, but their boat and all other boats were subject to inspection for tobacco and alcohol, presumably to determine if the required duty on these products had been paid. Odell mailed a letter to their backer, Mr. Smith.

The Tagish NWMP post was a major stopping point for stampeders. Boats that were not registered by the NWMP at Lake Bennett were required to register at the Tagish Post. John Godson, under orders of Colonel Steele of the NWMP, registered 2,344 handmade boats and barges at Lake Bennett, starting with boat number 1. NWMP Inspector D'Arcy E. Strickland was ordered to assign numbers to unregistered boats and barges as they stopped for inspection at the Tagish Post. Not knowing how many boats had been registered at Bennett, Strickland started registration with number 10,000. He registered an additional 4,736 boats. A total of 7,080 boats and barges were registered at both locations, with about 28,000 passengers.[141]

Odell received his first letter from home at the Tagish Post and mailed a letter to his father informing him that

> [w]e do not know just to what point we are going, perhaps to Dawson, perhaps closer on down to American Territory in far Alaska. We shall stop along at different places along Yukon river, see what we can see, hear what we can hear and get what we can get. We may try to go up the Stewart river, as we planned when with the other [Thompson] party. We have a good wind to sail by, the first in

five days, so I shall make this letter short. We will eat a cold lunch of bread, biscuit, flap-jacks and coffee and start on down March Lake [*sic* Lake Marsh], perhaps reaching Miles Canon at supper time. Do not worry any about Miles Canon and White Horse Rapids. There have been many accidents there this spring, but there are a lot of reckless, crazy idiots going down the trip. We shall probably pack our goods around and rope our boat down to run no risks.[142]

After setting sail again, Odell and Aldrich ran into their new acquaintance Tom Wood and met his partner Walter J. Hoglen.* Hoglen would soon become an important part of Odell and Aldrich's quest for gold. The Hoglen and Wood boat was registered as boat No. 13,997 at the Tagish Post.[143]

---

* Walter J. Hoglen's Yukon diary was included in Mark Odell's collection. The diary includes less than ten entries. The first entry, dated February 24, 1898, stated "Started for Alaska from Dayton O. 6:30 P.M. in company with Tom Wood & Bill Owens. Reached Chicago." Then, the Hoglen/Wood/Owens party took a train to Puget Sound passing through Edmonton, Alberta. They sailed on the Steamship *Lakme* from Seattle up the Inside Passage to Skagway before crossing into Canada over the Chilkoot Pass. Odell never mentioned Bill Owens in his diary and letters sent home. NWMP records show a "Owens, W" from Dayton, Ohio, with a boat registration no. 13,705. Presumably, Bill Owens had broken away from the Hoglen/Wood party.

This boat registration number was 42 lower than the Odell/Aldrich boat registration number.

Walter J. Hoglen, Dayton, Ohio, Odell Collection.

Tagish NWMP station, Odell Collection.

Joining with Walt Hoglen & Tom Wood

After Odell and Aldrich met Tom Wood's partner Walt Hoglen, it becomes increasingly clear from Odell's diary that the two groups of men sailed down the Yukon River together, although Odell did not specifically note the joining of the two groups. They sailed northward and camped together several nights in a row. Odell mailed this letter home on July 2.

> But just think, my boy, of five lake trout weighing over sixty pounds, and one of them over twenty and longer than your leg, with meat a delicate brownish pink, which melts in your mouth, and free from bones. Along here people are catching grayling trout on flies, but we have not tried it yet. Our **traveling companions** [emphasis added], a couple of fellows about our own age from Dayton, Ohio, whom we ran across the day I mailed the letter to you at Tagish and received your letter, caught these trout trolling. I presume we four will keep along together now. One of them is a Yale '96 man.[144]

Odell was upbeat, but still did not indicate in his diary their destination as they sailed northward into the Yukon gold fields. Potential prospecting sites included the fabled Klondike region near Dawson City, other sites along the Yukon River south of

Dawson City, or even further down the Yukon River into Alaska.

One Night's Troll, Lake Tagish, Odell Collection.

Miles Canyon

The men soon confronted a major physical barrier – Miles Canyon and two immediately following rapids, the somewhat dangerous Squaw Rapids shortly followed by the extremely treacherous White Horse Rapids. This was the second major physical barrier they faced and, by far, the most dangerous part of the sail northward down the Yukon River. The dreaded White Horse Rapids were named after "the foam upon them [which] resembled white steeds leaping and dancing in the sunlight."[145]

After about 200 boats were lost in one week attempting to pass through Miles Canyon and the White Horse Rapids in May of 1898, NWMP Superintendent Sam Steele ordered that an experience pilot had to guide each boat passing through Miles Canyon.[146] The famous author Jack London made his living for a while acting as one of these river pilots. Boats were lightened to increase their freeboard by removing goods. The goods were transported on the tramway around the three obstacles.

"Waiting for Pilot to Shoot the Miles Canyon & Whitehorse Rapids," Yukon Archives Print No. 1996, Vancouver Public Library.

View of the head of Miles Canyon on the Yukon River, Yukon Territory, 1898. Eric A. Hegg Photographs, HEG635, University of Washington Library, Special Collections.

Miles Canyon on the Yukon River, Eric A. Hegg Photographs, HEG097, University of Washington Library, Special Collections.

Pilots charged $25 or more to guide crafts through the White Hores Rapids, the northern most of these two rapids. Some stampeders tied their boats with ropes and let the boats drift through the rapids. P.B. Anderson and a seaman named Grant, who had accompanied the famous Yukon photographer Eric Hegg, also worked as pilots taking boats through Squaw Rapids and White Horse Rapids. [147]

Norman Macaulay, one of the many innovative Yukon entrepreneurs, built and operated a narrow gauge, hewed pole track, tramway line running some three miles along the sides of Miles Canyon, Squaw Rapids and White Horse Rapids. Horses pulled the improvised rail cars of goods over wood tracks. Some photographs show two parallel sets of tracks with rail cars running in different directions.

Macaulay's Tramway, Eric A. Hegg Photographs, H EG557, University of Washington Library, Special Collections.

The tramway ran from the foot of Miles Canyon, at Canyon City, on the eastern or right side of the Yukon River past White Horse Rapids. This Canadian Canyon City should not be confused with the Canyon City on the Alaskan side of the trail to Chilkoot Pass. The Canyon and White Horse Rapids Tramway opened in June of 1898, having taken only twenty-one days to be completed by eighteen workers.[148] Work began almost immediately after Superintendent Steele ordered the use of pilots to guide boats through the dangerous waters. Prior to the construction of the tramway, Macaulay operated a roadhouse at Canyon City, which he built in the fall of 1897 after leaving Dyea.[149]

An advertisement for the White Horse Rapids Tramway lists P.G. Shallcross, of the Chilcoot Trading Company, as the main contact for the tramway. Macaulay and Shallcross operated several business enterprises, including a hotel in Dyea.[150] Shallcross operated the Sunset Telephone Company, with telephone lines running from Dyea to Bennett.[151] Macaulay operated a bunkhouse at Lake Marsh, which Odell later described as "a bum bunkhouse".[152]

The tramway followed an ancient First Nation portage trail on the eastern side of Miles Canyon, Squaw Rapids, and White Horse Rapids. Archeological evidence found at Canyon City indicates that a First Nation campsite existed there some 2,500 years earlier. In 1883, early prospectors constructed windlasses and log "roll-ways" to aid their portage around the treacherous waters.[153]

William Ogilvie reported that, in 1887, miners hauled their boats on the western side, or opposite side from the later Macaulay tramway. The miners laid wooden rails in places and used windlasses to haul their boats.[154] By the late summer of 1898, John Hepburn constructed a rival tramway line running on the western side of the river through the canyon and past the rapids, presumably following the old rollway trail. His tramway also had wood rails with horses pulling carts of goods.[155] In June of 1899, Macaulay purchased the rival tramway for a reported $60,000 and operated both lines for a while.[156]

Macaulay charged 5¢ a pound for hauling goods on the tramway around Miles Canyon and the rapids.[157]

As the Yukon River flows northward, the riverbanks deepen and the river narrows to about one hundred fifty feet in width.[158] Just before Miles Canyon, the river widens with a bay on the eastern side and the high riverbank on that side suddenly drops close to the river level. Canyon City was located there and included a NWMP encampment, a hotel of sorts, and the headquarters of the rail tramway company.

The four men inspected the dangerous river. In letters home, Odell made two references to the danger of Miles Canyon and the White Horse Rapids.[159]

After mooring their boats at Canyon City, they hiked northward along the tramway route to the foot or northern end of White Horse Rapids. They decided that they would lighten each of their boats by 400 pounds, haul their goods around Miles Canyon, Squaw Rapids, and White Horse Rapids, and hire a pilot to take their two boats through these treacherous waters. Odell noted in his diary that the men camped at the southern end of Miles Canyon, presumably at or near Canyon City.

> Hired one Smith to pilot our boat to foot [or northern end] of [White Horse] rapids, other boat following to head [or southern end] of rapids, he returning to pilot theirs [the Hoglen/Wood boat] thru rapids. They stuck on Squaw Rapids finally off no damage. Lightened both boats at head of [the White Horse] rapids. Camped at foot of rapids. Tom [Wood] & I went up to head of canon for their

sleeping bags. Heard of Cornell's [crew] victory over Yale and Harvard.[160]

Boat Going Through Miles Canyon. Odell Collection

Boat Going Through Squaw Rapids. Odell Collection.

Shooting the Whitehorse Rapids. Asahel Curtis Collection CUR1435, University of Washington Library Special Collections.

Odell described the passage through the treacherous waters of Miles Canyon and White Horse Rapids in a letter he sent to his father.

> We shot the Canon - Miles Canon - and White Horse Rapids all safely yesterday afternoon and feel mightily relieved for they are nasty places, with the water going like hades at high water mark, so to speak. We lightened our boat some to do it, packing 400 pounds four miles and a half, and 800 pounds about half a mile.
>
> The mosquitoes are something terrible here at times. So bad that a person will stand in a choking, blinding smoke trying to eat his meals and cussing between mouthfuls and alternately rubbing the tears and cinders out of his eyes and scratching his bites....

Near us is a camp of men who are feasting on moose and bear meat. We may take day off and go back from the river a few miles and try it ourselves in a day or so.[161]

End, White Horse Rapids, Odell Collection.

Odell's diary and letters failed to mention the original White Horse town site at the northern end of the Macaulay tramway. This tent village was located on the eastern side of the river. The White Pass and Yukon Route company laid out a small community on this site below the White Horse rapids in the fall of 1899, and called the community Closeleigh. When the railroad arrived in 1900, the small village mostly moved to the western side of the river and the name of the village was changed to a single word -- Whitehorse.[162] Eventually, the small settlement become the largest city in Yukon Territory and replaced Dawson City as the territorial capital. Presumably, Odell felt the small White Horse encampment was too insignificant to mention after the men had faced the dangers of Miles Canyon and White Horse Rapids. This is an interestng fact to note.

After the pilot guided their boats through these dangerous waters, Wood, Hoglen and Odell hiked up to the head of Miles Canyon to retrieve their sleds and ferried the sleds down the river on a scow. Odell noted seeing the *Alemanda*, a paddle wheel steamship, arriving at the northern end of White Horse Rapids. The *Flora*, another paddle wheel steamship, had smashed its wheel on the bank, nearly sinking. The men loaded their boats and started down the river. They got stuck on a sand bar, worked three hours to free the boats, and camped for the night.

The next day they unloaded their boats and dried out their gear. Hoglen and Odell went hunting and saw tracks of many moose and other game, along with bear spoor and an animal den. They stayed at their camp for several days, waiting for better weather to dry out their gear. Finally, they packed up their gear and started sailing downstream, past the Takheena River, about 16¼ miles below the White Horse rapids. The following day they floated down the river, avoiding shoals and sand bars. They laid to, waiting for a head wind before rowing further down the river where they camped at a temporarily deserted Indian village and saw Dawson Jim's sign. Odell did not make any other identification of Dawson Jim.

Clearly, the four men had joined into, at least, an informal partnership.

Lake Laberge

After sailing further down Lake Laberge, their prospects rose as they entered part of the Yukon where gold was to be found. Aldrich noted that "flake gold is found all along the Yukon River, and I presume the same is true of the Yukon; but it is so light that it cannot be saved."[163]

Indian Village, Lake Laberge, Odell Collection.

The four men were alert to signs of potential mining sites. Odell's and Aldrich's boat leaked badly over the night, so they dried their goods again and waited for a lighter wind. They stopped at the mouth of the Hootalinqua River. Although Odell failed to note in his diary the NWMP post at this site, the police detachment probably inspected their papers and goods.[164]

Initial Mining Activity

The next day they sailed further down the river, stopped for lunch, and caught six Graylings. They sailed onward and stopped at Cassiar Bar where claims had been staked and men were working a water wheel and sluice boxes. Frederick Schwatka noted a mining encampment at Cassiar Bar when he passed down the Yukon River in 1891, stating that in 1886 six men had found gold at this site.[165]

This was the first sight of Yukon gold for the men. They stayed at Cassiar Bar for another day and a half, working to wash gold with a man name Fraser, and found small amounts of their first gold. The photo below is a rare photo of mining activity at Cassiar Bar.

Sluice Work, Cassiar Bar, Odell Collection.

Pushing Ahead to Fort Selkirk

After setting sail again, the men stopped at the Big Salmon River NWMP Post, several miles below Cassiar Bar. Again, it is probable that the NWMP checked their boat registrations and inspected their boats.

The men leisurely floated down the river and occasionally stopped to prospect, but "little colors" were found. They sailed northward to the Little Salmon NWMP post. Again, Odell made no mention of inspections by the NWMP.

Notes posted at Little Salmon River NWMP Post, Odell Collection.

This photograph of messages left at the Little Salmon River NWMP Post is very rare, depicting improvisation by stampeders in leaving notes on trees for their friends who would pass by later and pick up their communications at this location where the Mounties required all boats to stop and be recorded.

Odell walked up the Little Salmon River on an Indian trail where he saw grave cabins about a quarter mile up from the mouth of the river.* The men stayed the evening, where they met and played whist with Harry Granger. Harry Granger would soon become an important part of Odell and Aldrich's quest for gold.

Later photo of Harry Granger, Odell Collection.

The men continued sailing northward where they encountered many islands and channels, nearly grounding on a rocky bar. They reached Carmack's

---

* Gord Allison reports that "there are graves about a quarter mile up the Yukon River from the mouth of the Little Salmon River." However, Odell's diary expressly refers to the location of the graves he visited as being about a quarter mile "up the Little Salmon River."

Post and ate lunch above Five Fingers Rapids. After inspecting the rapids, they shot through the white water and camped about eight miles downstream across from a NWMP Post with a sawmill.* Odell noted that there were a considerable number of prospectors at this location living in tents.

Boat navigating Rink Rapids on the Yukon River, Yukon Territory, Eric A. Hegg Photographs HEG706, University of Washington Library, Special Collections.

They continued sailing northward, passing through Rink Rapids and stopped for lunch at Maris (probably Merrice) Creek. Odell noted that there were many tents at Maris (Merrice) Creek with men who had staked their claims and two "pretty women." The men were in the wilderness -- no shaving this time.

---

* Gord Allison reports that "[t]he post and sawmill were less than two miles down from Five Fingers Rapids. Rink Rapids is less than six miles from Five Fingers."

On July 26, thirty-three days after leaving Lake Bennett, they stopped at Steamboat Slough and then sailed on to the nearby Fort Selkirk. The route of the stampeders from Dyea to Fort Selkirk is a little more than four hundred miles long, all but the first thirty-three miles were over water. Odell and Aldrich met two men, Greir and White, at Steamboat Slough, a small somewhat sheltered cove indented into the shoreline three or four miles upstream from Fort Selkirk. During the winter months a few smaller paddle wheel boats were stored at Steamboat Slough.

Not much has been written about this Steamboat Slough.* A Canadian Development Company Post was located there. Odell mentioned Steamboat Sough five times in his diary, including New Year's Eve, 1898, when he and a friend ate dinner there. Presumably the attraction to Steamboat Slough was the quality of the food available, and not alcoholic beverages, as Odell was rabidly anti-alcohol. It is somewhat ironic that Odell mentioned Steamboat Slough with such regularity, but as mentioned above, had failed to note Closeleigh or White Horse in 1898 when he traveled past that area. As discussed below, Odell again failed to mention White Horse in 1899 when traveling out of the Yukon.

---

* Gord Allison discusses Steamboat Slough in his blog YukonHistoryTrails.com .

Just before arriving at Fort Selkirk, Odell noticed seeing two moose swimming across the river.

A photo of the dog that Hoglen and Wood brought with them was taken on the banks of the Yukon River at Fort Selkirk in 1898.

Arrival at Fort Selkirk – "Our dog, which one is the dog?" – Walt Hoglen. Odell Collection.

Aldrich described the beautiful scenery they saw during their sail downstream

> I shall not attempt to describe to you the scenery of this country. It is beautiful all along the way. The mountains are low and rolling. Wild flowers abound in summer and in places a whole mountain side will be covered with a pink flower called fireweed. Wild roses are plentiful,

and I have seen delicate little flowers which are new to me. The climate is most delightful surprising imaginable. The four seasons are easily distinguishable. The summer is warm, sometimes very hot; but spring and fall are as delightfully cool and pleasant, the weather about Selkirk reminds me of our New York fall.[166]

Chapter 8
Initial Efforts to Prospect at Wolverine Creek Headwaters

Although Odell and Aldrich were not aware of it when they arrived, Fort Selkirk would be as far north as they would venture into the Yukon.* Dawson City is north of Fort Selkirk, about 178 miles by water on the Yukon River.

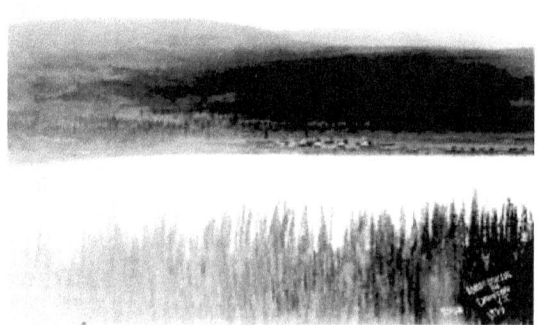

Fort Selkirk in distance, Larss & Duclos Photos, Yukon Archives Print No. 6288, Bill Roozeboom Collection.

---

* A discussion of Fort Selkirk is found in Appendix A.

Fort Selkirk, an old trading site, would become central to their prospecting and mining efforts in the Yukon. Odell, Aldrich, Hoglen, and Harry Granger would mine for gold and stay the winter in a cabin they built at the headwaters of Wolverine Creek, southwest of Fort Selkirk. They would make periodic treks from their cabin to Fort Selkirk where they would purchase supplies and break the tedium of a long winter in Yukon.

Fort Selkirk served as a civilized oasis for the men. In 1898, Fort Selkirk had a population in the mid-hundreds, including 200 members of the Yukon Field Force.* The population varied at any time, with prospectors coming and going.

Aldrich wrote home later describing their search for gold.

> All the way down the lakes and rivers we heard bad reports of the gold prospect and no news of any strikes outside of the Klondike, which as you know, is a very limited district. We have not allowed all this talk to dampen us and have rushed on with as much determination as before.[167]

They kept stiff upper lips and proceeded ahead.

Despair

Odell was not impressed with the potential for gold near Fort Selkirk and made note of "bad bars" in his

---

* The Yukon Field Force is discussed in Appendix A.

diary, which could refer to either saloons or sandbars. At Fort Selkirk, Odell and Aldrich rekindled their friendship with Greir and White, colleagues from Cornell whom they had seen earlier, and discussed prospective prospecting sites. They met Norman McCleod and his wife. McCleod advised them to keep their eyes on C.D. Emmons and his group to detect their prospecting plans. For several days, they followed this advice.

Odell's diary noted that he and Aldrich were disgusted with the "Pelly & McMillan Rivers, whole country, queen, Dominion govt, everything & everybody in general." The men could not decide what to do. Had they come this far, and endured so much, without any good potential prospecting sites? Thousands of prospectors had sailed north on the Yukon River weeks before them. The mining areas with better potential had already been taken.

After several days of considering their options, Odell and Aldrich decided to continue sailing down the Yukon River with Greir and White. Odell and Aldrich loaded their boat and broke camp, ready to leave.

Just before they left, Aldrich met another prospector named Al Yeaton, who with others was going back into mountains and prospect for gold. Odell and Aldrich quickly decided to join Yeaton, rather than proceed down the Yukon River with Greir and White. The decision proved to be serendipitous.

Getting to Wolverine Creek Headwaters

Odell, Aldrich, Hoglen, and Wood arose at 4 a.m. the next morning and started out on their prospecting adventure at the headwaters of Wolverine Creek with at least six other men, led by Conrad Huntley.

The trail was wet and swampy. They were "tired as blazes" and camped at night in a fine grove of trees on the big creek, presumably Wolverine Creek. Odell caught 18 Grayling, but lost Tom Wood's revolver.

Aldrich's letter to the *Brooklyn Daily Eagle* also described this "trail," but the newspaper editor summarized this portion of his letter.

> The letter contains much more than can be given here and enters into details regarding the unsuccessful attempts of the writer and other prospectors whom he met to discover gold in paying quantities. The difficulties which were encountered, the quicksands and trails knee deep with mud [getting to their camp on Wolverine Creek], the tedious shaft sinking and the ultimate erection of winter quarters, preparatory to the long wait for spring, are vividly described by the old High School boy, and they afford a comprehensive idea of the hardships endured by scores of Klondike miners.[168]

Other prospectors joined the men at their first night's camp short of their objective on Wolverine Creek. Huntley and Odell left camp and reached the site identified by Al Yeaton. The mining site was at the "headwaters" of Wolverine Creek where it runs in a south/north direction from its source, before the creek turns and runs in a west/east direction and eventually enters the Yukon River south of Fort Selkirk.

Soon, the others arrived. The growing party included Mark Odell, Ellis Aldrich, Thomas Wood, Walt Hoglen, Al Yeaton, Alec Harbinson, Dan McShane, Conrad Huntley, Diron McLennon, Archie McLennon, and someone named Donahue.

Wolverine Creek is the first significant creek south of or upstream from Fort Selkirk that enters the Yukon River from the west. The creek flows northward out of the Dawson Range southwest of Fort Selkirk, west of Wolverine Peak and northeast of Prospector Mountain, for about fifteen miles past Mount Pitts, and then turns eastward and flows about twenty miles entering the Yukon River.

Seven years earlier, on July 9 and 10, 1891, Frederick Schwatka in his last Yukon expedition traveled on what he described as an Indian trail from Fort Selkirk to Wolverine Creek. This was the same trail that Odell and the other prospectors would have taken from Fort Selkirk to Wolverine Creek. The Schwatka party appears to have camped near where Odell, Aldrich, and the other men decided to mine in 1898.

Schwatka described this old Indian trail as being difficult to follow. He described the trail as difficult to follow. The Schwatka party found groves of conifers, moss, and boulders along the trail and, in places, sank in soft mud with every step taken.[169]

Schwatka was disdainful of this and other Indian trails. He found it "incomprehensible" that these trails varied from being plainly marked and well defined in densely wooded areas or rough mountainous areas to being much more obscure when passing through open country. In open country Indians would spread out and even stoop to their knees when faced with a tree branch, and crawl under the branch, rather than cutting down the branch. Schwatka considered Indian trails to hardly vary from game trails of migratory animals.[170]

Dr. Charles Willard Hayes, a geologist and mineralogist who accompanied Schwatka on his 1891 expedition, described the trail between Fort Selkirk and Wolverine Creek as having scattered spruce trees and generally following sparsely wooded valleys over grass, moss and moose brush.[171]

This "Indian trail" that Odell, Aldrich, and the others followed from Fort Selkirk to the headwaters of Wolverine Creek was the northern end of the cattle trail used by Jack Dalton in 1897 to drive cattle to Fort Selkirk. Apparently, Dalton never used that trail again. This cattle trail is sometimes confused with the Dalton Trail.

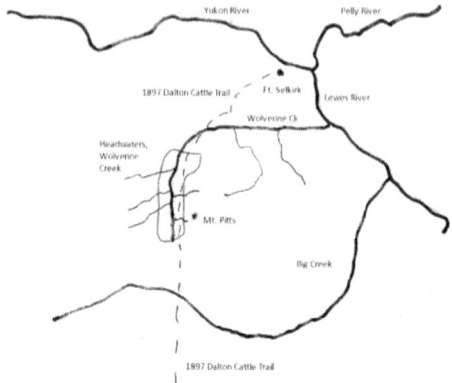

Area of mining site at headwaters of Wolverine Creek.

Gold and Drift Mining Techniques

Two types of gold mining were practiced.

One method is hard-rock or quartz mining where gold is found in veins or in rock, the rock is dug from the ground, and then crushed to separate the rock from gold deposits. The other method is placer mining. Most of the initial mining in the Yukon was placer mining, also called "poor-man's" mining since less equipment is necessary, and a placer mining operation could be performed by as few as two men with minimal equipment and no large machinery.[172]

Placers are stream-bed deposits of gold. Yukon prospectors sought gold nuggets, gold flakes and gold dust that had eroded from a lode or vein of gold and slowly moved by water downstream over geologic time. Gold is heavy, so nuggets, flakes and gold dust gradually moved toward the bedrock as a stream traveled downstream over millions of years.

The hope for placer mining is to find a likely mining site, often in the old stream bed just outside of a bend of a current stream. Prospectors panned the current stream looking for "colors," or gold dust, hinting that gold may be found nearby. If sufficient colors were found, they would dig a vertical shaft in the old stream bed down to the bedrock, above which placers would hopefully be found. This part of the shaft was optimistically called the paystreak. Then, horizontal shafts or drifts were dug fanning out from the bottom of the shaft just above the bedrock.

Placer mining was also known as drift mining or winter drift mining, signifying that the technique allowed the prospectors to work their claims during the long, dark winters rather than just idling away in their cabins and waiting for summer. The basic idea was to accumulate a pile of paydirt over the winter and sluice in the summer. However some miners, including Odell and his partners, used small rockers in their cabins to separate the gold from the muck and rock. The technique had been perfected on the Yukon's Fortymile River earlier in the 1890s.

Permafrost was found throughout much of the Yukon. It is a permanent feature in the northern parts of the Yukon, and extends southward in patchy areas. Where found in the more southern areas, permafrost is often a foot or two below the surface in the during the summer, so prospectors set fires to melt the frozen ground and then dug out the thawed muck and gravel. The mine shaft was quickly abandoned after a fire was set and the miners waited until the fire died out and the smoke and noxious gases gradually cleared out of the shaft before they could dig out the muck and gravel. This was a slow and laborious procedure, repeated in monotonous repetition over and over, with the shaft gradually being lowered only a few inches after each burning and digging sequence.

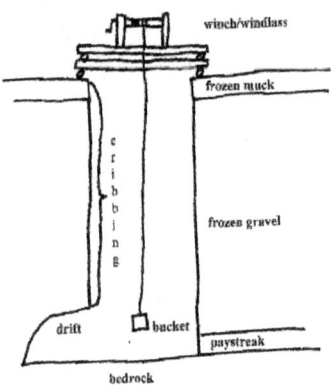

Sketch showing placer mining technique

Structural siding (called cribs) was erected or placed along the walls of the vertical shaft, hopefully to keep the shaft from collapsing. The cribbing could also be used as a ladder to climb up and down the shaft. Once the shaft was over the head of the miners, gravel and muck were winched out of the shaft to the surface in a bucket with a rope attached to a hand cranked windlass or winch. The gravel and muck were set aside for later panning, rocking or sluicing.

Washing procedures were used to separate gold from the muck and gravel. The muck and gravel were inspected by panning or using a small rocker or larger sluice box with ridges on the bottom, where gravel would be washed through the sluice box by diverted stream water. Gold, whether in the form of nuggets, flakes, or dust, sank to the bottom of the pan, or bottom of the rocker or sluice where it was trapped by the ridges or riffles. During the winter, some prospectors washed the muck and gravel by panning or using small rockers inside their cabins. Others stored the muck and gravel for panning, sluicing or rocking when the weather warmed in the spring.

Placer mining was grueling and exhausting work with little chance of success and was soon abandoned in favor of steam-powered machinery in the more productive mining areas by 1899.[173] Some environmental damage arose from the primitive placer mining, but nothing like the widespread damage caused from industrial mining techniques using steam-powered machinery and eventually large dredges.

Initial Mining Efforts

After finding colors on Wolverine Creek at the site Al Yeaton had identified, Odell, Aldrich, Wood, and Hoglen sank a vertical shaft in the old stream bed. In

1896, William Oglivie reported that there was gold in Wolverine Creek.[174]

They hit permafrost at two feet, and lit a fire to melt the frozen earth. The thaw from their first firing was eight inches deep. They did not see any "colors" or gold dust and the sides of the shaft kept caving into the bottom of the hole. Odell noted in his diary that their grub supply was getting low and they had no remaining salt. His face was "poisoned" by gnat bites.

The other prospectors worked on their own shafts.

After several days of frustration, diminishing supplies, and grim prospects, Odell and Diron McLennon left the campsite and headed back to Fort Selkirk. Odell's moccasins & socks wore through, so he wrapped flour sacks around his feet to complete the journey.

Meanwhile, the remaining miners erected cribs on the sides of their vertical shafts, trying to keep the sides from caving in, but these efforts were of no avail and the sides kept caving. Odell and McLennon returned to the camp with new supplies. The men kept setting fires to melt the permafrost, digging, and adding to the cribbing as the holes got deeper. They changed the channel of the creek but to no avail. Then Odell records on August 13, 1898 – "Heavy marching orders. Break camp and depart for Selkirk all hands."

All the men left their mining sites at the headwaters of Wolverine Creek for Fort Selkirk. On the way back to Fort Selkirk, they passed the Emmons party that was starting for the White River with eleven horses. The Emmons party would have followed the route from Fort Selkirk that Odell and his party had used to reach Wolverine Creek. However, where Wolverine Creek bends from flowing in a south/north direction to a west/east direction, the Emmons party would have continued westward across a marshy area that appears to drain both into Wolverine Creek and Selwyn Creek. They apparently used this route to reach the White River that enters the Yukon River west of Selwyn Creek.

Odell and his dejected prospecting party reached Fort Selkirk that evening at 6 pm.

Everything was a disaster. The despair and indecision were evident from Odell's diary. They discussed following the Emmons Party to the White River, but some of the men backed out. For two days, "everyone in air." H.H. (Old Man) Pitts talked about trying to locate a copper ledge.

By August 18, Odell and Aldrich had "decided to give up the trip. Up in the air what to do." On August 19, Tom Wood decided to "hit the trail for home." Odell and Aldrich faced dim prospects after they had expended money, time, and effort to reach the Yukon gold fields. The next day, August 20, Hoglen, Aldrich and Odell decided "to go back to our prospecting place for winter."

Odell crossed the Yukon River and purchased a horse, a young buckskin they named "Buck."

On August 25, Tom Wood "hit the Dalton trail* for the coast." Odell did not identify the route Wood took from Fort Selkirk to reach the Dalton Trail. Three potential routes were: (1) By boat from Fort Selkirk up the Yukon River to Yukon Crossing and then by a trail along the west side of the Yukon River to Carmack's Post; (2) hiking along the eastern side of the Yukon River (following the route Jack Dalton used to drive cattle to Slaughter Slough in 1898) to Tantalus Butte and crossing the Yukon River to Carmack's Post; or (3) hiking along the very rough northern cattle trail that Jack Dalton used to drive cattle to Fort Selkirk in 1897 and joining the Dalton Trail at Hutchi.

If Wood had much money, he probably would have purchased passage by boat from Fort Selkirk to Carmacks Post. If he chose to hike to Carmacks Post, the easiest and shortest route would have been following the route along the eastern side of the Yukon River where Jack Dalton had driven cattle to Slaughter Slough earlier that year. However, Odell noted in his diary that when he, Aldrich, and Hoglen returned to their old mining site on the headwaters of Wolverine Creek, they found a note that Wood had written to them. This indicates that Wood took this strenuous and little used route to reach Carmacks Post that Jack Dalton had used in 1897 to drive cattle to Fort Selkirk.

---

* A description of the Dalton Trail is found in Appendix C.

Chapter 9

Mining at Wolverine Creek

Before Odell, Aldrich, and Hoglen left Fort Selkirk for their old prospecting site, they went to see Indians at what Odell described as their "dirty camp" and ate "delicacies." After enjoying the delicacies, the three men returned to their old stomping grounds near the headwaters of Wolverine Creek, build a cabin, and resumed their mining efforts over the winter.

Initially, entries in Odell's diary were upbeat but become darker as the men experience the long, monotonous, and cold winter and they become sick. In his October 4, 1898, letter home Aldrich wrote:

> If we should strike anything it will be the result of tender foot luck and nerve.... It is a mistake for a man to come to this country for one year. It takes all that time to get used to the country and to get well located. I believe that this is a rich country minerally, but I should be unwilling to spend more than one year here and take the small chance that a man has of finding that wealth.[175]

Building a Cabin at Wolverine Creek Headwaters

The men had to organize and rapidly implement a strategy to prepare for the severe Yukon winter. Their first task was to build a cabin.

Odell and Aldrich decided to buy a horse to pack their gear. They crossed the Yukon River and purchased a young buckskin horse from William's cattle camp for $60, aptly naming the horse Buck. After returning to Fort Selkirk, they started back to their old prospecting site and stayed the night at their friend Alec Harbinson's hay camp.

Aldrich (left), trusty horse Buck, Odell (right), "Off on prospecting trip out of Ft. Selkirk," Odell Collection.

The above photograph shows the firm tundra or taiga and the size of the trees near Fort Selkirk. The firm tundra may not have been typical, as Odell and Aldrich mentioned much quicksand and deep mud on the trail. Note the large box strapped to Buck, presumably a tool box.

Odell and Aldrich pulled their boat up from the river's edge and retrieved their cache of goods. They kept losing their new horse Buck on the trail back to Wolverine Creek. The trip to the old campsite took three days. Along the way back, they hunted for hay to harvest at the "junction" of a big meadow and Wolverine Creek, but without success.

They stayed at their former camp ground on a little creek and then finally reached their old stomping grounds where they found a note left by Tom Wood. The note was not included in Odell's records, and he did not describe the message in his diary. The three men pitched a tent at their old prospecting site.

The men worked around the campsite and made trips back to Fort Selkirk for supplies. On September 8 Odell returned to Fort Selkirk. On the way back to their camp, he killed a grouse with a hatchet.

At Fort Selkirk, Harry Granger joined Odell, Aldrich, and Hoglen to mine at Wolverine Creek. Odell had met Granger on the sail down the Yukon River at the Little Salmon NWMP Post where he played whist with Granger and his partner Tyler. Odell noted in his diary that a flock of 124 sand hill cranes flew by overnight when they camped by the first swamp on the trail from Fort Selkirk to their old prospecting grounds. Granger had a horse named "old Sleigh Bells."

Originally, Granger and his partner Tyler had planned on prospecting up the Little Salmon River, up the Yukon River from Carmack's Post. Although Odell did not use the precise words, it is clear from his diary entries that Granger had joined with Odell, Aldrich, and Hoglen to stay the winter and mine at the Wolverine Creek site. Granger's partner, Tyler, was at Fort Selkirk as Odell's entry for the next day mentioned that he purchased a scythe and rifle from him. Presumably, the Granger/Tyler partnership had broken up.

The four partners hiked through swampy areas covered with muskeg -- a mix of water and dead vegetation frequently covered by a layer of sphagnum and other mosses.

Winter comes early in the Yukon. The men acted with dispatch to build a cabin, bunks, chairs, tables, and shelves. This work took place from September 13 until October 28.

Trees were cut, sawed to correct lengths, rolled or pulled to the cabin site, and notched at the ends so a log running perpendicular to the first log would fit together with the first log. They cut a road from the cabin site to their logging site. Gradually levels of the logs were placed on top of each other, eventually nine levels high. Trees at this northern latitude were small and sparse. They erected gables and cut, peeled, and erected ridge poles. The weather became colder during the days, and they had to maintain a brisk working effort to keep warm.

They put up peak poles and cleared out the inside of the cabin. They dug moss and jammed moss between the log courses to keep out the wind and cold. A door opening was cut, roof poles were added. They dug more moss and jammed the moss between the logs on the roof. A course of dirt was applied over the roof logs as a final barrier. The cabin floor was dug out and sealed. They set up two stoves and built bunks, tables, chairs, and shelves. Hay was gathered for their beds. A door was hung. At least one window, and perhaps as many as four windows, were installed, as the men previously had purchased four panes of glass at Ft. Selkirk. A floor was added with planks sawn in a saw pit they constructed. They could cut six to seven boards out of one good log. A porch was added outside the door.

With pride, Odell hung his red and white Cornell pennant on a cabin wall.

A water hole was dug. Perhaps due to Victorian modesty, Odell failed to mention the digging of a latrine. It was quite common for Yukon prospector records not to mention their latrines.

Odell's records did not describe where the cabin and mining area were located, much less name the creek where the cabin was located. The only clue he left came decades later, when he wrote "Headwaters, Wolverine Creek" on the edge of a photo of this site that he gave one of the authors. Odell wrote that the distance from the cabin to Fort Selkirk was about 35 miles. In several instances, he noted in his diary that the hike took from 11 to 14 hours. However, in one instance, Odell's diary indicated that he made this trip in 9 hours and 20 minutes. It is inconceivable that he could have snowshoed 35 miles in that short of time. Perhaps the cabin was more like 25 miles from Fort Selkirk.

Rear of cabin on Wolverine Creek. Odell Collection.

Work area behind Wolverine Creek cabin, Harry Granger. Odell Collection.

The men built a shack midway between their cabin and Fort Selkirk that was used when they could not

Trail from Fort Selkirk to cabin on Wolverine Creek. Odell Collection.

Another photo of t'rail from Fort Selkirk to their cabin on Wolverine Creek. Odell Collection.

Wolverine Creek as it bends from running from a south/north direction to a west/east direction along the trail to Ft. Selkirk, described as the "Big Bend." Also described as "Camp on Stone Creek," probably where the shack was located. Odell Collection.

make the hike in one day. It appears that this cabin was located on the plain above or north of the major bend in Wolverine Creek when it changes from running in a south/north direction to a west/east direction. On a list of photos, Hoglen noted that the shack was located on what he called Stone Creek.

Periodically, two of the four men hiked to Fort Selkirk and returned to their Wolverine Creek cabin with supplies.

Odell and Aldrich's horse Buck, Harry Granger's horse Sleigh Bells, and a third horse named Nellie, kept wandering off and they had to stop working and search for them. Their "little roan mare" Nellie was ailing, so they shot and skinned her, presumably butchering her for meat.

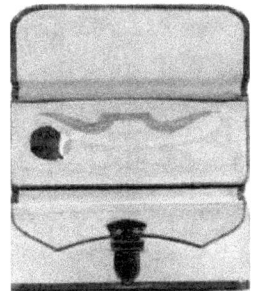 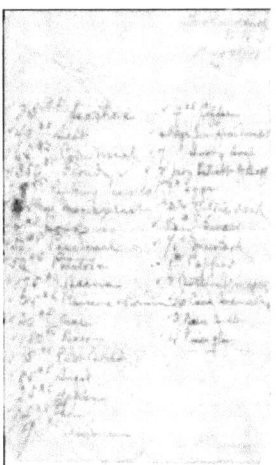

Inside of Odell wallet and shopping list for Ft. Selkirk. Odell Collection.

"Grampa's Wonder" is pine tar soap, produced since 1876, supposedly good for skin ailments such as psoriasis and still is sold today.[176] Note four panes of glass were purchased, presumably for a window or windows in their cabin. Nothing but first-class accommodations. Glass paned windows were somewhat rare in the early years of the Yukon gold rush and were installed by "aristocrats or cheechakos." More commonly, a window was made from "empty stout and ale bottles" that were stacked with the bottoms facing inwards.[177]

The next major task was to cut trees down and saw the logs into shorter lengths to burn in their stove and in the mine shafts. It was estimated that two men would need at least thirty cords of cut wood to fuel their stove and fires in their mine shaft over a winter.[178] Presumably something less than twice this amount of wood would have been needed by four men living together, but the amount of wood that was needed to be cut was still prodigious.

On one of their trips to Fort Selkirk in late October, Odell noted in his diary that he and Walt took Buck and Nellie down below the big creek where Walt fell into the water. Odell built a fire to dry Walt out and remarked that it was cold enough to wear moccasins. Mittens were worn in the winters rather than gloves, as your fingers could freeze if glovers were worn.[179]

In his later years, Odell told his grandsons stories of the Yukon winters being so cold that the prospectors wore moccasins over two pairs of thick German socks. It was too cold to wear boots. He kept his last pair of moccasins at his Seattle house years after returning from the Yukon. The moccasins were identified by an expert as a style common to a First Nation group from Quebec. If this is accurate, presumably the First Nation people in Quebec made the moccasins for a trading company that sold them to Odell at Fort Selkirk.

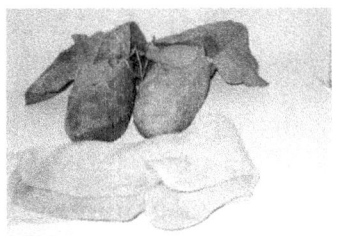

Odell's last pair of moccasins and German socks.

In early October, Odell noted that the days were getting shorter and it was dark at 5:30 pm. For several days after they had finished their cabin, the men washed and mended their clothes.

Return to Mining Efforts

The four men finally returned to mining on November 4, and began working on Alec Harbinson's hole. The built a windlass and dug to a depth of 15 feet from the surface.

Odell did not mention claims for their mining sites being filed with Canadian authorities. However, it is difficult for the authors to believe that the cautious Odell would not have filed a claim. In 1987, a staff person at the Yukon Archives in Whitehorse told one of the authors that records of early claims filed on Wolverine Creek and other sites in this mining district were destroyed in a fire in the 1950s.

Odell's diary describes the monotonous placer-mining work, repeated over and over, day after day. Fires were lit on the floor of the mineshaft to melt the frozen ground. The miners would wait for the noxious smoke to clear, and then dig out the mud and gravel. The abbreviations "B & D" were often used to describe burning and digging.

Several times their hole would fill with water, and they had to bail up to ten feet of water out of the hole.

Placer mining shaft & windlass, Wolverine Creek. Odell at left. Granger at right. Odell Collection.

The burning and digging process continued day after day. Finally, on November 16, they had their first success at finding gold in clay-like soil with crushed rock when they washed a pair of nuggets from the debris.

Odell and Aldrich started digging a second shaft after they hit a big boulder in their main shaft. Progress in burning and digging on the second shaft went faster than their original shaft, as the new hole was eleven feet deep after two weeks of work. Then, they hit a boulder in the second shaft, broke the boulder loose from the ground and lit a fire to split the boulder into pieces. The next day, they found that the fire had broken up the boulder. However, the sides of the new shaft caved in. They straightened out the sides and dug six inches of clay from the second shaft from which they washed a pan of debris and found four flecks of gold.

Odell noted in his diary that their water hole kept backing up.

Frequent Snowshoeing to Fort Selkirk

They continued a tradition of two of the four men snowshoeing from their cabin on Wolverine Creek into Fort Selkirk every other week. They would rest at Fort Selkirk and purchase additional supplies.

When conditions were not good, or the men became tired, they stayed overnight at the "shack" they had built along their route between the Wolverine Creek cabin and Fort Selkirk. A special treat was to enjoy cigars at Wade Blaker's Hotel Selkirk.*

Hotel Selkirk, Fort Selkirk, University of Washington Roll, Yukon Archives, Print No. 1323.

They would dine and camp with their friend Norman McCleod and his wife.† Food and other supplies were

---

* Stampeders frequently used the term "cigar store" referring to small cribs where prostitutes plied their trade in alleys of Dawson City. (Gates, *History Hunting in the Yukon*, 178.) However, it is highly doubtful that the straight-laced Mark Odell was referring to the enjoyment of prostitutes in this diary entry and instead was referring to the enjoyment of smoking wrapped tobacco found in cigars. Odell was a life-long smoker of tobacco, mostly enjoying pipe smoking and cigars.

† The McCleods probably ran a hotel or a restaurant at Fort Selkirk. H.M. McLeod was one of the men who signed an application on behalf of R. Wade Blaker in January of 1900 for a liquor license at Fort Selkirk. Others who signed the application were H.H. Pitts, who was a merchant at Fort Selkirk; A. Mogridge, who managed the Savoy Hotel; and C.D. Emmons, who is mentioned in Odell's diary. These men appear

purchased at Harper's trading post, run by "old man" Pitts. Harper's trading post was established in 1889. Harper left the Yukon in 1897 and died that year in San Francisco.

H.H. Pitts, operated Harper's post at Fort Selkirk, in 1897 and 1898.[180] Tappan Adney noted that Pitts had resided in the Yukon for 25 years and was told by him that the Yukon was prospectors' country where the only people to succeed are calculating and have grit and determination.[181]

Odell mentioned Pitts in several diary entries. One entry was on August 15, 1898, when Pitts talked about sending a guide out to locate a copper ledge. Another entry was on November 11, 1898, when Odell noted that it was 45 degrees below zero in Fort Selkirk when he and Aldrich passed by Pitts' shack.

Odell recorded extreme temperatures in his diary. One entry was particularly chilling – "Holy Smut .... find it was 51 degrees below last night!!!!!!" He also recorded temperatures of 40 below zero and 45 below zero. The diary entry for the corresponding day with the extreme temperatures that Odell described as being "colder than blazes" and he was not able to sleep. Walt had a chill, so they kept a fire going all

---

to have been other businessmen at Fort Selkirk. (YRG I, Series 1, vol. 75, Applications for Liquor licenses, 1898-1901, file 20. R. Wade Blaker, Yukon Archives.)

night in the stove. Odell also noted that it averaged 40 to 45 below zero for several days.

Odell's Descriptions of First Nation Peoples

Odell noted Native peoples in his diary while at their cabin on Wolverine Creek, which described a tragedy.

> Indian hunting camp at first meadow down [below the cabin]. Squaw and boy pulling sick boy on sled below down. Grave foot of shack meadow.

On New Year's Eve, Odell and his friend Alec Harbinson visited Steamboat Slough, presumably to enjoy good eats. Odell recorded that he, George, and Ellie visited Indian cabins at Fort Selkirk. It is not clear who this George was. In another entry, Odell noted – "At night 12 Selkirk Indians in whom we fed. Great event." The next day

> [w]ole crowd of Indians here from morning til one o'clock 9 bucks, about 15 boys and papooses, 6 or 8 squaws. We traded for moccasins, bead work jewelry.

Immediately prior to Odell and Aldrich leaving the Yukon, they traded a little with Indians at Fort Selkirk. On their trek out of the Yukon over the Winter River Trail, Odell and Aldrich stopped at Jim Boss's bunkhouse on Lake Laberge where Odell considered purchasing a quiver and arrows but decided against this added expense.

Cabin Life at Wolverine Creek

Their diet was quite varied, given the remoteness of their cabin. At times Odell noted in his diary that he had baked bread, presumably sourdough bread. They would also eat caribou, ptarmigan, rabbit, various stews, dried potatoes, and other vegetables. For Thanksgiving, 1898, Odell noted a special meal of President's cake and roast beef pie. President's cake is an extravagant cake made with a variety of dried or candied fruits and a variety of nuts and was enjoyed at festive occasions. For Christmas, 1898, he noted they

> had great old Christmas dinner. Plum pudding, pies, cake, game stew. Think my first Christmas away from home.

Odell's records include a potato recipe. Hoglen's diary included recipes for corn bread, fruit pudding, an unnamed potato dish, and for making baking powder.

Odell did not describe the long, and dark, winter days at Wolverine Creek, a little south of Fort Selkirk. Dawson City is north of Fort Selkirk and has only six hours of daylight during the months of December and January. Fort Selkirk would have had slightly longer day light hours, but the dominant nature of a Yukon winter is the interminable darkness and cold. The ever-present darkness was psychologically wearing on the men. This limited amount of daylight contrasts with Odell's description of sunlight on Lake

Lindeman lasting eighteen hours, from 3:30 a.m. until 9:30 p.m.[182]

Odell made only a few entries in his diary mentioning the pervasive darkness. He noted on January 4 that – "Sun almost in sight in forenoon." On January 11, he noted "saw the sun for first time here since Nov." This must have been quite an event for the four partners. The moon was much more evident, as for several days of each month Odell mentioned the moon and moonlight. Each snowshoeing trek from their cabin on Wolverine Creek to Fort Selkirk, and back again, was partly in the dark and they probably relied on moonlight for much of the trip.

> Reach camp about 8 by moon light.
>
> Start back at 4:10 [a.m.] moonlit all way to shack 7:45 [a.m.], Reached cabin little before four [p.m.].

Odell mentioned the beauty of the moonlight.

> Fine moonlight night with wind howling up to N.W.
>
> Beautiful moonlight.

Injury was a major worry for the men, located at their cabin 25 or more miles from Fort Selkirk, where the Yukon Field Force had at least some medical facilities. Odell noted with much foreboding their worst accident.

> Rope on sack broke & let 2 heavy logs fall on Walt's shoulder. Very fortunately only bruising him.

Presumably, the accident occurred when the men were lowering logs into a mine shaft that were to be burned to melt the frozen ground.

The four partners stayed in their cabin most of the time, attending to chores and continuing their mining activities. They read, played cards, and talked about their past lives and plans for the future. Daily chores were very time-consuming and involved cutting trees and chopping wood used for cooking, heating, and burning in the mine shafts, cooking, cleaning, and maintaining their cabin and environs. They also washed or searched for nuggets and gold dust in the gravel and muck retrieved from the mine shafts.

Periodically, Odell mentioned washing and mending clothes. Aldrich shaved on December 26, 1898. The Odell diary included some mention of chores, but mostly described mining activities and treks back and forth to Fort Selkirk. The men appeared to make ready for the long winter season by washing and mending clothes on October 31, and November 1 and 3. The next entry for these chores was on December 18, then January 15 and 22, when Odell noted that he mended clothes all day.

The four partners were sore much of the time and had a run of sickness in late November and early December of 1898. Odell complained of having tender and cracked feet like chapped hands. He wrote about the men having bad colds and coughing like blazes, with a head ache and general lassitude. "All four have the distemper nicely." Odell noted "feel quite bum as usual" on December 2. "Lay around feeling all hands" on December 4. On January 28, Odell felt "rather bum." As discussed below, Aldrich was quite ill in late January when Odell decided to have him taken out of the Yukon.

The four men worked on at least three shafts, perhaps more. One shaft was mined primarily by Odell and Aldrich, and another shaft was mined primarily by Hoglen and Granger. However, on at least one occasion (early December of 1898), Odell and Aldrich stopped working on their shaft, as they encountered a large rock that was not affected by burning a fire above, so they temporarily abandoned that shaft and began another across the creek from their cabin. They found cobbles and small boulders in the new shaft.

Some nights the fire in the shaft went out, so they had to relight the fire and hope for the best. Other nights the fire in the shaft kept burning.

Their good friend, Alec Harbinson who Odell notes in his diary as operating a "hay camp" farm outside of Fort Selkirk, visited the four men for an extended stay in December. Presumably, Harbinson harvested wild hay from meadows near Fort Selkirk. They celebrated Christmas. Harbinson helped them work on an old hole, presumably the hole he had started several months earlier. The men made curtains for the "south window," hunted rabbits, and set snares, and Granger made Odell somewhat presentable by cutting his hair. Mentioning the south window, rather than just a window, infers that the cabin had more than one window.

Odell noted some of their tiredness and wear.

> Walt & I start for cabin [from Fort Selkirk] at 7:25 [a.m.] just showing signs of coming down. 45 degrees below as we passed Pitts shack cold. Leave 12:30 hour later Walt gets feet wet on creek. Build fire and dry. He tires out after leave Big Crossing. Stop, build fire toast little bread left. Rest 2 or 3 hrs push on slowly to cabin about 10 [p.m.].
>
> Trail [to Fort Selkirk] drifted badly. Difficult to follow. About 23 below. Selkirk about 5 [p.m.]. Very tired. I snowshoed from where I left off last night.
>
> Start 7:40 [a.m.] for cabin new snow hard walking. Reach cabin about five [p.m.], little after mighty tired. Cloudy gray and gloomy all day.

Odell noted in his diary that he wrote to Mr. Smith, the man who financed their Yukon prospecting adventure, on December 11, 1898, but did not describe the contents of the letter. It is possible that Odell informed Smith of his desire to leave the Yukon when they could get out later in the winter or early spring. However, Odell's diary does not mention such a decision at that time. The last entry in the diary mentioning burning and digging was on January 24, 1899.

Decision to Get Aldrich Out of the Yukon

By the end of January 1899, the men were worn out and sick, especially Aldrich who was a physically and emotionally beaten man, ready to return home with the assistance of others. Odell was tired and emotionally beaten, but not sick at that time.

While at Fort Selkirk, Odell and Aldrich decided that Aldrich should leave the Yukon. They went to see W.H. (William) Swinehart, who operated a farm a few miles west of Fort Selkirk, and arranged for Swinehart to take Aldrich out of the Yukon. Odell returned to their camp and brought some of Aldrich's gear to Fort Selkirk. The day before, Odell had retrieved their sled and "cut it off" ready to take it back. It is not clear what "cut it off" meant, other than perhaps removing the sled from its storage site.

Presumably, Odell also retrieved their trusty horse Buck from Swinehart's farm. Odell and Hoglen returned to their cabin to collect Aldrich's possessions. On their way back to Fort Selkirk.

> Walt gives out almost after yet half way to Selkirk so take 5 hours to come last 2 hours distance. Get here at dark Walt gives out completely after reach flats 10

minutes from here. Stop, build fire and rest.

On February 2, 1899, Aldrich left Fort Selkirk with William Swinehart and others heading out of the Yukon. Odell remained at Fort Selkirk – "I hang around town not very cheerful." His best friend and partner was leaving the Yukon, while Odell was to remain in the Yukon.

Aldrich was so exhausted on the trek from Fort Selkirk to the Lewis bunkhouse that he had to leave his sled five miles below Lewis Bunkhouse the night he started his journey out of the Yukon. The Lewis Bunkhouse was located about 18 miles upstream from Fort Selkirk. Swinehart met his partner (probably Ham Kline or William "Billy" Thompson) the next day and decided to return to Fort Selkirk, leaving Aldrich at the Lewis Bunkhouse.

Chapter 10

Grueling Trek Out of the Yukon Over the Winter River Trail

There was no other option. Odell would take Aldrich out of the Yukon.

On February 4, Odell and Swinehart left Fort Selkirk to retrieve Aldrich from the Lewis Bunkhouse and bring him back to Fort Selkirk. They returned with Aldrich on February 5. Perhaps as a bad omen, Odell lost his watch while retrieving Aldrich.

Odell and Aldrich, two exhausted Sourdoughs, were about to start a grueling 400-mile trek out of the Yukon over the Winter River Trail.

Preparing for the Trek to the Outside

The task of leaving the Wolverine Creek site was more difficult than hiking into the site.

Odell and Aldrich left Fort Selkirk on February 7 and returned to their cabin on Wolverine Creek with their empty sled – "mighty tired."

Odell, Aldrich, Hoglen, and Granger ate their last supper together in the Wolverine Creek cabin. A time-lapsed photo of Walt Hoglen was taken eating his dinner at the cabin, which he entitled "lonely supper." Much of the cabin's interior is visible in this photo – a stove, a table, a chair, shelves, small diameter roof poles (on top of which the men had piled dirt for protection from the environment), what looks like the end of a bed, and a curtain (presumably covering one of the windows in the cabin).

"Lonely supper", Walt Hoglen eating meal in partners' Wolverine Creek cabin. Odell Collection.

On February 8, Odell and Aldrich settled, or divided up their gear and supplies, with Walt Hoglen. No mention was made of settling with Harry Granger.

The Odell Collection includes two photos of Odell and Aldrich's gear loaded on a sled ready to haul to Fort Selkirk.

"'97 comes back – Feb. 9, 1899, Headwaters Wolverine Creek, Yukon Ty." Odell Collection. From left – Mark Odell, Ellis Aldrich & Harry Granger. Odell Collection.

Sled ready to leave. Odell Collection.

Odell identified himself in the first photo by drawing an "X" over the man at the left standing behind the sled lighting his ubiquitous pipe. The notation at the bottom of the photograph "Headwaters Wolverine Creek" is the only record Odell left about the location of their cabin and mining area.

This second photo of the men shows two men pulling the sled with gear and equipment that Odell and Aldrich would take to the Outside. Hoglen etched the description "My pards leaving the Country. Going out." into the photo. Odell wrote the following description of the photo:

> A third fellow [Odell] is just bidding us good bye and telling us to "lean into the collar boys." Perhaps that has been an unspoken slogan of '97 [the year Odell and Aldrich graduated from Cornell] – 'Lean into the collar.'

Walt Hoglen, near Wolverine Creek cabin. Odell Collection.

Harry Granger is wearing snowshoes, near Wolverine Creek cabin. Odell Collection.

Odell's and Aldrich's horse Buck was not included in the two photos of the sled and gear. However, it is hard to believe that Buck wasn't with the men – why pull their sled without the assistance of their horse? As discussed below, Buck pulled their sled, with a lighter load after they sold some of their goods, from Fort Selkirk out of the Yukon over the Winter River Trail.

Odell, Granger, and Aldrich finally left their Wolverine Creek cabin for Fort Selkirk on February 9, hauling the Odell/Aldrich sled fully loaded with provisions and equipment. Odell and Aldrich would never see the cabin or Wolverine Creek again. The three men were not able to reach their midway shack on Stone Creek with the heavy load, so they abandoned the sled and hiked to the shack and spent the night there. Odell noted that it was very difficult work, and they left their sled between "Willow & big creek" before reaching their shack midway between their cabin and Fort Selkirk.

The next day, the three men returned and retrieved the Odell/Aldrich sled, hauling it to the "crest of divide," and returned to the shack to stay the next night. The next day, the three men "took loads to Selkirk three days regular horse work."

Once at Fort Selkirk, the Odell and Aldrich sold some of their goods and gear. Granger returned to the Wolverine Creek cabin. Odell and Aldrich would never see him again. The men sold much of their goods and gear, traded with Indians, and made their sled and gear ready to start up the frozen Yukon River the next morning with a significantly lighter load on their sled.

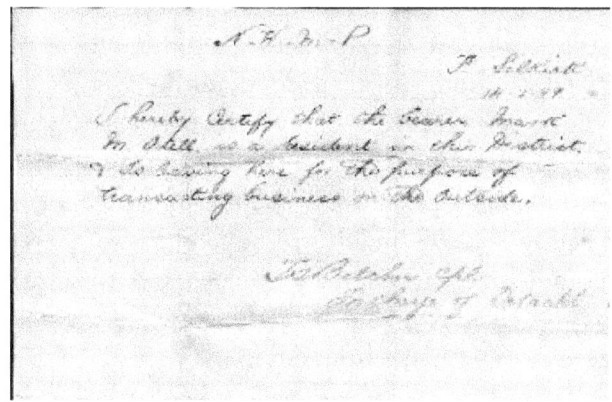

Pass or authorization for Odell to leave the Yukon, Odell Collection.

No mention was made in his diary, but Odell and Aldrich obtained written authorizations or passes from the Fort Selkirk detachment of the NWMP authorizing them to leave the Yukon.

400 Mile Trek to Outside Over Winter River Trail

On February 15, 1899, Odell and Aldrich began their 400-mile hike out of the Yukon – destination Skagway, Alaska, and the Outside.

Odell did not name the trail they followed out of the Yukon. However, the trail was called the Winter River Trail* as it ran over the frozen Yukon River waterway winding in a generally southerly direction towards Bennett City. After reaching Bennett City, they hiked overland to Log Cabin near the US/Canadian border, over White Pass, and alongside the newly laid narrow gauged railroad track from the summit to Skagway.

For the most part, ice on the Winter River Trail provided a smooth surface for sleds to traverse. It was described near Dawson City as being "smooth as marble."[183] However, the conditions were not uniform. A description of the Winter River Trail the year before in 1898 mentioned huge blocks of ice in places, hidden open water, and the necessity to zigzag across the river to avoid dangerous areas.[184] It was dangerous to leave the beaten trail over the ice.[185]

Traffic on the Winter River Trail was described as "brisk" throughout the winter of 1898-99.[186]

---

* The Winter River Trail is discussed in Appendix E.

Always cautious, Odell and Aldrich would keep to the beaten trail over the ice. Odell noted two instances when the men took "cut offs" from the frozen waterway to reach their night's destination at a bunkhouse. Presumably, these cut offs allowed people to avoid large pile ups of ice or dangerous patches of thin ice over raging water, or the cut offs essentially allowed them to avoid the winding portion of the river and take a more direct route:

- South of Five Fingers Rapids, where Odell and Aldrich "go over cut off to the B.L.&K. [Bennett Lake & Klondike Navigation Company] house [road house]"
- South of Miles Canyon when the "Make foot Lake Marsh about 5 oclock [sic]. Good 24 miles by cut off and stay at a bunkhouse operated by Norman Macaulay."

A United States Army officer, Lieutenant J.C. Castner, led a small party over the Winter River Trail one week before Odell and Aldrich taking the same two cut offs.

> We left Hootalinqua and followed up the Thirty-Mile River [between Lake Laberge and the junction with the Teslin River]. This stream proved a stumbling block to many Klondike gold seekers last year. More lives were lost on it than on any other in this region. It is open in many places in winter. Several portages were made to avoid its snake-like windings....

> Eighty-five miles above Hootalinqua we went around the famous White Horse Rapids by a well-established road, striking the river again above Miles Canyon. Here a tramway 4 miles in length permits the gold seeker to transfer his impedimenta around the rapids.[187]

Presumably, the cut off trail around Miles Canyon and the White Horse Rapids followed the route of Norman Macaulay's tramway line.

During the winter of 1898-99, the Winter River Trail was the only route available into or out of the Yukon interior. At that time, a land-based trail did not exist between Lake Bennett and Dawson City. A series of bunkhouses and small communities were constructed in 1898 on the shoreline along the frozen waterway. These sites were spaced on average every 18 or so miles apart, where shelter, food and supplies were available. NWMP outposts were located at some of these stops. Some stops were constructed as mail stops but others sprung up as well. They were used by travelers in and out of the Yukon to purchase food and shelter in lieu of begging for food from the NWMP as they had during the winter of 1897-98.[188]

Bunkhouse conditions varied. Most were crude. A nicer bunkhouse at Hunker Creek, outside of Dawson City and not part of the Winter River Trail, was described as consisting of one large room with three stoves and twenty-four bunk beds, but guests had to supply their own blankets.[189] Men slept two to a bunk.[190] Lesser accommodations at the Brimstone bunkhouse, also outside of Dawson City and not part of the Winter River Trail, were described as a very rough place with men crowded together in a single room with their dogs, gear, and sacks of food.[191] One wonders if there was fire to accompany the brimstone?

The odor in most of these bunkhouses was dreadful and the noise was distracting. "There was an endless chorus of snores, belches, farts, and moans, and the anguished cries of those lost in nightmares."[192] Presumably, wood smoke, body odors, bad breath, and steaming, wet clothing added to the stench.

There were two notedly bad parts of the Winter River Trail. One bad spot was immediately south of Fort Selkirk, from the Fort to Hootchiku. The other bad spot was on the last ten miles of Thirty Mile River.[193]

By trekking to the Outside over the Winter River Trail, Odell and Aldrich essentially followed the same route they had sailed from Lake Bennett to reach Fort Selkirk, but moved in the opposite direction, up the Yukon River and then the series of lakes and short channels in a general southern direction toward Bennett. For the most part, the trail had already been broken by others, but in one instance they held up for several days at a bunkhouse waiting for a storm to abate but the trail had already been broken by the time they restarted their trek. At this time of year, the men would have hiked during both daylight and darkness.*

Odell's records provide somewhat rare details about the Winter River Trail and the bunkhouses along the route. These records include daily diary entries describing their trek. A short table at the end of the diary noted the location of the bunkhouse or stop where they stayed, mileage between the stops, and the date the men stayed at the bunkhouse. Lieutenant Castner noted essentially the same stops over the Fort Selkirk to Bennett City portion of the route as Odell recorded, traveling this same area about one week before Odell and Aldrich.[194]

One record of these bunkhouses along the route states that they were first developed "after 1899."[195] However, as the records of both Odell and Lt. Castner reveal, as well as NWMP records, this system of bunkhouses existed at least by late 1898 and were in use during the winter of 1898-99.

After disposing of some of their gear and equipment at Fort Selkirk, their sled had a much-lightened load. They brought out a tent, sleeping bags, fire wood, cooking equipment, some tools, perhaps a change of clothes, Odell's Yukon Diary, Odell's Cornell pennant, and food for themselves and their horse

---

* A discussion of the development of the Winter River Trail into what became the land based Overland Trail is found in Appendices A, E, and F.

Buck. They also would have taken any gold they had found.

The above photos of their sled with its load, taken when Odell and Aldrich left their cabin and mining site on Wolverine Creek, show the load to be about two and a half to three feet in diameter and eight to nine feet long. However, this was before they sold much of their gear at Fort Selkirk. The load was wrapped in what looked like a heavy tarp, presumably made of canvas.

> We brought it [Odell's Cornell pennant] out with us on our four hundred mile walk [out of the Yukon].[196]

Buck pulled their sled, with the two men helping to pull or push when needed. Part way out of the Yukon, the men added a dog to provide greater pulling power.

Odell and Aldrich would take about one month, during February and March of 1899, to complete the 400-mile distance trekking on snowshoes out of the Yukon from Fort Selkirk to Skagway. They hiked between four and 32 miles each day, stopping at night to stay in crude bunkhouses along the trail. Each bunkhouse charged from 75¢ to $2 to stay overnight. Food was extra. Presumably the charges noted by Odell were for both Odell and Aldrich, although this is not made clear in Odell's Yukon diary. Odell described some of the bunkhouses as being dirty and cramped. Aldrich was ill, and both Odell and Aldrich became very sore on their grueling trek back to civilization.

The men's good friend, Alec Harbinson, left the Yukon at the same time. Harbinson is mentioned in several entries in the Odell Yukon diary during Odell's and Aldrich's trek to Skagway. His name appears several names before Odell and Aldrich in the NWMP exit ledger at Tagish Post listing people who exited the Yukon.[197]

The temperature during their trek out of the Yukon was well below zero, causing them much discomfort. After reaching the States, Aldrich reported that on their trek out of the Yukon the thermometer dropped to 68 degrees below zero in one instance and for two weeks, the temperature averaged about 45 degrees below zero.[198] Much of the time, the men would hike in darkness.

Finally, Odell and Aldrich were ready to leave Fort Selkirk on their trek to the Outside.

On February 15, 1899, Odell and Aldrich left Fort Selkirk a little after 9 a.m., and reached the Lewis Bunkhouse, 18 miles up the river at 3:45 p.m. The ice was hard, but bad in many places for a sled.

On February 16, they left the Lewis Bunk House at 5 a.m. and hiked about 12 to 14 miles to the AEC bunkhouse, arriving at 2 p.m. They stayed the night in a shack with six other "travelers" – the manager of the AEC, three of his companions (one of which was a Mr. Gnole), and two others. The wind blew hard that last night drifting on the trail and packed hard.

On February 17, Odell and Aldrich left the AEC facility at 9 a.m. and made Goring's bunkhouse by 2 p.m. They met ten dog teams and one horse just below Big Horn. The wind blew

> down the river sharp chilled my thumb putting on sweater. Cold as or colder than yesterday.

Odell noted four sleds going northward with mail and two going southward with mail.

The men left Goring's at 7:30 a.m. and reached Five Fingers Rapids a little after noon. They stayed at the B.L.&K.N. bunkhouse. The diary refers to this bunkhouse as "Sirgel's Bunk House" run by a person named "Passage Union '98 from Schenectady." Presumably, Odell meant that Passage Union was from the Cornell class of 1898. There may have been two bunkhouses at Five Fingers. In the table at the end of his diary, Odell notes an AEC facility operated by McDonald at Five Fingers Rapids. Along the way to Five Fingers Rapids, they passed more mail teams. The weather was good, but a strong wind began blowing in the evening that "filled" the track on the trail. So, they decided to stay at the bunkhouse on February 19.

This decision was wise, as it blew and snowed all day – "worst storm of the year." They helped Passage Union bring in and cut wood. Presumably, the men earned their room and board by these actions, but Odell did not make note of that. In the evening, they were joined by Coleman, Jim and Bill Butler (of Dawson City and St. Paul), and P.D. McKellar (of Dawson City and Whatcom County, Washington). McKellar was the person who had told Odell at Fort Selkirk to watch Emmons and his group. Odell and Aldrich stayed over another day on February 20 waiting for the trail to clear. A druggist named Kelly and his partners came down at night with tales of a "terrible trail." This was probably Charles E. Kelly who operated a drug store in Skagway.

They left Sirgel's bunkhouse at 7:30 a.m. on February 21. Coleman and others had started out earlier in the morning but soon returned – "dogs sorefooted." Odell noted that the trail was well broken, but their sled dragged "mighty hard." He and Aldrich stopped to get warm in cabins seven miles down from Five Fingers. Their progress was slow. They had intended to make the next BL&KN bunkhouse but could not make the distance, so they stopped at Burn's bunkhouse that was kept by someone named Ferguson. The men were "mighty tired." They met the NWMP hauling mail. Five men on foot, two dog teams, and one sled were ahead of them. Odell noted that Five Fingers Rapids were frozen over.

The next day, February 22, Odell and Aldrich "go over cut off" trail to the BL&KN bunkhouse, kept by L.C. McCarty, and find Blanc and Chisholm there who wanted the men to take their dog out to

Skagway. This proved to be a godsend as they could make further distances with the combined power of both a horse and dog pulling the sled. It appears that at least one other bunkhouse was located at this site, as the table at the end of Odell's diary noted an AEC facility at this location. "Old Hart and Marx come along also."

Odell and Aldrich started early on February 23 and made the mouth of the Little Salmon, some 16 miles south, at 5:15 p.m. He noted the dog was a considerable help. Their friend, Alec Harbinson, came along. It was a very cold day. They paid $2 to stay at the bunk house.

On February 24, they made 14 miles to "Brincis cabin" by 1 p.m. and stayed over with five others, along with Marx and Hart. In his table of bunkhouses, Odell referred to this establishment as "Bruces." They paid 40¢ for dog food and $2 for staying the night at the bunkhouse.

On February 25, Odell and Aldrich made the Cassiar Bar Bunk House, three miles above the mouth of the Big Salmon River by about 6 p.m. the next day. They had scheduled 28 miles for the day. Half of the way to the Big Salmon River, they ate lunch at Walch's old cabin. Purchases at Big Salmon included five pounds of beans at 50¢, two pounds of sugar at 75¢, and 50¢ worth of dog feed, for a total of $5.50. Odell noted that five friends stopped at the same bunk house.

On February 26, they made the confluence of the Hootalinqua (Teslin) River and Yukon River about 6 p.m. The men had lunch at an old cabin with police who were hauling the mail. They stayed at Hadock's purchasing nine pounds of beef dog meat for $2.25, five pounds of buns at 20¢ apiece, and one pound of potatoes at 75¢. Along with paying $2.00 for staying at the bunk house, the total expenditure was $6.00. Odell noted that his feet were very sore, and he was very tired.

On February 27, they made "half way houses" 17 miles up at the Thirty Mile River and paid $2.00 to stay overnight in one of the cabins. "Feet very sore & legs lame."

On February 28, they made it to the north end of Lake LaBerge about 2 p.m. and purchased seven pounds of flour at 50¢ per pound, a can of baking powder for 50¢, and moccasins for their dog at 50¢. They also paid $2.00 for bunks. A "windy chap" also stayed at the bunkhouse. It was stormy that evening.

On March 1, they reached a First Nation village at the head, or southern end, of Lake LaBerge, "long 30 miles or more", and together with two other men stayed with Jim Boss. Boss was a hereditary chief of the Southern Tutchone peoples living on Lake Laberge who operated a bunkhouse.[199] Odell saw a quiver and arrows that he wanted very much, but apparently did not purchase them. They paid $2.00 for bunks. Odell's feet were still very sore.

On March 2, they made Miles Canyon, about 30 miles distance. They stopped to eat lunch about eight miles below McCarthey's Bunk House at Miles Canyon where they stayed the night at a cost of $2.00 – "a real bum place." Their purchases included milk for 50¢ and two pounds of sugar for $1. The bottoms of Odell's feet were blistered. He could hardly walk the last twelve miles. Just as Odell had failed to mention the townsite of White Horse on his way into the Yukon gold fields, he again failed to note White Horse on the trek out of the Yukon. Lt. Castner also failed to note White Horse in his report. These failures to mention White Horse must reflect its insignificance in early 1899. Again, these are interesting omissions.

On March 3, they made Lake Marsh at 5 p.m., a good 24 miles by a cut off trail, and stayed in "bum bunk house" owned by Macauley at a cost of $2.00. This would have been Norman D. Macauley who owned and operated the Canyon City tram railway. They bought one pound of potatoes for 50¢ and five pounds of flour for $1.50. Odell noted that it was 44 degrees below zero that morning.

On March 4, Odell and Aldrich made the foot of Tagish Lake between 3 and 4 p.m., bought bacon for 60¢, and stayed at another bunkhouse at a cost of $2.00. Although Odell did not make note of it in his diary, records show that the men passed through the Lake Tagish NWMP Post at this date and were recorded in a NWMP ledger as leaving the Yukon.

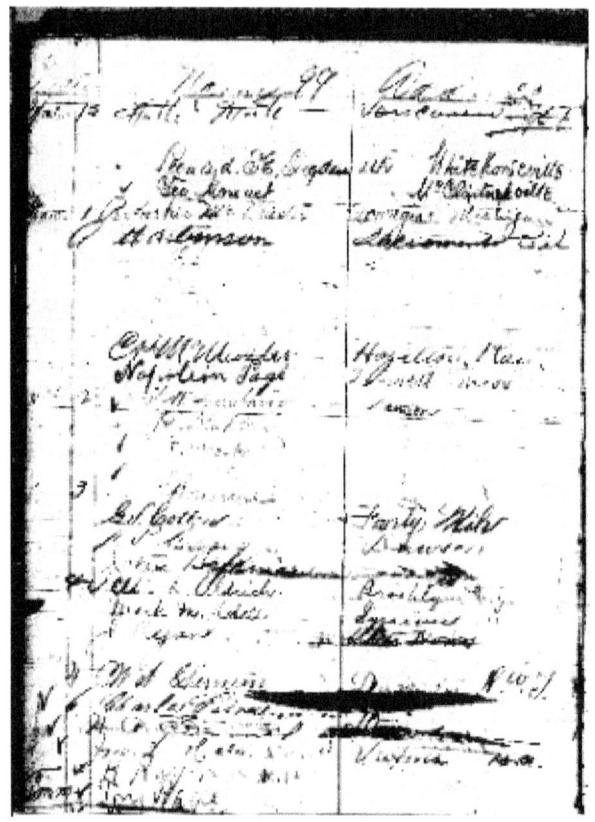

Records Leaving Yukon Territory, Tagish NWMP Post, March 2, 1899. Aldrich and Odell 3/4rs down the page, #4 for this day. A. Harbinson 1/4 down the page, #1 for this day.

On March 5, Odell and Aldrich made Cariboo Crossing by 3 p.m. Odell noted that it had snowed all day and there was a "hard head wind" from Windy Arm. The men stayed at the Hotel Maine, paying $2.00 for bunks and $6.00 for supper and breakfast.

On March 6, they had clear weather and at 5 p.m. they had reached the townsite of Bennett at the southern end of Lake Bennett. They had hiked 32 miles to reach Bennett townsite where they ate dinner at the Last Chance for $2.00, and stayed at the Hotel Klondike at a cost of $1.00 for bunks and $4.00 for meals. This ended the Winter River Trail portion of their trek out of the Yukon. The remainder of the trail to Skagway was over land.

Hotel Klondike, Bennett City, Yukon Archives Photo No. 50, Vogee Collection.

On March 7, they left at noon and stopped at the Old Log Cabin Hotel for the night at "Bennett." The hotel was located seven miles south of the head of Lake Bennett, near the Canadian entrance to White Pass. There was a bad storm and wind all day. They paid $2.00 to stay at the hotel and paid $4.00 for meals and 75¢ for freight. Odell and Aldrich were exhausted.

The WP&YR railway charged 3½¢ per pound to haul freight from Log Cabin, British Columbia, to Skagway.[200] Presumably, the freight was hauled by the

Red Line Transportation Company (a subsidiary of the WP&YR) from Log Cabin to the summit of White Pass where the rail line had reached by this date. No mention was made in his diary, but the construction on the railway was proceeding in this area when they arrived. On February 18, 1899, the narrow-gauged railroad had reached the summit of White Pass, a few miles south of Log Cabin.*[201]

On March 8, Odell and Aldrich left the Old Log Cabin Hotel and headed for the ill-defined border between Canada and Alaska. They hiked alongside the new railroad tracks and arrived at Skagway later that day. Hallelujah!! Finally, out of the wild and into civilization and its creature comforts.

The two exhausted and sore Sourdoughs had finally hiked out of the Yukon over the Winter River Trail and then overland, almost one year after they entered the Yukon as eager Cheechakos.

Skagway

The men had faced bad winds and a storm at their backs all day while hiking from White Pass to Skagway. They paid $1.50 for freight and left their trusty horse Buck at what appears to be the Manhattan, a hotel in Skagway. No mention was made about the dog they brought out. The freight charges must have been for the railroad hauling some

---

* A discussion of the White Pass and Yukon Route railway is found in Appendix E.

of their supplies from White Pass to Skagway. Celebrations were in hand. They obtained rooms at the Dewey Hotel, located at the northwest corner of 7th Avenue and Broadway. Clearly the finest overnight accommodations they had in a year, ate dinner at the Summit Restaurant, and bought tobacco.

Advertisement, Dewey Hotel, Skagway, Alaska.

The next day, March 9, they took baths, shaved, bought new clothes, and cleaned up. This entry revealed how tired the men must have been – after their long trek out of the Yukon, they waited until the day after arriving at Skagway before bathing, probably for the first time in almost one year, apart from using bucket water to wash in their cabin. Or perhaps hot water was not available in the evenings.

Odell purchased drugs for 50¢, spent $1.50 for a bath, probably at the Hotel Dewey that was famous for its Turkish Baths, and bought clothes – pants for $13, shoes for $7, shirts for $3, socks for 85¢, suspenders for 75¢, a hat and tie for $3. Presumably their old, worn, and smelly clothes were tossed. He expended $1.60 for meals that day and 50¢ for a bunk, presumably moving out of the Hotel Dewey.

The final entry in Odell's diary was on March 10, 1899, listing the cost for meals and a bunk, as well as 75¢ for socks and a tie, handkerchiefs for 50¢, and a cap for 50¢. He needed to start looking like a cultured "man of books."

Odell and Aldrich soon set sail to Seattle aboard the S.S. *Laurada*. She was the first ship to leave Skagway in 1899 taking prospectors out of the North.

Did Odell and Aldrich Return with Gold?

The extent of the gold Odell and Aldrich brought out of the Yukon is shrouded in mystery. Until recently, the authors were under the impression that Odell and Aldrich had found very little gold in the Yukon. After returning from the north, neither Odell nor Aldrich spoke about hitting it rich in the Yukon. They denied finding much gold for the rest of their lives. Odell's Yukon Diary only contains a few entries mentioning the men finding "colors" or a "pair of nuggets."

To the authors' knowledge, the only physical evidence of gold that Odell had found in the Yukon was a very small amount (perhaps the size of two or three BB's) that he kept in a vial stored in the basement of his Seattle house. When requested, Odell would show his grandchildren this small vial who were in awe of this "treasure."

On October 4, 1898, Aldrich wrote a letter to a friend stating that their hopes for easy gold had not materialized – "Alas, how rudely at times are our fondest hopes blasted, and how harsh is reality when experience causes the scales to fall from our eyes."[202] The letter was written prior to Odell's and Aldrich's primary mining efforts on Wolverine Creek.

However, the March 23, 1899, edition of *Seattle Daily Times*, at page 5, included an article describing a secret cargo of gold that arrived in Seattle on board the steamship Odell and Aldrich sailed on from Skagway.

MANY WEALTHY MINERS

The Laurada Brought $150,-000 From Alaska on Her Last Trip Down.

The text of the article was:

> The Steamship *Laurada*, which arrived nearly a week ago from the North, was the first Klondike treasure ship to arrive

this year although the fact that a large quantity of gold was on board was kept so quiet that the fact did not leak out until the arrival of the *City of Seattle* yesterday. Men who came out with the rich miners gave their secret away.

They place the amount of gold on the *Laurada* at $150,000. The gold was in possession of Purser Donnelly but he had his instruction to keep quiet about it. The exact amounts that the rich miners had are not known, but their names are. A woman was one of the lucky gold holders. It is said in Alaska that she brought out a sack of gold as long as her stocking. She is Tonny Page, a very clever Dawson woman who has made good money through her friendship with Dawson miners and who knows how to keep her money.

H. Sullivan of Gold Run Creek also had considerable dust. D. Clark, W.H. Parsons and H. Raymond brought some Circle City gold out with them. **M.M. O'Dell [sic] and E.L. Aldridge [sic] are two New Yorkers who brought out considerable dust.** [Emphasis added.]

The *Laurada* was not able to get water at Skagway and on the trip to Juneau the passengers drank champagne or beer in its place. It is said that the richest of the Klondikers washed his face in the sparkling liquid.[203]

Almost two weeks after the *Seattle Daily Times* article, the *Cornell Daily Sun* reported that the *Laurada* arrived in Seattle with $150,000 of Yukon gold and that Odell and Aldrich each came out with between $15,000 and $20,000 in gold.[204]

It is possible that the reporters writing these newspaper articles were caught up in the frenzy over the Yukon gold rush and were mistaken about gold found by Odell and Aldrich. Clearly, the news articles were not part of Odell's earlier self-publicity efforts, as Odell would have spelled their last names correctly had he written a press release upon which the articles were based. Presumably someone other than Odell or Aldrich leaked this story about the gold coming out of the Yukon.

The authors have some doubts that Odell and Aldrich each returned with this amount of gold. Fifteen to twenty thousand dollars of gold in 1899 is worth a considerable amount in current dollars. Further, any gold that Odell and Aldrich brought out of the Yukon would have been the property of their backer or backers who "grub staked" their prospecting efforts. The men were to receive "liberal compensation" for their efforts, whether successful or not. Any compensation would be given after the backers were reimbursed for the men's expenses and took a larger share of whatever remained.

William Shape wrote that the per person cost to finance a trip into and out of the Yukon was about $1,000,[205] so a substantial portion of the value of any gold brought back to the states would have been used to reimburse the backers for these costs. As mentioned below in "Afterwards," Walt Hoglen left the Wolverine cabin one month after Odell and Aldrich left the camp for the Outside. It makes little sense for Hoglen to have left the cabin if the mining shafts on Wolverine Creek were producing significant amounts of gold.

The *Seattle Daily Times* of March 17, 1899, listed "L.C. Smith of Osceola" as staying at the Hotel Diller in Seattle.[206] The Diller Hotel was a luxury hotel in Seattle with running water, toilets, and the first elevator in the city.[207] This possibly was the same Mr. Smith who financed Odell's and Aldrich's trip to the Yukon. Osceola may have been a winter home allowing L.C. Smith to avoid the cold season in Syracuse, New York. Very probably, Mr. Smith would have traveled by train to meet Odell and Aldrich when they returned with gold.

Odell was aware of the newspaper articles and disputed the tale of a horde of gold. In the undated letter he wrote from Seattle to his sister Ida in upstate New York, Odell mentioned that it was

> with a grim amusement that I read in clippings from New York, Syracuse and Eastern papers, that I was worth several thousand dollars, this while I was sneaking around to the cheap Japanese restaurants and eating ten cent meals. I had enough left when I reached Seattle to live on about a month. Fortunately I got

a good place to work, am getting better known and eat better meals.[208]

However, he asked his sister to inform him about "the amount of my indebtedness to you" and that he had fifty dollars to send her, but "wanted to wait and send it all if possible."[209]

It is possible that Odell was secretive about the gold by disputing the story of his riches to his sister but he also failed to note any major gold strike in his diary.

Aldrich was also aware of the newspaper reports, and was quoted by a reporter in Ithaca, New York, in mid-April 1899, denying becoming wealthy.

> Mr. Aldrich remarked that the statement in some of the papers to the effect that they returned with fabulous wealth is false. The men who made money were those that were there in the great strike of '96.[210]

A newspaper article, published five months after Odell and Aldrich returned from the Yukon, stated that

> As for Odell he struck nothing but bad luck. He was accompanied by Aldrich, also a Cornell man, and instead of finding gold they found nothing but hardships and privations. They had been fitted out by Ithaca parties who offered them one-half of what they made. They came back without a cent, notwithstanding the flowery accounts sent from the coast to the effect that both men had struck it rich.[211]

Entries in Odell's Yukon diary during the winter of 1898-1899 reflected the darkness and gloom of the Yukon winter days. Odell, Aldrich, Hoglen and Granger were worn out and often sick. The only upbeat entries in the diary during this period occurred in late January of 1899, when First Nation visitors arrived at their cabin. They talked, had several meals, and a general "great event."[212]

At that date, Odell's and Aldrich's primary mine shaft was more than thirty feet deep, near or at the level of the bedrock where gold was more likely to be found. It is possible that they found substantial gold at this level, but, again, the Odell diary does not include any note of significant amounts of gold being found.

On January 29, 1899, a few days after this "great event" celebrating with First Nation visitors, Odell arranged for sick Aldrich to be taken out of the Yukon and returned to Skagway. Would Aldrich have brought out the "considerable gold" alone, or was he being taken out solely because of his illness? Or perhaps Odell would have retained the gold himself? The first effort to get Aldrich out failed. It is clear from his diary that, by at least February 8, 1899, Odell had decided to take Aldrich out of the Yukon himself.

Odell and Aldrich would have been secretive about finding any gold in the Yukon, at least until they were safe in Seattle with the gold. Presumably, the most pressing issue would be how to keep the gold secure when they returned to the Alaskan panhandle, especially in the infamous Skagway. The Yukon was a relatively law-abiding area with Mounties providing security. However, Alaska was less secure, even after Skagway's notorious Soapy Smith was killed earlier on July 8, 1898. Prospectors would have kept quiet. Any gold brought out along the Winter River Trail would have been kept on their persons or hidden in their sled load. The news stories seem to ring true about any news of the gold on the *Laurada* being kept quiet for almost one week after the vessel had docked in Seattle.

Canada imposed a 5% gold royalty tax on gold removed from the Yukon.[213] The authors were unable to find records of these royalty payments for 1899. A newspaper article in the *Seattle Daily Times* recounts how miners exiting the Yukon were compelled to pass through inspection by Canadian officials and "human nature" would lead these prospectors to avoid a 5% gold royalty tax by minimizing the amount of gold they reported.[214]

Afterwards

Mark Odell, Ellis Aldrich, Walt Hoglen and Harry Granger went their separate ways after Odell and Aldrich left the Wolverine Creek mining area and headed for the Outside over the Winter River Trail.

Pierre Berton wrote about how the Klondike or Yukon experience had a major impact upon those who made it to the goldfields.[215]

From the perspectives of his grandchildren, Odell retained at least some of these feelings. Tom Wood kept a lust of gold searching for gold in Nome, Alaska. Walt Hoglen and Harry Granger remained in the Yukon for several years after Odell and Aldrich had left. Odell and Aldrich did not return to the Yukon. Walt Hoglen retained the greatest fire for the Yukon among Odell and his partners. Decades after leaving the Yukon, Hoglen returned and lived the last years of this life in the Yukon. He still had the call of the north in his later years.

Little remains of the structures and improvements Odell and his partners saw in the Yukon and Alaskan panhandle. Many thriving settlements soon disappeared, including the town of Dyea, camps or "towns" along the Chilkoot Trail, the two towns or cities at the southern ends of Lake Lindeman and Lake Bennett, mining sites along the Yukon River, and the rest stops or bunkhouses along the Yukon River. The tiny settlement of Closeleigh, that became Whitehorse, was so insignificant that Odell and others failed to take note of the settlement when passing it by in 1898 and 1899.

Whitehorse is now the Territorial capital with an estimated population of almost 28,000 people in 2023, 62% of the population of Yukon Territory. Moving the capital from Dawson City to Whitehorse seems to have been inevitable. Whitehorse is located north of the most difficult parts of the Yukon River to navigate, allowing boats to enter the Yukon River from the Bering Sea to reach Whitehorse. The railway ended at Whitehorse rather than further north at Fort Selkirk as originally planned. Construction of the Alaskan Highway during World War II, that didn't reach Dawson City, also helped secure the move of the capital to Whitehorse.

Odell and Aldrich never reached Dawson City that had become the largest Yukon settlement and site of the most extensive mining activities during the fabled gold rush. Dawson City remains, but is sparsely populated out of the tourist summer season with a population of 1,375 people. Skagway has a population of 968 people, but becomes more populated during the summer tourist season, especially when cruise ships arrive. Fort Selkirk is abandoned but remains as an historic site with archeological crews living onsite during the summer work season. Tourists frequently stop on their way down the river during the summer.

Ellis Aldrich

Within a few days of their arrival in Seattle, Odell saw Aldrich off to travel by train to New York. This was the last time the college chums saw each other until their fiftieth Cornell reunion in 1947.

After seeing his family in Brooklyn, Aldrich visited Cornell University in Ithaca, N.Y., where he spoke about Odell's and his adventures in the Yukon, stressing that their experiences resembled descriptions in many magazine articles about other prospectors.[216] Aldrich's father died in 1899, the same year Ellis returned to New York from the Yukon, so it is possible that Aldrich was able to see his father when he returned to New York in March of 1899. Aldrich returned for his last quarter of law school at Cornell and graduated with a Bachelor of Law degree after the fall term of 1899. He was admitted to the practice of law in New York City in 1900 and had a successful law career practicing in Manhattan. Aldrich married Jane E. Norton in 1901. They had two children – Janet and Sherwood.[217] The family moved to Maine in 1923.

In the 1900 U.S. Census, Ellis was enumerated as living with his mother, Josephine Aldrich, a widow, in Brooklyn. He appeared in the 1905 New York

Census as living in Brooklyn with his wife and daughter. Aldrich was listed as living in Montclair Township, Essex County, New Jersey in the 1910 and 1920 Decennial Censuses.

He was recorded in the 1930 and 1940 Decennial Censuses as living in Topsham, Maine where he practiced law and served in the Maine State Senate as a Republican in 1931 and 1932. Aldrich purchased the historic Topsham mansion in Lewiston, Maine. This colonial mansion was built in 1802 and was once the home of William King, the first governor of Maine.[218]

Odell remained in contact with Aldrich until Odell's death in 1963. Both Aldrich and Odell attended their 50-year Cornell reunion. Aldrich died in September of 1968.

Years ago, in a telephone conversation with one of the authors, Aldrich's daughter-in-law, Constance Aldrich, indicated that she and her then deceased husband Sherwood had encouraged Aldrich to write about his Yukon adventures. These efforts bore no fruit. However, the Cornell University Archives records indicate that in 1947 Aldrich wrote a paper describing his Yukon adventures for his fiftieth college reunion. Unfortunately, this paper has been misplaced. As mentioned above, a long letter written by Aldrich in October of 1898 was published in the *Brooklyn Daily Eagle*. The family was not aware of this news article, or the paper Aldrich had written for the 1947 reunion.

Ellis Aldrich later in life. Courtesy of the McKenzie Family Collection.

Walt Hoglen

Walter J. Hoglen remained in the Yukon for at least two years after Odell and Aldrich had left. Mark Odell's collection includes a diary book that Hoglen had kept, but very few entries were made. In March of 1899, Hoglen moved from the Wolverine Creek cabin to Fort Selkirk. This was a little less than one month after Odell and Aldrich left on their 400-mile trek out of the Yukon. Hoglen hunted for bears up the Pelly River. On May 30, he began working as a cook for the Yukon Lumber Company. On June 21, Hoglen started for Dawson City.[219]

Walter J. Hoglen, age twenty-nine, was enumerated in the 1901 Canadian census as living in Dawson City. He was listed as a miner employed for wages. Online Yukon genealogy records list Walter J. Hoglen as leaving the Yukon Territory on June 11, 1904, for Circle City, Alaska.[220] Hoglen was listed in the 1910, 1920, 1930, and 1940 Decennial Censuses as living in Los Angeles, variously listed as a common laborer or an engineer.

The Odell Collection includes a photo of Odell and Hoglen sitting at desks in a Seattle business office, presumably sometime from 1905 to 1909. Odell helped Hoglen obtain employment at the construction firm where he worked. Hoglen soon moved to California. He and Odell remained close friends.

Left, Mark Odell; right Walt Hoglen, *circa*. 1905 in Seattle. Odell wrote "me" under his image photo and "Walter" under Hoglen's image. Odell Collection.

The lure of the north remained with Hoglen for the rest of his life. He returned to the Yukon in June of 1946. Before leaving for the Yukon, he stayed at Odell's home in Seattle, opened a bank account in a Seattle bank, and leased space to store his personal effects. Presumably, this was where Holgen left his photos of the Yukon and diary from 1898.

From these accounts, Odell and Hoglen had maintained a close but distant friendship since their days mining at the headwaters of Wolverine Creek in 1898-99.

After he returned to the Yukon, Hoglen lived at Fort Selkirk for about a year. It is possible that Hoglen hiked to the old cabin at the headwaters of Wolverine Creek. In April of 1947, he was taken to the Whitehorse General Hospital for treatment of "frozen feet" and died on May 1, 1947. Hoglen is buried at the Pioneer Cemetery in Whitehorse, Yukon Territory.[221] He noted in his information provided to the Whitehorse General Hospital that he had no close relations but Mark Odell was his best friend. After his death, hospital Odell seemed to have functioned as the executor of Hoglen's estate in the Yukon.

Harry Granger

The authors do not have records of Harry Granger, but he appeared to have remained in the Yukon for a while. Canadian customs at White Pass listed "H. Granger" as leaving the Yukon on July 14, 1900. The 1901 Canadian census enumerated "Henry Granger," age 24, in the Upper Eldorado part of the Yukon. Either entry could be the Harry Granger who mined at Wolverine Creek with Odell and Aldrich in 1898 and 1899.

Tom Wood

In late July of 1898, Tom Wood hiked from Fort Selkirk out of the Yukon over the Dalton Trail. As discussed above, Wood could have taken one of three routes from Fort Selkirk to reach the Dalton Trail.

By 1899, gold had been discovered on the beaches near Nome, Alaska, beginning a new gold rush.* Wood joined in this frenzy to find gold.[222] While in Nome, he both worked at and held ownership interests in various mines, stores, road houses, express companies, hotels, and boats, and worked with the Canadian Customs. Wood had "flush days and bust days," that included making trading trips to Siberia.[223] RCMP records listing people entering the Yukon, show Thos. J. Wood, from Dayton, Ohio, entering

---

* The Nome Gold Rush lasted from 1899 to 1909, after gold was discovered in the beach sands near the town of Nome at the outlet of the Snake River on the Seward Peninsula at Norton Sound on the Bering Sea. By 1899, Nome had a population of 10,000, many of whom had arrived from the Klondike Gold Rush area, and the population later swelled to 20,000. At the height of the gold rush, hundreds of tents extended for 15 miles along the beach west of town. During the summer of 1899, $2 million of gold was recovered from the beaches using shovels, rockers, wheelbarrows, and buckets. Nome was much easier to reach than the interior gold fields of the Klondike Gold Rush, and some misleading ads made it sound as if nuggets could be picked off the beach. Absentee investors ultimately took over the mining operations using hydraulic mining techniques and dredges. Total production from the Nome district was around 3.6 million ounces of gold. *(Northwest and Arctic Gold 1897 - 1927,* Alaska History and Cultural Studies, *Nome Gold Rush,* Wikipedia.)

on boat number 44 on May 20, 1900.²²⁴ Presumably Wood visited Hoglen at that time.

Wood returned to Dayton, but after few months moved to Idaho where he farmed at the small community of Farnum, Fremont County, Idaho.

Mark Odell

Soon after arriving back in Seattle, Odell was hired as an agent for the White Pass & Yukon Route (WP&YR) railroad company.* In mid-April of 1899, Aldrich reported that Odell had decided to remain in Seattle and go into business. A Syracuse newspaper noted that Odell had returned from the Yukon gold fields, was living in Seattle, and was the secretary of a freight and transportation company running from Seattle to Skagway, Alaska.²²⁵ Odell remained in Seattle during May. An article in the *Gazette and Farmers' Journal* indicated that Odell was working as a contracting agent for the WP&YR railway in Seattle.²²⁶

Later in 1899, Odell returned to Skagway and continued working for the WP&YR.²²⁷ He also obtained employment as a ticket agent for the Alaskan Steamship Company.†

---

* A discussion of the White Pass and Yukon Route railroad is found in Appendix E.

† On August 3, 1894, six men under the leadership of Charles Peabody formed the Alaska Steamship Company, raising

By December of 1899, Odell had returned to Seattle where he continued working for both the WP&YR and Alaskan Steamship Company. In 1900, the two companies coordinated efforts by offering trips to the Klondike with steamship travel to Skagway and train travel into the interior of the Yukon. Seattle was still experiencing a period of phenomenal growth fueled by Klondike and Alaska gold.

In late May and early June of 1900, Odell again returned to Skagway and Lake Bennett to observe and report on the state of freight transportation facilities. He traveled by train from Skagway to the summit of White Pass and "looked with interest from the car windows upon the old trail that he plodded over a year and a half ago" and then by the Red Line Transportation Company's stage to Lake Bennett.[228] Odell credited M.J. Heney for keeping freight moving.

$30,000 by selling 300 shares of stock at $100 each. The company was reorganized in 1897 and its fleet was expanded rapidly as the Klondike gold stampede created a huge demand for transportation north. In 1909, an Alaska Syndicate, using funds from J.P. Morgan and the Guggenheim Company, bought the Alaska Steamship Company for use in its copper mine in the Wrangell Mountains, and merged the company with the Northwestern Steamship Co. Limited, keeping the Alaska Steamship Company name. The merger gave the new company a near monopoly in the Alaska shipping industry. (Grace, Michael L. *History of the Alaska Steamship Company, Seattle, 1895-1971.*)

Odell's Cornell years continued to be an important part of his life. He wrote to his sister Ida, in an undated letter, that his old red and white Cornell pennant

> now faded and grimy it adorns my rooms here in Seattle, a remembrance of happy days in college, of wild free life in the Yukon wilderness, and above all of love for Alma Mater and brotherly affection between boys of a fraternity.[229]

Like many others who sought their fortunes in the Yukon, Odell made his home in Seattle after returning from the gold rush. His success in Seattle was emblematic of the huge economic boom Seattle experienced from the Yukon Gold Rush. Seattle's population surged and construction boomed, cementing its position as a major west coast port city.

Perhaps symbolic of Seattle's relationship with Alaska and the Yukon, a group of Seattle businessmen "removed," *i.e.*, stole, a 60-foot totem pole from Fort Tongass, Alaska, and erected the totem pole in Seattle's Pioneer Square in 1899. The totem pole became Seattle's emblem and symbol of riches found in Alaska during the gold rushes.*

---

* The business leaders took the totem pole honoring Chief-of-all-Women while townspeople were away fishing. Almost immediately, the business leaders were indicted in federal court for stealing the totem pole. The charges were dismissed in 1900

Taking part in this flurry of economic activity arising at least in part from the Yukon goldrush, Odell was employed in 1901 by the Whitmore Concrete Company that focused on concrete construction.[230] By 1908, he was a partner in the firm that was renamed the Whitmore and Odell Company.[231] In 1911, Odell incorporated his own concrete and general contracting company.[232] Newspaper accounts at times refer to Odell as being a civil engineer, and in one instance an architect, but he did not have formal training in these professions.

Odell participated in numerous public and private construction projects. He rebuilt Bainbridge Island's Port Blakely lumber mill after the mill was destroyed by fire in 1907, at that time the largest lumber mill in the world. Odell paved many sidewalks in Seattle, especially on First Hill. He built the Canadian Pacific steamship wharfs and railroad station in Vancouver, B.C., between 1913 and 1916.

Odell also played a role in the development of the University of Washington. He helped start the University of Washington's crew program. In 1906, Odell and another experienced rower from the East were unpaid coaches for the school's new crew program. Odell assisted Hiram Conibear, who was hired in 1907 as the head crew coach. It is said that Conibear did not know how to row when he was

---

"by a friendly judge on consideration of" money being paid to the Tlingits. (Ketcherside, 51.)

hired. Odell taught the "American stroke" rowing technique to Washington rowers and Conibear. This technique was developed by Cornell's Coach Courtney and dominated college rowing for two decades after the Cornell crew won the national championship in 1897. Conibear is credited with developing the "Washington Stroke" that is partially based upon the American or Cornell stroke he learned from Odell.*

---

* Hiram Conibear died in 1917 after falling out of a plum tree. In the 1920s, there was an effort by those associated with Washington rowing to have the stroke used by the school named after Conibear. In a 1923 article, Walter McLean, "an old coxswain" on Washington's crew, gave his ideas about "what we shall call our justly famous stroke." When "Connie" took over as crew coach in 1907, his rowers had learned their skill from Washington's earlier coaches, and those rowers passed on their knowledge to their new coach. McLean wrote: "[Conibear] would be the last one to deprecate the help received from his men, not only in the first year but in all succeeding years ... Since then, many oarsmen have contributed their earnest thought and experience to the development of our stroke ... among whom the writer remembers vividly the strident-voiced P.D. Hughes and *silent Mark Odell* [emphasis added], all contributed their mite to its refinements.... Let us call it 'the Washington stroke' for all of those who have helped evolve it, and so that if there are improvements yet to be made, we may encourage enterprise and incorporate them without changing the name." ("Walter G. McLean Strongly Favors Naming Stroke After Washington." *The Seattle Daily Times.* August 20, 1923, Sports Section, 1.)

A recent book on the history of rowing describes how Odell taught the Cornell rowing technique to Conibear and Washington rowers.

> Many have described George Pocock as the sole author of the Conibear Stroke, but history demonstrates that this is less than the full story. Conibear's descriptions of the ideal stroke differed substantially from George Pocock's written descriptions of the Thames Waterman's Stroke. It would be more accurate to recognize that the Conibear Stroke was the result of crucial early consultation with Charles Courtney reinforced **by having former Cornell rower Mark Odell as a volunteer assistant in Washington program**. [Emphasis added.] Add in the influence of George Pocock, and Conibear had everything he needed to supplement his own innate intelligence.[233]

University of Washington crews became dominant in college rowing, and its rowers have coached several crew programs throughout the country, spreading Washington rowing techniques throughout the United States. In 1936 the University of Washington men's rowing team won the gold medal for men's eights at the Olympic Games that were held in Berlin. Daniel James Brown wrote a best-selling book celebrating the team.[234] George Clooney made a movie about the Washington crew based upon the Brown book.

In 1910, Mark Odell married India Bell Poulson, a Seattle public school teacher. Poulson was born on July 16, 1875, in Lincoln Township, Audubon County, Iowa. They had two sons and a daughter – Mark Jr, Burr, and Margaret (the authors' mother).

Mark and India Bell Odell were part of Seattle's upper crust society with huge aspirations for wealth and position. India was a member of the first faculty at Lincoln High School in Seattle but stopped teaching when she married. The Odells enjoyed social prominence in Seattle, but much of this prominence vanished with Mark's untimely loss of his construction company.

The authors' mother spoke of her father going broke in 1926 "trying to pave Snoqualmie Pass" over the Cascade Mountains east of Seattle.[235] He was out of work for several years and the family was supported by India's successful career selling life insurance policies for the Banker's Life Company. Eventually, Odell became a general insurance agent and remained in that occupation until his death in 1963. Although the Odell's maintained friendships with members of the Seattle society, they never recovered their financial stability.

Odell retained his conservative opinions as he aged, but as an old man he no longer openly expressed these opinions. Perhaps time had mellowed or tempered his opinions. Perhaps he had just learned that he should keep these opinions to himself.

During the infamous 1919 Seattle General Strike, Odell was one of the hundreds of local businessmen and students from the University of Washington who were deputized to help "maintain" the peace during the strike, which was the first general strike in the nation. Odell would show his grandchildren two artifacts from this period. One was a six-pointed badge star imprinted with "Special Deputy" with a three-digit number somewhere in the hundreds. The other was a pistol kept in a holster attached to a belt with loops to hold bullets, but no longer had any bullets. To his grandkids, this looked like a relic from Dodge City or Tombstone where people were disarmed and required to hang their holstered weapons on a hook before entering town. When asked how he had obtained these relics, Odell would talk about being deputized and assigned to the top of a building where he would watch and report on what he termed "bad men" below on the streets.

Odell attended his fortieth year and fiftieth year Cornell University reunions at Ithaca in 1937 and 1947. The returning alums who were members of the famous 1897 Cornell crew celebrated both reunions by rowing in a shell on the Cayuga River. It is quite common for returning crews (sometimes with current crew members) to row a shell during their reunions. Odell noted in Cornell Alumni records in 1937 – "Main interests – Keeping feet on the ground and head above water."[236]

In 1952, when his wife India was hospitalized after having a stroke, Mark walked with the authors around the First Hill area of Seattle, where most of the hospitals in Seattle were located. He talked about paving the sidewalks, but noted with pride that he did not allow his name to be imprinted onto the sidewalks, as was the practice by most contractors. He did not want people walking on his good name.

India Bell Odell died in 1953. She had been employed as a salesperson for the Bankers Life Insurance Company where she became one of its top producing agents and qualified for membership in the company's highest honor group, the President's Premier Club.

Mark Odell remained an enigma. He was a rural farm boy who, as a principal of a local public school, won a state scholarship to attend Cornell where he received a bachelor's degree and was one quarter short of earning a law degree. Evidence of the newly acquired Ivy League elitism was evident from Odell's writings in the Yukon. He took care to identify fellow collegians in his diary and wrote to his father describing himself as a "man of letters" in the wilderness.

The authors knew their grandfather as an older, very formal gentleman. He always wore a tie and three-piece suit, with a gold pocket watch attached to his vest by a watch chain. The authors still have Odell's formal, dress gold watch and chain, as well as his everyday gold watch and chain. Odell normally wore a fedora when outside, but in summer months he substituted a stovepipe straw hat. His focus on being well dressed even included times when he did yard work wearing an old three-piece suit, but no tie. He was hard of hearing in his later years and used a hearing aid.

Odell always wore a one piece, union suit – long john underwear featuring a button up backdoor. He normally wore long sleeved long johns, but in the warm months he wore thinner long johns with three quarter length sleeves.

Odell in later life.

Under Odell's Victorian views, men could smoke, but not women, and no one should imbibe alcohol. He smoked cigars as a young teenager with tobacco grown by his father on his upstate New York farm. A later owner of this farm told one of the authors that in 1949 he took his young daughter to see the last harvest of tobacco in the area. Odell's ever-present pipe is seen in almost every non-posed photo. In later years Odell enjoyed smoking Revelation tobacco in his corncob pipe.

Every morning Odell followed the same shaving routine. He stropped his straight razor, soaked his face with hot water, lathered up Williams mug shaving soap (known since 1840 "for a lasting lather") in a shaving brush bowl, applied the lather using a brush with badger hair bristles, and shaved. Although his hands shook, as his writing was shaky, he never nicked himself when he shaved.

In the late 1950s his son Burr gave Odell a television set with earphones to lessen impacts from hearing loss. Odell would sit directly in front of the television and watch baseball games, telling his grandkids that when he was a youth playing baseball, there were no called strikes and the batter would tell the pitcher the location and speed of the pitches he desired. One can only wonder at his awe over television broadcasts, as Odell was 37 years old when the first radio program broadcast was made in 1906 and 51 years old when the first radio news program was broadcast in 1920.

Odell, circa., 1958.

Odell was a proud, educated man, with any vestige of temper blunted by advanced age, life's experiences, and most of all his financial ruin in the mid-1920s. In his later years, his hobbies were reading and working crossword puzzles. Burr Odell, his last surviving child, mentioned to one of the authors that he felt his father was "a defeated man." Presumably, Burr was referring to his father's financial losses in the mid-1920s and a resulting loss of social prominence.

Still every inch a Victorian gentleman, Odell tripped and broke his hip in 1963 while opening the front door for a young woman at the Coleman Office Building in downtown Seattle where he still had his office working as a general insurance salesman. After this injury, and the subsequent removal of his prostate gland, Odell still had the strength to walk using crutches. He died on June 26, 1963, at age 94, about a month after his accident.

Odell remained modest and unassuming about his accomplishments, as seen from his description of his adventures in the Yukon as being very commonplace in old Seattle.

Each working day before his injury, Odell walked from his home on Capitol Hill several blocks to a bus stop and rode the bus to his office in downtown Seattle. His gait was slower, but the walk was easier for the 94-year-old, somewhat hard of hearing, former Sourdough than his 400-mile trek out of the Yukon over the Winter River Trail with his old college chum, Ellis Aldrich, in 1899.

Appendices

Appendix A - Fort Selkirk

Prior to the Klondike gold rush, Fort Selkirk was one of the most significant white settlements in what became the Yukon Territory. That status soon vanished as prospectors flocked to what became Dawson City and the nearby Klondike gold fields. Although Fort Selkirk retained some level of importance, its significance had greatly ebbed.[237]

Today, the old Fort Selkirk trading post is an abandoned archeological site, a faded memory and mere shell of itself. The diminished status of Fort Selkirk arose from three factors: (1) The lack of a major, gold strike near Fort Selkirk; (2) the failure to extend the WP&YR railroad from White Horse to Fort Selkirk, as had been originally planned; and (3) the location of the Overland Trail across the Yukon River from Fort Selkirk rather than on the same side of the River as Fort Selkirk.

Fort Selkirk is located on the left bank of the Yukon River as one travels downstream, immediately beyond the confluence of the Pelly River and Yukon River. For centuries, Northern Tutchone peoples hunted large game, trapped smaller fur bearing animals, and fished at the site that became Fort Selkirk. During their seasonal visits, Native peoples lived in temporary brush shelters, covered with moose hide or caribou, which were open at one side towards fire pits.

What is now known as Fort Selkirk was also a major meeting and trading site for Native peoples. For centuries, coastal Chilkat Tlingits traveled into the Yukon interior to Fort Selkirk and traded with Northern Tutchone peoples, a branch of the Athapascan peoples. Tlingits brought goods from the coast to trade – shells, walrus ivory, seaweed, herbs, and roots. Tutchone peoples brought goods from the interior to trade – furs, hides, and clothing. Later, Tlingits brought European goods to be traded – guns, wool blankets, tea, and tobacco. Tlingits and Tutchone people often intermarried. Archeological artifacts from thousands of years ago have been found at what became Fort Selkirk.

In 1848, Robert Campbell constructed a Hudson's Bay Company trading post about two kilometers up the Pelly River from its confluence with the Yukon River. He named the trading post Fort Selkirk. After spring floods damaged the post, Campbell moved the trading post downstream to the historic trading site of the Native peoples, and the current site known as Fort Selkirk. Some gold was found near the new site of the trading post.[238]

The move had dire consequences. Chilkat Tlingits resented the intrusion of the trading post on their historic trading grounds. On August 18, 1852, a party of Chilkat Tlingits attacked and pillaged the trading post. Campbell fled and was saved by Chief Hanan, of the Selkirk band of Tutchone peoples. The Hudson's Bay Company abandoned its trading post at Fort Selkirk. Three basalt chimneys were the only remains of the old Hudson's Bay trading post when Frederick Schwatka passed by the abandoned site in 1883.

Arthur Harper, a native of Antrim County, Ireland, who arrived in the Yukon in 1873, built a new trading post at Fort Selkirk in 1889. The new Fort Selkirk trading post was one of several trading posts that Harper, and his partners Jack McQuesten and Al Mayo, constructed for the A.C. (Alaska Commercial) Company along the Yukon River. Fort Selkirk grew as gold was discovered along the Yukon River and became a major trading and supply center. Schwatka mentioned Harper's trading post at Fort Selkirk during his 1891 expedition, noting that Harper's log-house was located alongside the ruins of the three stone chimneys from the earlier Hudson's Bay trading post.[239]

An Anglican mission was established at Fort Selkirk by Reverend T.H. Canham shortly after Harper established his trading post.

E.A. Hegg photo of Fort Selkirk, 1898, Yukon Archives Print No. 6287, Bill Roozeboom Collection.

Harper's Post, Fort Selkirk, Yukon Archives, E.A. Hegg Collection.

By 1898, Fort Selkirk was a hub of activity with hotels, restaurants, and several trading posts.

The North-West Mounted Police located at Fort Selkirk a few months before Odell and Aldrich arrived in late July of 1898. In March 1898, the Yukon Field Force was created by the Canadian government to reinforce and assist the NWMP in maintaining law and order in the Yukon. The Yukon Field Force consisted of 203 volunteers from Canada's Permanent Militia who initially were dispatched to Fort Selkirk, arriving on September 11, 1898.

Canadian Army Yukon Field Force at Fort Selkirk, Eric A. Hegg Photographs. HEG 424, University of Washington Library, Special Collections.

Only a few small buildings were constructed at Fort Selkirk by the NWMP, but the Yukon Field Force constructed eleven large log cabins to house its officers and enlisted men. Six women accompanied the Yukon Field Service into the Yukon, four of whom were nurses. One was married to a soldier. Another was a reporter for the *Toronto Globe*. [240] The Yukon Field Force left Fort Selkirk for Dawson City in the spring of 1899 and the NWMP took over two of the larger Yukon Field Force cabins. By June of 1900, the Yukon Field Force were withdrawn from the Yukon.[241]

Probably reflecting its diminished importance, the 1898 NWMP Annual Report did not include a separate estimated population figure for Fort Selkirk and instead included the population of the settlement with populations of other, nearby areas.[242] Ironically, the community probably had its greatest population that year, numbering in the mid-hundreds, including 200 members of the Yukon Field Force. The number of prospectors would have varied dramatically, as these argonauts transited back and forth to prospecting grounds and their cabins.

At least by 1898, sternwheelers made regular stops at Fort Selkirk when the Yukon River was clear of ice. During winter months, supplies, mail, and travelers between Whitehorse and Dawson City traveled over the Winter River Trail on the frozen Yukon River.* Long-distance travel over the ice trail diminished when the new Overland Trail was built between Whitehorse and Dawson City, and passed near Fort Selkirk on the other side of the Yukon River. The Winter River Trail remained in use for traveling over shorter distances.

In 1898, Fort Selkirk was briefly considered as a possible site for the capital of the newly created Yukon Territory. However, the more northern

---

* Discussion of the Winter River Trail are found in Chapter 10 and Appendix E.

Dawson City was selected. The capital was moved from Dawson City to Whitehorse in 1953. Fort Selkirk initially had been planned as the northern terminus of the White Pass and Yukon Route (WP&YR) railroad. However, after reaching White Horse in 1900, plans were abandoned to extend the line to Fort Selkirk.

Fort Selkirk lost population when mining activity lessened and the NWMP detachment left in 1911. However, mining activity picked up in the 1930s, and Fort Selkirk's population grew again. A smaller Royal Canadian Mounted Police detachment returned to Fort Selkirk in 1932, staying until 1949. In 1935, the detachment became a one-man operation with Corporal Gordon Irwin (G.I.) Cameron providing all the governmental services. His wife, Martha, and their daughter, Ione, lived with him at Fort Selkirk. Ione Christensen, nee Cameron, later represented Yukon Territory in the Canadian Senate.

The Hudson's Bay Company returned to Fort Selkirk in the 1930s and opened a new store. However, the company's presence at Fort Selkirk did not last long. Most of the commercial traffic between Whitehorse and Dawson City continued being hauled by sternwheeler boats and Fort Selkirk was a major stop. After World War II, a highway between Whitehorse to Dawson City was constructed bypassing the Fort Selkirk area and the old trading post dwindled in significance.* Almost overnight, Fort Selkirk was abandoned. Sandy Sinclair reported that Fort Selkirk was abandoned in 1956 when he visited the site.[243] Today, restoration work at Fort Selkirk proceeds year around and sometimes archeological digs occur. Occasional tourists visit Fort Selkirk during summer months.

---

* The highway did not follow the same route as the famous Overland Trail, by running along the right side of the Yukon River, as it passed by Fort Selkirk. Instead, the highway moved away from the Yukon River miles south of Fort Selkirk.

Appendix B - Postal Service

Mark Odell had planned on using the postal service to keep in close touch with his family, friends, and financial backer Mr. Smith. He had intended on writing long letters to his home in Baldwinsville, which would be published in the *Gazette & Farmers' Journal* to supplement his finances, as he had done during his college years.

First Letters from Odell

Odell mailed letters to home at the beginning of his expedition. He mailed short letters from Seattle and Skagway to his friends and family, and a very long letter from Sheep Camp describing his experiences on the Golden Stairs and Chilkoot Pass. A letter mailed from Dyea on April 4, 1898, was printed in the April 28 edition of the *Gazette & Farmers' Journal*. A letter mailed from Sheep Camp, Alaska, on April 11, 1898, was printed in the May 5th edition of the *Gazette & Farmers' Journal*.

Once he reached Canada, it is evident that Odell's plans to mail frequent, lengthy letters home had to change. He complained about the private postal system operating at Lake Lindeman. The private postal service was improvised like many activities in northern Canada during the gold rush. Private carriers hauled letters from regular postal facilities in Alaska over the Coast Range into Canada and Lake Lindeman, or in the reverse direction from Lake Lindeman over the Coast Range into Alaska. The NWMP operated the regular postal facilities in northern Canada beginning in October of 1897, but did not provide postal service at Lake Lindeman.[244] While camping at Lake Lindeman, Odell was not aware of the nearby NWMP postal service provided at Lake Bennett.

Most letters mailed from the continental United States to the Yukon passed through the U.S. postal service to a Pacific coast city, were shipped by steamer north to Alaska, hauled over the Coast Range into Canada, and finally taken down the Yukon River into the Yukon gold fields – by boat during warm weather or by dog sled during colder months. Some letters would have been shipped from a Pacific coast city by steamer to St. Michael, and off loaded onto paddle wheel boats and shipped up the Yukon River to the Yukon. In February and March of 1899, Odell mentioned several times meeting the "police with mail" when he took the Winter River Trail out of the Yukon.

One of the major difficulties with the postal service was due to "inadequate arrangements" between the United State postal service and the Canadian postal service. Bags of mail for American stampeders piled up in Seattle, Juneau, Skagway, and Dyea.[245]

Cost and Postal Locations

Odell complained about the cost of sending a letter out of Canada.

> It costs considerable to get a letter out of here. There is no post office this side of Dyea, some thirty-five or forty miles away, and we pay some private person who is going through to carry them. This is the first letter I have written since coming here. I hope to write three or four more this afternoon, put them all in one envelope mailed to *The Gazette* and thus pay carriage on only one letter. If I had known it I could have had letters mailed to me at Sheep Camp, or Lake Lindeman. They would have come to Dyea by the U.S. mail service and then on to these other places to a sort of private enterprise post office.[246]

> It costs like sin to send a letter out from here, so I will enclose two or three in this one to you, and ask you to mail them from there.[247]

He described locations of Canadian post offices along the route into the gold fields.

> I find that the Canadian Government has established a post office at Lake Bennett, B.C., and one at Lake Tagish, N.W.T..... I learn that a post office has also been

established at Fort Selkirk, N.W.T. Write to me there until further directions after writing to Lake Tagish.[248]

These locations were in addition to the postal facilities at Dawson City, where he had told his family and friends to send their letters to him.

The time it took for a letter mailed from northern Canada to reach its destination in the States varied greatly. Odell mailed two letters from Lake Lindeman, British Columbia, on May 7, 1898. The second letter, mailed later in the day than the first letter, arrived in Baldwinsville, New York, and was printed in the May 26, 1898, edition of the *Gazette & Farmers' Journal*. However, the first letter arrived in Baldwinsville almost a week later and was reprinted in the June 2, 1898, edition of the *Gazette & Farmers' Journal*.

A letter mailed to Lake Lindeman normally was hauled by the United States Postal Service to Skagway and then taken to Sheep Camp. Private entities transported letters from Sheep Camp to Lindeman, where stampeders had to pay an extra 15¢ to receive each letter.[249]

Later Letters

A letter mailed from the foot of Lake Tagish on June 28, 1898, was printed in the August 18 edition of the *Gazette & Farmers' Journal*. It arrived in New York several weeks after a letter mailed from the foot of the more northern White Horse Rapids arrived on July 2, 1898.

The first letter Odell received while he was in the Yukon was a letter from his father, that he received on July 28, 1898, at the Lake Tagish NWMP Post on the sail down the Yukon River.

Odell mentioned mailing letters to his family and friends when he arrived at Fort Selkirk on July 26, 1898, and another letter to his father from Fort Selkirk on September 27, 1898. The last letter Odell mentioned mailing from Fort Selkirk was to his backer Mr. Smith on December 11, 1898.

Odell received letters at Fort Selkirk from his brother Burr and a friend on September 6, 1898. He received another letter at Fort Selkirk from his brother and another friend on September 26, 1898. Odell wrote in his diary on September 28, 1898, that a Captain Burstall would receive Odell's mail at Dawson City and send the letters south to Fort Selkirk.* On November 19, 1898, he received two letters at Fort Selkirk from friends. On December 18, 1898, Odell noted in his diary that his mail was forwarded from Dawson City to Fort Selkirk, which included letters from family and friends in New York, as well as a

---

* Captain H.E. Burstall was a member of the Yukon Field Force. (Dobrowolsky, 135.) He arrived at Fort Selkirk on September 11, 1898, and eventually became a Lt. General in the Canadian Army. ("LGen Sir HE Burstall KCB, KCMC (1870-1945)," Royal Canadian Army Museum website.)

letter from Tom Greir that was mailed to him from Lake Tagish in June. On January 26, 1899, he received three letters at Fort Selkirk, one written by a friend in May, one from his brother written on November 7, 1898, and one from W.J. Thompson written to him from the Yukon Territory in April of 1898. Ellis Aldrich received twelve letters that same day.

On October 4, 1898, Aldrich mailed a letter from Fort Selkirk to a friend of his in New York City. The letter which bore a Canadian stamp, but no postmark, did not arrive in New York until a week before Christmas, some two and one-half months later.[250]

Tale of a Missing Letter

A newspaper account described the long and tortuous journey of an undelivered letter mailed to Odell by a law school classmate from Cornell that followed Odell in and out of the Yukon, before being returned to the sender a year and a half after being mailed.[251]

The letter was mailed on March 21, 1898, from Ithaca, New York, to Odell in Seattle. It reached Seattle in April of 1898, but Odell had already sailed north to Alaska. From Seattle, the letter was forwarded to Dawson City, Yukon Territory, and then forwarded onto Dyea, Alaska, eventually returning to Ithaca, and then to Le Roy, New York, the hometown of the letter sender in late August of 1899. The envelope was "plastered over with stamps and directions for forwarding."[252] Notwithstanding

Odell's complaints, the amazing movement of this letter into and out of the Yukon illustrates how elaborate the postal system was.

The postal system may have been slow, erratic, and costly, but it worked.

North-West Mounted Police

In earlier years, private parties, including Captain William Moore hauled mail into and out of the Yukon over the Coast Range.

However, once the NWMP arrived in the Yukon, that force took charge and began hauling the mail. At least for a while before July 1, 1898, the NWMP was the "exclusive" provider of mail service between Skagway and Dawson City. The Canadian Department of Interior let a contract to a Mr. Richardson, of Seattle, who was to provide this mail service for four years, presumably to commence on the first of July. Richardson subcontracted this responsibility to the Arctic Express Company (AEC), but the AEC was unable to provide the service, so the NWMP continued hauling mail into and out of the Yukon. The mail service could not be provided for several months a year – during the period late in the year when ice was forming on the inland waterway, and paddle wheel boat were no longer able to ply the waters, and at the end of the winter season when it became unsafe to travel over dangerous ice.[253]

Appendix E describes mail being hauled over the Winter River Trail during winter months when Odell and Aldrich trekked out of the Yukon.

As part of these mail hauling responsibilities, the AEC was required to construct "stopping places every thirty (30) miles from Dawson to Bennett" along the Yukon River. The NWMP was unable to determine if the AEC had built these stopping places by the time of its Annual Report for 1898, but the Report noted several stopping places provided by others – Normal Macaulay had stopping places at White Horse Rapids, presumably his bunkhouse at Canyon City, and at McClintock River. T.N. Campbell operated a stopping place north of the Police Reserve near Dawson City. Mr. Williamson operated another stopping place at Cariboo Crossing.[254]

The NWMP continued performing "mail duties" for the Canadian Development Company during the cold season of 1898-99, through June of 1899.[255] By June, of 1899, the CDC operated postal system in the Yukon.

Appendix C - Dalton Trail

The Dalton Trail was several trails used for many centuries by the Chilkat Tlingit peoples of the Alaskan coast to enter southwest Yukon and trade with the interior Athapascan peoples known as the Southern and Northern Tutchone. They met and traded goods and food at what is now Fort Selkirk.

The old trail started from Pyramid Harbor, on the Chilkat Inlet of the Lynn Canal, not far from the Haines Mission (now Haines, Alaska), and ran northwest into the Yukon interior. After crossing what is now the Canadian/United States boundary, the trail ran northward past Dezadeash Lake and Champlain's Landing (called Champagne today), to Hutchi. The trail continued northward following the Nordenskjold River to the Yukon River at Carmack's Post.

Control over what became known as the Dalton Trail, and other trails from the coast into the interior, was maintained by Native peoples until Europeans began exploring the interior.

Jack Dalton first arrived in Alaska and the Yukon in 1885. In 1886, Frederick Schwatka hired Dalton and other guides for his expedition into the interior.[256] In 1890, Dalton, Edward J. Glave, and others were part of the Frank Leslie Newspaper Expedition that explored the Yukon. The expedition split into two groups, one of which explored the Yukon interior.[257]

During the 1890's, Dalton improved the trail that eventually bore his name. He constructed a trading post in United States' territorial portion of the trail, about one hundred miles from Pyramid Harbor, with the idea of opening a major trade route into the interior. By 1896, Dalton "became increasingly proprietary about his trail and protective of his control over it."[258]

In the summer of 1897, Dalton drove cattle from Pyramid Harbor north on what became known as the Dalton Trail to Hutchi. Instead of continuing northward on the Dalton Trail to Carmacks Post, he drove the cattle to Fort Selkirk. The cattle trail ran west from Hutchi and then north, passing west of Aishihik Lake and east of Sekulmun Lake, leading to the village of Aishihik, and then north to Fort Selkirk.

Ironically, J.J. McArthur, a Canadian government surveyor, accompanied Dalton on this cattle drive, surveyed this direct route to Fort Selkirk, and identified this route as part of the Dalton Trail. He described the route from Hutchi to Fort Selkirk as being a well-defined trail.[259]

Michael Gates, the living historian with the greatest expertise on the Dalton Trail and other Yukon history, refers to this route as the route of Dalton's 1897 cattle drive, rather than a little used or secondary branch of Dalton's Trail.[260] In 1898, Inspector A.M.

Jarvis, NWMP, noted that Dalton never again used this northern cattle trail that ran over a 5,500-foot mountain range. Javis described the cattle trail as being "something awful."[261]

Dalton improved the portion of the Dalton Trail located in the United States and charged tolls for using the portion of the Dalton Trail that he had improved on the American side of the border. In 1899, the tolls were $2.50 for a horse, cow, mule, or burro; $2.50 for an unloaded sled with one horse; $1.50 for a dog sled with two dogs, and an additional 25¢ per dog; 1¢ per pound of merchandise; and $1 for a foot passenger with a pack of 25 pounds or more.[262]

In 1898, the NWMPs established a detachment at Pleasant Camp on the Dalton Trail (not to be confused with the Pleasant Camp on the US side of the Chilkoot trail), built the Dalton Post on the Canadian side of the trail, and patrolled the Canadian side of the trail.[263]

In 1898, Dalton drove more cattle up the Dalton Trail to Carmacks Post, crossed to the eastern side of the Yukon River, and drove the cattle northward along the eastern side of the Yukon up to a place across the River from Fort Selkirk. The site became known as Slaughter Slough, as the cattle were slaughtered there.

Slightly more than 1,000 people traveled over the Dalton Trail in 1898, most traveling from Pyramid Harbor into the Yukon, but nearly 300 who took the trail out of the Yukon to Pyramid Harbor.²⁶⁴ Tom Wood, Walt Hoglen's original partner, was one of these approximate 300 people who took the trail out of the Yukon in 1898.

By 1900, the White Pass and Yukon Route railroad became the dominant route into and out of the Yukon and the Dalton Trail stopped being an economically viable route into the Yukon.²⁶⁵

Appendix D - White Pass and Yukon Route

The White Pass and Yukon Route (WP&YR) railroad company became the major transportation company in the Yukon.

In July of 1898, the White Pass & Yukon Railway Company, Ltd., a British based holding company owned by the Close Brothers (an English investment bank), acquired the rights of three other companies to construct a railroad from Skagway, Alaska, passing over White Pass into the interior of the Yukon to Fort Selkirk.[266] These three other companies were the

>(1) Pacific and Arctic Railway and Navigation Company, with a charter to construct a railroad in Alaska from Skagway to the summit of White Pass. The line would be 20.4 miles long.
>
>(2) British Columbia Yukon Railway Company, with a charter to operate a railroad from the summit of White Pass across the narrow strip of northern British Columbia separating the summit and Yukon Territory. The line would be 32.2 miles long.
>
>(3) British Yukon Mining, Trading, and Transportation Company, with a charter to operate a railroad in Yukon Territory.

259

This portion of the railroad was planned to terminate at Fort Selkirk, but was only extended as far as Whitehorse, 58.1 miles from the territorial boundary.[267]

Each of the acquired companies was listed under the main WP&YR masthead on stationery Odell used in 1899 or 1900 to write to his sister about his Yukon adventures.

WHITE PASS & YUKON ROUTE
Pacific & Arctic Railway and Navigation Co.
British Columbia Yukon Railway Co.
British Yukon M. T. & T. Co.

S. M. IRWIN
Traffic Manager
Seattle, Wash.

TRAFFIC DEPARTMENT

Masthead of WP&YR stationery, 1899. Odell Collections.

The Close Brothers incorporated the Pacific Contract Company, Ltd., to construct the railway.[268] Construction of the rail line began on May 28, 1898, and tracks were laid up Broadway in Skagway on June 15, 1898.[269] The Red Line Transportation Company was incorporated to haul freight and workers ahead of the rail lines.[270]

Some $10 million was spent building the narrow-gauge railway.[271] Progress occurred in steps, with rail service being provided from Skagway to each significant new location and the Red Line Transportation Company hauling freight and passengers beyond the end of the track. The location of the end of the track kept moving further into Canada as the railway construction proceeded. By February 20, 1899, the railroad reached the summit of White Pass, climbing some 3,000 feet in elevation from Skagway over twenty miles, with grades of up to 3.9% and turns of up to 16%.[272] In March 7, 1899, Odell and Aldrich passed through the nearby Log Cabin settlement on their way out of the Yukon and shipped some of their outfit to Skagway. The railroad reached Bennett City by July 6, 1899.[273]

Construction of the railway effectively ended the use of both the Chilkoot Pass and Dalton Trail for people and supplies entering the Yukon.

The next phase of constructing the railroad was accomplished by laying tracks in two directions -- south from the newly established town of White Horse and north from Bennett City. The two tracks met at Carcross on July 29, 1900.[274]

Location of the railway terminus at White Horse was a major factor in this new settlement eventually becoming the major population center of the Territory. Plans were dropped to extend the railroad from White Horse to Fort Selkirk. Passengers, supplies, and mail were offloaded at White Horse and shipped by paddle wheel steamboats down the Yukon River to Dawson City and other mining areas when the rivers were free of ice. During the cold, winter months, supplies and people moved by dog sleds and sleighs from White Horse to Dawson City first over the Winter River Trail and then over the all-land Overland Trail that soon replaced the Winter River Trail.

The WP&YR became the major integrated transportation company in the north providing varied freight and passenger transportation services into and out of the Yukon. Eventually, the company provided docks, train service, stage service, sleigh service, paddle wheel boat service, hotels, buses, trucks, ships, airplanes, and oil pipelines.[275]

The WP&YR purchased the three companies operating aerial tramways along the Chilkoot Trail – the Chilkoot Railroad & Transport Company, the Alaska Railroad and Transportation Company, and the Dyea-Klondike Transportation Company. All three companies had merged into the Chilkoot Route before the WP&YR purchased the combined tramway company.[276] The WP&YR railroad became the dominant route into and out of the Yukon.

As part of its efforts to consolidate all means of transportation, in August of 1899 the WP&YR acquired the two tramways running parallel with Miles Canyon that Macauley owned for $185,000.[277] Canyon City was soon abandoned.

In 1901, the WP&YR began operating paddle wheel steamboats on the Yukon River. Its river division was called the British Yukon Navigation Company.

The WP&YR was awarded a contract to haul mail into and out of the Yukon in 1902. It built what became known as the Overland Trail and the system of roadhouses along the route. In 1955, a highway was constructed between Whitehorse and Dawson

City, effectively ending the use of the old trail and much of the paddle wheel boat traffic.[278]

The railroad suspended its operations in 1982, when mining operations in the Yukon collapsed because of low mineral prices. Limited service reopened in 1988 – basically providing seasonal tourist service, which included hauling some freight, such as canoes, to Bennett and beyond to Carcross.[279]

Appendix E - Winter River Trail

During the winter of 1898-99, Odell and Aldrich followed the Winter River Trail or the "trail on the river" out of the Yukon.

Little has been written about this route even though the route over the frozen Yukon River was the sole route into and out of the Yukon during winter months before: (1) The WP&YR railroad from Skagway into the Yukon reached Lake Bennett in 1899 and White Horse in 1900; and (2) the Overland Trail between Whitehorse and Dawson City was completed in 1902. The Winter River Trail continued being used for short-distance trips during the winter months after these major transportation improvements opened.

Use and Development of the Winter River Trail

The Winter River Trail was the traditional route used by Native peoples to travel up and down the frozen Yukon River during cold months. Traveling on the Winter River Trail was by foot or dog sled. Newly arrived prospectors also used the Winter River Trail, but added horses to pull their sleds, and constructed riverside improvements in the form of bunkhouses along the route.*

The Winter River Trail was the basic route for relatively long-distance travel, generally running in a north/south direction into and out of the Yukon Territory for five to six months a year during the cold months.[280] During the few warm months, walking on land trails for short distances and travel by canoes, sailboats, and rafts (and later by paddle wheel boats) on the Yukon River for longer distances were the primary modes of travel.† Traffic into and out of the Yukon stopped twice a year, at the beginning of the long cold season while ice began forming until the ice cover became sufficiently thick to allow safe passage over the Winter River Trail, and at the end of the cold season when the ice on the Winter River Trail was melting and not safe to traverse.

Prior to the Klondike gold rush, very few modern facilities existed on the Winter River Trail – only a few trading posts were constructed on the banks of the Yukon River. The Hudson's Bay Company established Fort Selkirk as a trading post in 1848 but

---

* Gord Allison, an historian who lives in Haines Junction, Yukon Territory, created a blog about historic Yukon trails and has taken several trips on the Yukon River in search of many of these abandoned bunkhouses. He discusses this on his website.

† For millennia the Yukon River was the major route or highway that First Nation peoples used to travel throughout the Yukon. Beaumont, Jody and Michael Edwards, *An Introduction to First Nations Heritage Along the Yukon River*, 83 & 105.

abandoned the trading post in 1852. In 1874, the Alaskan Commercial Company opened a trading post called Fort Reliance, located about eight miles downstream from what eventually became Dawson City. The post was abandoned but reopened in 1886, and soon abandoned for a second time. In 1889, Arthur Harper built a new trading post at Fort Selkirk for the Alaskan Commercial Company.

In 1895, the North-west Mounted Police opened Fort Constantine on the Fortymile River. This was the first NWMP facility in the Yukon. Three other NWMP posts were established in 1897 – the Tagish Post, the Lower LaBerge Post, and Fort Herchmer at Dawson City.

One of the earliest documented passages over the Winter River Trail was during the winter of 1896-97, when Captain William Moore traveled by dog sled over the Winter River Trail from the Yukon interior to Skagway.[281] Other than Fort Constantine on the Fortymile River and Harper's post at Fort Selkirk, no cabins or facilities were available on the Winter River Trail.

Another early recorded passage over the Winter River Trail was by Joe Meeker, a prospector, who drowned on the Winter River Trail attempting to leave the Yukon during the winter of 1897-98. He was lost under an ice shelf at the White Horse Rapids, along with his poke or "precious bag of gold dust."[282] These rapids were dangerous all year.

In late November of 1898, a member of the NWMP nearly died in an accident on the ice hauling mail out of the Yukon

> Corporal Richardson [and another NWMP officer] ... made good until he reached the eight mile cabin near Hootalinqua Post, when as he was about to go ashore with his outfit, the ice in the river began to move, broke up into pieces and swept the men down the stream, this occurred on the 30th of November. The men narrowly escaped with their lives by hanging on to the limb of a tree – though every effort was made, the mail could not be recovered.[283]

Facilities were gradually constructed along the Yukon River. Before the winter of 1898-99, the only facilities on the Yukon River were several NWMP posts or detachment cabins and a few small, wood cutting camps. The wood cutting camps provided fuel for the voracious boilers of steamboats plying the Yukon River in summer months.

During the winter of 1897-98, the few NWMP detachments "were put to so much trouble and annoyance" by prospectors leaving Dawson City for the Outside "buying or begging food," that the NWMP instituted a policy of refusing to give away or sell provisions during the following winter season. However, "absolutely destitute" people were allowed to perform manual labor for meals and sufficient food to get them to the next detachment. Over the summer of 1898, a series of private, way stations, bunkhouses, or stopping places were constructed over the length of the Yukon River where travelers could purchase supplies and overnight accommodations.[284] Odell and Aldrich would stay at many of these way stations on their trek to the Outside.

Locating both inns or stopovers, and forts or military stations, at periodic distances, basically one day's travel apart, along a route or road, is an age-old practice. The Romans located both types of facilities along the eastern leg of a major road stretching from Rome to Constantinople.[285]

Various Annual NWMP reports described the Winter River Trail between Dawson City and Bennett or White Horse. The 1898 Annual Report, written in the late months of 1898, described the trail as being over the ice.

> The Arctic Express Company were to have built stopping places every thirty (30) miles from Dawson to Bennett, and took some men down to put up buildings. I am unable to report what they have done as communication with the interior ceased soon after they commenced operations.
>
> Mr. McCauley has stopping places at the White Horse Rapids and the McClintock River, Mr. T. N. Campbell has one north of the Police Reserve at this place, and a man named Williamson has one at the Cariboo Crossing, near the police

detachment. So from the White Horse to Bennett accommodations can be had every twenty five (25) miles.[286]

However, many of these stopping places along the Yukon River were constructed in 1898. Odell and Aldrich would stay at many stops on their trek out of the Yukon over the Winter River Trail in February and March of 1899.

By February 1899, when Odell and Aldrich travelled over the Winter River Trail, two cut offs over land were in place along the route. The first cut off was a little south of Five Fingers Rapids. The second cut off was on the east bank of the shoreline following the Macaulay tramway route and avoiding the treacherous White Horse Rapids and Miles Canyon.

Traffic on the Winter River Trail "was brisk" during the winter of 1898-99 when Odell and Aldrich left the Yukon for the Outside.[287] Supplies moved into the Yukon, mail moved into and out of the Yukon, and prospectors moved in and out of the Yukon over the Winter River Trail.

The 1899 NWMP Annual Report described how improvements to the trail were gradually made on the frozen river and then were made on dry land after the winter of 1898-99. In addition, these two cut offs from the frozen river were described.

> A land trail was built last summer from Hootchiku to Lower LaBarge by the Department of the Interior, saving a

> distance of 65 miles, and from White Horse to Cariboo [Crossing] by the White Pass Railway, saving 45 miles, thus reducing the distance from Dawson to Bennett by 110 miles. The land trail should be completed by next summer. There is now a very good trail from Dawson to Dominion Creek, forty miles of which was built by the Territorial Government, this should be extended to Selkirk next year, which would reduce the distance to that point at least 50 miles. From Selkirk to Hootchiku a land trail can be built without much difficulty, and from Lower LaBarge it could be continued to White Horse.[288]

The statement about completing the land trail from Dawson City to White Horse was optimistic and the trail was not completed for a few years.

A table listing the different stops along the Winter River Trails is shown below.

More fully, the 1899 report continued describing stopping places along the improved trail.

> Sixteen stopping places and way stations have been established by the Canadian Development Co., between Bennett and Dawson; these buildings are mail stations and boarding houses combined.
>
> There are also three bunk houses at Cariboo Crossing, one at Tagish, near the confines of the Police Reserve, one at the

mouth of the McClintock River, one at the Canyon, and three at the White Horse Rapids.

The stopping places established by the B.L. and K.N. Co. At LaBarge, Hootalinqua and Five Fingers are now closed down. Whether it is the intention of this company to open them again during the coming winter I cannot say.

One bunk house is being erected at Five Fingers by a private individual, and will be open by the first of the year.

Owing to the number of stations established by the Canadian Development Co. along the line route, I am under the impression that our detachments will not have as much trouble in boarding civilians (per order) as in the past year.[289]

The shutdown of the B.L.&K.N. Company's bunkhouses was a result of the newly constructed Overland Trail bypassing these stops along the Yukon River. Eventually, some of the NWMP posts along the Yukon River were also abandoned, as the new overland trail bypassed these important locations.

Improvements were also made to the southern portion of the trail as track for the WP&YR railway was laid. By the summer of 1899, track had been laid from Skagway, over White Pass, to Bennett. By the summer of 1900, track was laid from Bennett to

White Horse, avoiding the dangerous White Horse Rapids and Miles Canyon.

In 1900, the Canadian Development Company (CDC) was awarded a contract to improve the winter trail, carry mail and freight from Whitehorse to Dawson City, and to construct roadhouses along the route. The WP&YR company purchased the CDC in 1901, along with other transportation companies in the Yukon, as part of its efforts to monopolize these modes of travel.[290] The CDC used the old winter trail for one year in 1901, before building a new and much improved Overland Trail in 1902. Mail, supplies, and people were hauled over the trails during the winter months. Eventually the Overland Trail had a twelve-foot width, so wheeled coaches were used at the beginning of each winter season and sleighs were substituted when more snow fell. Horses pulled the wheeled coaches and sleighs. The drivers were called "skinners."

A 1901 news article lists the stopping places on the Winter River Trail between Dawson City and White Horse, stating that "at each place mentioned there are from one to three roadhouses where travelers can secure comfortable lodgings and good meals at reasonable rates."[291] A few of the stopping places were the same names as the bunkhouses listed below on the Winter River Trail from 1899 and 1900.

In 1902, the Winter River Trail had been replaced by the Overland Trail connecting Dawson City to the railway at Whitehorse.

> The new winter trail (i.e., the Overland Trail) to White Horse, just completed, will necessitate the establishment of new detachments as, with three exceptions, it does not pass anywhere near any of our summer outposts on the river.
>
> I did not make any changes in our detachments until it developed whether the overland route was to be used or not. Many people will for a time patronize the old road which has a police post, post office and telegraph every 30 miles or so.[292]

The 1902 North-West Mounted Police Report continued in greater detail describing the new improved Overland Trail.

> At last Dawson is connected with the outside world during the winter months **by a road other than over the ice on the river.** [Emphasis added.] Its completion, like that of the telegraph line three years ago, is a source of great satisfaction. The grading was finished about the end of September and the trail reported to be in very good condition considering that there has not been much traffic over it. The grades are easy and few in number.
>
> The total length is about 323 miles, being about 46 miles shorter than the all-water route.

The road runs from White Horse in a westerly direction about three miles, thence north to the Takhini River, from whence it follows the valley of the Little River to the divide between it and the Nordenskiold; crossing the latter it follows the old cut-off [trail] to Mackay's and crosses the Yukon at that point. Then keeping along the eastern bank of the river for some distance it gradually trends a little east and crosses the Pelly River about one mile from its mouth. From there it proceeds inland almost due north leaving the Yukon some miles to the west of it, crossing the Stewart and Indian Rivers about 50 miles from their mouths and so on through the mining centers of Eureka, Eldorado and Bonanza to Dawson.

One great advantage attached to this road will be that people from the creeks south and east of Dawson will not be compelled to come there before going out or coming in, but will be carried right to their very doors, as the road traverses the very heart of the country embraced in the main mining district.

Road houses, where extremely good accomomdations [*sic*] can be obtained at very reasonable rates, have been established all along its route. Under the new Liquor License Ordinance these stopping places, if licensed premises, as most of them are, must have at least six comfortable bed rooms, and a sitting room and dining room entirely distinct from the bar room. This ensures good accommodation for all the travelling public....

Two ferries have also been established at the crossings of the Stewart River, one near its mouth, affording the miners on Henderson a means of communication with Stewart City, and the other where the new trail to White Horse crosses the river.

A ferry has also been placed at the Pelly River crossing of the New Winter Trail, also over the Indian River on the White Horse trail....

First class stages ply between White Horse and Dawson and the fare for the through trip, not including meals and lodging, is at the present time of writing, $50.

At the close of 1900, there were only 75 miles of road; during the season of 1901, 144 miles of road and trail were added, and during the past season the number of miles constructed was no less than 407 1/2.

The following statement shows the roads and trails constructed by the Department of the Interior, and the Government of the Yukon –

Dawson and White Horse winter road (new road built from Eureka Creek to White Horse) ....283 miles....[293]

The new, all-land trail was known as the ***Overland Trail***, Dawson Overland Trail, and the Whitehorse-Dawson Trail. The Winter River Trail continued to be used for shorter-distance travel along the Yukon River as the Overland Trail was developed into the primary long-distance travel route.

Gradually, the WP&YR company constructed or purchased stops along the new, all land route. Stops became known as "staging posts." Eventually the compound at a post would include a roadhouse or hotel, stables, storehouses, and cabins. New road houses often were two-story tall with separate outhouses for men and women. They were much improved over the crude lodgings Odell and Aldrich used in during their trek out of the Yukon in the winter of 1898-99. Once the road had been sufficiently improved, stages would stop at two or three staging posts a day. A meal cost $1.50 and a bed cost $1.00 per night.[294]

During warm months, passengers and freight were hauled by horse-drawn wagons. Horse-drawn sleighs were substituted during cold months. Before the construction of wood bridges over some creeks with ferries used to cross the four major rivers. During warm weather, passengers and freight were off-loaded at the banks of a river, ferried across the water in canoes, and loaded onto new wagons. A technique called "booming" was used during the cold weather to create safe ice by corralling the ice floes and adding water to thicken the corralled ice. Freshly cut branches and bushes were strewn over the frozen river crossing and then sprinkled with water to create a smooth surface over which sleigh runners would glide.[295] Ferries were used to cross major rivers a few bridges were built across creeks.

In a recent news article in the *Yukon News*, Michael Gates noted that in the fall of 1911, Charles G. Percival and George D. Brown drove an Abbot-Detroit 'Bulldog' automobile from Skagway to Dawson City.[296] They drove over the newly laid railroad tracks across White Pass to Carcross and then over the "old government overland trail to White Horse" and then onto Dawson City over the "Dawson Trail," later returning to Skagway over the same route. In 1955, a highway was constructed between Whitehorse and Dawson City, effectively ending use of the old trail and much of the paddle wheel boat traffic.[297]

Table with Details about the Winter River Trail

The table included below includes a comprehensive list of stops found on the Winter River Trail and the mileage between the stops. Six different sources used. NWMP detachments are also listed. Soon, most of these facilities were abandoned as an all-weather, overland route was constructed between Dawson

City and Whitehorse, the terminus of the newly constructed WP&YR railroad.

The sources for this table are:

- Diary entries from, and a table found at the end of, the 1898-99 Odell Yukon Diary.
- A report of the trip along the route by Lt. J. C. Castner, United States Army, 1899.
- A list of Canadian Development Company stops along the route detailed in the 1899 NWMP Annual Report.
- A list of NWMP forts or detachments along this watercourse that appeared in the 1898 NWMP Annual Report, 1899 NWMP Annual Report, and a website on "The Force in the North," prepared by the MacBride Museum in Whitehorse, YT.
- A list of stops included in the Bartsch family's 1900 diary.
- A 1901 newspaper article from *The Whitehorse Star*.

Mileage figures show the distance from one stop to the next stop, generally in a southerly direction, along the Yukon River.

A party led by Lieutenant J. C. Castner, an American Army officer, followed the Winter River Trail from Circle City, Alaska, through the Yukon Territory, to Bennett City in early 1899. Odell and Aldrich hiked over the southern portion of this trail out of the Yukon a few weeks after Castner in February of 1899. After reaching Bennett City, the Castner Party, and Odell and Aldrich, followed the overland route of the soon to be constructed WP&YR railroad from Bennett City to Log Cabin, British Columbia, and then followed the recently built railroad route over White Pass and on to Skagway.

Stops, Bunkhouses, or NWMP Posts on the Winter River Trail over the Ice out of the Yukon, 1898 – 1901 Circle City, Alaska, to Bennett City, British Columbia

Stops, Odell Diary Winter 1898-99	Miles from last stop	Stops, Lt. Casther Winter 1898-99	Miles from last stop	Canadian Development Company Stops, NWMP report 1899	Miles from last stop	NWMP Post	Miles from last post	Stops Bartsch Diary 1900	Miles from last stop	Stops Whitehorse Star, 1901	Miles from last stop
		Circle City, AK									
		20-Mile House	20								
		Webbers	22								
		Coal Creek	22								
		Jim the Indian	25								
		Ivy City	25								
		Nation City	28								
		Star (75-Miles	29								
		Eagle City, AK	21								
		Steamer Arnold, YK Transfer	24								
		40-Mile	22			Ft. Constantine					
		Station No. 2	18								
		Station No. 1	20								
		Dawson City	18	Dawson		Ft. Herchmer (Dawson)	48	Dawson		Dawson	
								12 Mile House, 10 ft on mainland	12	12 Mile House	12
										Cozy	3
		Ainsley	21					Ensley Roadhouse, to left on island	6	Ainslee	1

280

		Indian River	28	Indian River – south of McCabe Creek	31		10	Indian River	12
Indian River	11					Indian River, left on mainland		Indian River	
Reindeer	9							Lansdowne	1
								Reindeer	6
Cabin	4					Log Cabin, left on mainland	14	Log Cabin	5
								Ogilvie	9
								Mrs. Burns	9
60-Mile	9	60-Mile	20	Ogilvie, 60-Mile	20	60 mile Pass, left on mainland	6		
						9 Mile, n on island	9	9 Mile House	1
Stewart City	16	Stewart	23	Stewart River, Ft. Nelson	24	Stewart River, left on mainland	16	Stewart River	14
Kerry Mill	9								
White River	3					White river, left on island	9	White River	13
Thistle Creek	13					Thistle Creek, left on mainland	10	Thistle Creek	7
						Kirkman left on mainland	9	Kirkman's	9
				Halfway	36	Halfway Post, right on island	1		
Steamboats	10								
Tulare Creek	10	Tulare	35			Tulare Island, right on island	5	Tulare	6
								Coffee Creek	3
Arctic Express Company (AEC)	7					Island Post, left on island	7	Island post	4
						Clerk's Place, left on island	2	Clark's Roadhouse	2

Bertha Creek	7					Big Four	9	
Big Four	10					Sleepy Hollow	3	
						Ritchie's	6	
Northwest Express (NWE)	22							
Selwyn Rim	5	Selwyn	36	45	Selwyn	Selwyn, right on mainland	10	Selwyn
						Woodchopper's cabin, right on island	4	
						A.B.C.	5	
Holbrook	12					Ritchie Island	6	
						Captain Whalen's Place, right on Island	13	Captain Whalen's	6
Halfway House	7							Tent	9
Ft. Selkirk	18	Selkirk	30		Selkirk	Selkirk, right on mainland	17	Selkirk	9
						Canadian Development Company (CDC) Post No. 9	4	CDC Post No. 9	3
								Eldorado Steamboat	5
								Meat Cache	5
Carsens	17					Patterson's	8	Patterson's	4
		Minto	24		Minto	Minto	12	Minto Ranton	7
Lewis Bunk House	18								

							Hootchikoo	
AEC	14	AEC	13					10
Big Horn	12	Big Horn	12				Aurora No 5	6
Goring	3	Goaring's House	4					
BL&YN bunkhouse				Mackey (R mi< 5 miles above)	24		Mackey's Post	4	Mackey's	8
5-Finger AEC. McDonald; Sugel's bunkhouse kept by Passage Union	16	Five-Finger Rapids	17			Five Fingers – near Yukon Crossing	18	5-Finger Post	4		
							Taylor & Robinson's	18		
									Willson's	10
									Miller's	2
				Carmack's (½ mile from river)	24	Tantalus Butte - just north of Carmacks	20	Carmack's	2	Carmack's	10
									Model Roadhouse	1
NW Express	20	NW Express	22						Robertson's	11
AEC; and BL&YN kept by McCarty	4	Arctic Exp. Co	5	Montague	24			Montague	20	Montague	14
									33 Roadhouse	8
				Chico (forks of Nordenskiold R.)	23			Chico	22	Chico	12
Little Salmon	30	Little Salmon	35			Little Salmon					
Bruces/Brices cabin	15	Bank House	16								

Big Salmon	24	Big Salmon	25			Big Salmon			
Cassiar Bar bunkhouse		Cassiar Rk.	3						
Wood choppers	3	Wood-choppers	1						
Haddock's (1/2)	16								
Hootalinqua Davis	16	Hootalinqua	33			Hootalinqua – mouth of Lewes or 30 Mile River			
Half way house cabins	17	Cabin (½ Way House)	17					Midway	12
Lake Lebarge	14	NW Express	17	Lower Lebarge	23	Lower Lebarge	Foot of Lebarge	25	Lower BaBarge	10
								Middle LaBarge	15
								New Island Roadhouse	6
Across Lake Lebarge, Jim Boss bunkhouse	32	Cabin	34	Upper Lebarge	30	Upper Lebarge	Head of Lebarge	30	Upper LaBarge	9
								Tahkanna	12
								Seven Mile Tent	7
				White Horse	25	White Horse Rapids (in 1899 at Canyon city)	White Horse	25	White Horse	7
Miles Canyon		Miles Canyon	28						
				Lewgan	20				
Macaulay's/McCarthery's bunkhouse	30								
Marsh Lake bunkhouse, Macaulay	25	Marsh Lake	25			McClintock – near Tagish			
Tagish (foot) bunkhouse	24	Tagish House	25			Tagish			
Cariboo, Maine Hotel	22+	Cariboo, Crossing	22	Cariboo	22	Cariboo	22		
Bennett, Klondike Hotel	32	Bennett City	34	Bennett	28	Bennett	28		

Log Cabin, Old Log Cabin Hotel	Log Cabin, BC	12		Log Cabin		
	Summit, AK	15				
Skagway, AK, Dewey Hotel	Skagway, AK	20				

Bibliography

Books

Adney, Tappen. *The Klondike Stampede*. Harper & Brothers Publishers, New York, 1900.

Bagley, Clarence B. *History of Seattle, from the Earliest Settlement to the Present Time*. J. Clarke Publishing Company, Chicago, IL, 1916, Volumes 1 & 2.

Barrett, Anthony A. and Rhodri Windsor Liscombe. *Frances Rattenbury and British Columbia, Architecture and Challenge in the Imperial Age*. University of British Columbia Press, Vancouver, BC, 1983.

Becker, Ethel Anderson. *Klondike '98*. Binfords & Mort, Portland, OR, 1949.

Berton, Pierre. *The Klondike Fever, the Life and Death of the Great Gold Rush*. Alfred Knopf, New York, 1958.

Beschloss, Michael. *Presidents of War*. Crown Publishing Groups, a division of Penguin Random House, New York, 2018.

Binns, Archie. *Northwest Gateway, the Story of the Port of Seattle*. Doubleday, Doran & Company, Inc., Garden City, NY, 1942.

Bolotin, Norm. *Klondike Lost, A Decade of Photographs by Kinsey & Kinsey*. Alaska Northwest Publishing Company, Anchorage, AK, 1980.

Brown, Daniel James. *The Boys in the Boat, Nine Americans and Their Epic Quest for Gold at the 1936 Berlin Olympics*. Viking, New York, 2013.

Coates, Ken S. *Best Left as Indians, Native-White Relations in the Yukon Territory, 1840-1973*. McGill-Queen's University Press, Montreal, QC, 1991.

Coe, Harrie B. *Maine Biographies*, Vol. 1 - *A History*. Clearfield Press, Clearfield, PA, 1928.

Cohen, Stan. *The Streets Were Paved with Gold, a Pictorial History of the Klondike gold rush, 1896-1899*. Pictorial History Publishing Company, Missoula, MT, Fifth Edition, 1993.

Department of Interior, Information Respecting the Yukon District from the Reports of Wm. Ogilvie and from other sources, Ottawa, Government

Printing Bureau, 1897, The Yukon District Historical Sketch, Mr. Ogilvie's Exploration of 1887, Later Reports from Mr. Ogilvie, Cudahy, November 6th, 1896.

Dobrowolsky, Helene. *Law of the Yukon, A History of the Mounted Police in the Yukon.* Lost Moose, Madeira Park, BC, 2013, revised edition.

Ficken, Robert E. *Unsettled Boundaries, Fraser Gold and the British-American Northwest.* Washington State University Press, Pullman, WA, 2003.

Gates, Michael. *Dalton's Gold Rush Trail, Exploring the Route of the Klondike Cattle Drives.* Harbour Publishing Co. Ltd., Madeira Park, BC, 2012.

Gates, Michael. *History Hunting in the Yukon.* Lost Moose/Harbour Publishing, Madeira Park, BC, 2010.

Gray, Charlotte. *Gold Diggers, Striking it Rich I the Klondike.* Counter Point Publishing, Berkeley CA, 2010.

Haliday, Stratford and Robert Louis Tollemache. *Reminiscences of the Yukon.* London, Edward Arnold, 1912

Harris, Arland S. *Schwatka's Last Search, The New York Ledger Expedition Through Unknown Alaska and British Columbia.* University of Alaska Press, Fairbanks, AK, 1996.

Johnson, Karen L. and Dennis M. Larsen. *A Yankee on Puget Sound, Pioneer Dispatches of Edward Jay Allen, 1852 - 1855.* Washington State University Press, Pullman, WA, 2013.

Ketcherside, Bob. *Lost Seattle.* Pavilion Books, London, 2013.

Kirchhoff, M. J. *Dyea, Alaska, the Rise and Fall of a Klondike Gold Rush Town.* Alaska Cedar Press, Juneau, AK, 2012.

Kirchhoff, M. J. *The Founding of Skagway.* Alaska Cedar Press, Juneau, AK, 2015.

Larsen, Dennis M. *Slick as a Mitten, Ezra Meeker's Klondike Enterprise.* Washington State University Press, Pullman, WA, 2009.

Lynch, Jeremiah. *Three Years in the Yukon.* Dale L. Morgan, editor, The Lakeside Press, Chicago, 1967, (originally published London: Edward Arnold, 1904).

Mallory, Peter. *The Sport of Rowing, Two Centuries of Competition in Four Volumes.* River & Rowing Museum, Mill Meadows, UK, 2011.

Martensen, Ella Lung. *Trail to North Star Gold – A True Story of the Alaska-Klondike Gold Rush.* Metropolitan Press, Portland, OR, 1969.

McCune, Don. *Trail to the Klondike.* Washington State University Press, Pullman, WA, 1997.

Mighetto, Lisa and Marcia Babcock Montgomery. *Hard Drive to the Klondike: Promoting Seattle During the Gold Rush.* National Park Service, Columbia Cascades Support Office, Seattle WA, 1998.

Minter, Roy. *The White Pass, Gateway to the Klondike.* University of Alaska Press, Fairbanks, AK, 1987.

Morgan, Murray. *Skid Road*, revised edition. Comstock Edition, Inc., Sausalito, CA, 1978.

Myer, Melanie J. *Klondike Women, True Tales of the 1897 - 1898 Gold Rush.* Swallow Press, Athens, OH, 1989.

Neufeld, David and Frank Norris. *Chilkoot Trail, Heritage Route to the Klondike.* Lost Moose Publishers, Whitehorse, YT, 1996.

NWMP Annual Report, 1898, Part III, Yukon Territory, Report by Superintendent S. B. Steele, Commanding North-west Mounted Police in the Yukon Territory, Appendix A, Report of Superintendent Z. T. Wood; Appendix C, Report of Inspector C. Starnes; Appendix F, Annual Report of Inspector D'A. E. Strickland; Appendix G, Annual Report of Inspector Belcher; and Appendix H, Annual Report of Inspector A.M. Jarvis; S.E. Dawson, Printer to the King's Most Excellent Majesty, Ottawa, ON, 1899.

North-west Mounted Police Annual Report, 1899, Part II - Yukon Territory, A. Bowen Perry, Supt. Commanding Yukon District, Appendix A, "Report of Superintendent Z. T. Wood," Appendix A; and Appendix B, Report of Superintendent P. C. H. Primrose, Dawson District, 48, S.E. Dawson, Printer to the Queen's Most Excellent Majesty, Ottawa, ON, 1900.

Ogilvie, William. *Early Days on the Yukon: and the Story of Its Gold Finds.* John Lane Company, Toronto, ON, 1913.

Ogilvie, William, Dominion Land Surveyor, Department of Interior. *Information Respecting the Yukon District.* Government Printing Bureau, Ottawa, ON, 1897.

Oppell, Frank, compiler. *Tales of Alaska and the Yukon.* Castle, Secaucus, NJ, 1986, including an essay by Frederick Schwatka, entitled "The Great River of Alaska", printed in the Century Magazine, Volume XXX, September 1885.

O'Reilly, Shauna, and Brennan O'Reilly. *Alaska Yukon Pacific Exposition.* Arcadia Publishing, Mount Pleasant, SC, 2009.

Report of the North-West Mounted Police, 1902, Part III Yukon Territory, Report of Assistant Commissioner Wood. S. E. Dawson, Printer to the King's Most Excellent Majesty, Ottawa, ON, 1903.

Sale, Roger. *Seattle Past to Present, an Interpretation of the History of the Foremost City in the Pacific Northwest.* University of Washington Press, Seattle, WA, 1976.

Satterfield, Archie. *Chilkoot Pass, the Most Famous Trail in the North.* Northwest Publishing Company, Anchorage, AK, 1983.

Sharpe, William. *Faith of Fools, a Journal of the Klondike Gold Rush.* Washington State University Press, Pullman, WA, 1998.

Sinclair, James M. *Mission: Klondike, From Lawless Skagway to Bennett and Dawson.* Mitchell Press Limited, Vancouver, BC, 1978.

Sinclair, Sandy. *Inside the Rainbow.* Old Salty Publishing House, Olympia, WA, 2013, Third Edition.

Speidel, Bill. *Doc Maynard, the Man Who Invented Seattle.* Nettle Creek Press, Seattle, WA, 1978.

Speidel, William C. *Sons of the Profit, or There's No Business Like Grow Business, The Seattle Story.* Nettle Creek Press, Seattle, WA, 1851-1901, 1967.

Stein, Alan J. & Paula Becker, *Alaska - Yukon - Pacific Exposition.* University of Washington Press, Seattle, WA, 2009.

Swan, James G. *Almost Out of the World.* Washington State Historical Society, Tacoma, WA, 1957.

Swan, James G. *The Northwest Coast, Or, Three Years' Residence in Washington Territory.* Harper Brothers, New York, 1857.

Waszkis, Helmut. *Mining in America: Stories and Histories.* Woodhead Publishing Company, Cambridge, UK, 1993.

Wilson, Graham. *The White Pass and Yukon Route Railway.* Whitehorse, Yukon: Wolf Creek Books, Inc., 2002, Fourth Edition.

Young, Charles Van Patten. *Courtney and Cornell Rowing.* Cornell Publications Printing Company, Ithaca, NY, 1923.

Articles and Other Publications

"Baldwinsville Paragraphs," *The Post Standard*, Syracuse, NY, April 23, 1899, 4.

Bartsch, Chris, "Our Trip Out Over the Ice - Dec. 12th, 1900," included in Rob Ingram's, "Yukon Roadhouses, An Historical Survey," 1 March 1988, Appendix 1.

Beaumont, Jody and Michael Edwards, *An Introduction to First Nations Heritage Along the Yukon River*, 83 & 105.

"The City of Dyea, at the Gate to the Gold Fields it is Building. A Hive of Industry," *Dyea Trail*, Dyea, AK, January 19, 1898, 1.

"Col. Aldrich Sued for a Separation," *New York Times*, New York, July 12, 1925, 3.

Cody, H. A., "Alaska-Yukon Overland Mail, Past and Present," *Pacific Monthly*, Vol. 20, No. 6, pages 641-648 (December 1908.)

The Cornell Era, Volume XXX, No. 2, October 2, 1897, Ithaca, NY, Andrus & Church, 1898.

"Cornell Students from the Klondike," *Cornell Sun*, Ithaca, NY, April 6, 1899, 2.

"Correspondence Pleasant Valley," *Gazette & Farmers' Journal*, Baldwinsville, NY, May 27, 1886, 165.

"The Dawson City ice guessing pool goes back to Gold Rush days, Breakup also used to be how Dawson got rid of its sewage and trash, which is gross," *Yukon News*, Whitehorse, YT, Canada, May 3, 2018.

Decennial Record of the Class of 1896, Yale College, De Vinne Press, New York, 1907.

"The Diller Hotel", Wikipedia.

Docevski, Boban, "Via Egnatia – The Ancient Roman Road That Connects Rome to Constantinople," The Vintage News.

"Enjoying Whitehorse Trails, a Guide to the Yukon River trails to Schwatka Lake, Miles Canyon and Canyon City," Yukon Energy Corporation, 2000,

"Fort Selkirk," a guide published by Yukon Tourism, Heritage Branch, undated.

"Fort Selkirk," Yukon Department of Tourism and Culture.

"Forty Mile," Yukon Department of Tourism and Culture.

"From Trail to Tramway – The Archaeology of Canyon City," Yukon Department of Tourism and Culture.

Gates, Michael, "History Hunter: Early Yukon auto trek was a publicity stunt," Yukon *News*, Whitehorse, YT, Canada, November 1, 2018.

Gates, Michael, "History Hunter: Every photo has a story to tell, sometimes more than one," *Yukon News*, Whitehorse, YT, Oct. 20, 2023.

Gates, Michael, "History Hunter: When was the first recorded river break-up?," *Yukon News*, Whitehorse, YT, Canada, April 11, 2019.

Gates, Michael, "The Dawson City ice guessing pool goes back to Gold Ruch days," *Yukon News*, (Whitehorse, YT, Canada), May 3, 2018.

Gates, Michael, "When the miners' committee ruled," *Yukon News*, (Whitehorse, YT, Canada), November 13, 2015.

"Gold! Gold! Gold! Gold!" *Seattle Post Intelligencer*, (Seattle, WA), July 29, 1897, Latest News from the Klondike, 9 O'clock Edition, 1.

"Gold Near Fort Cudahy," *The Morning Olympian*, Olympia, WA, October 31, 1896.

Hammer, Thomas J., "On the Periphery of the Klondike Gold Rush: Canyon City, an Archaeological Perspective," Master of Arts Thesis, Simon Fraser University, 1999.

"History," White Pass & Yukon Route Railroad, 2009-2015.

"The Hotels", *Seattle Daily Times*, Seattle, WA, March 17, 1899, 8.

Ingram, Rob, "Yukon Roadhouses, An Historical Survey," 1 March 1988, included on the Yukon, Department of Tourism and Culture website, 1.

"In Alaskan Gold Fields, An Unprecedented Rush of Miners This Season, Not Transportation Enough for the Men Going to the Yukon, Juneau, and Cook's Inlet Districts," New York Times, Sunday, April 5, 1896, 29.

"Jack Dalton and the Dalton Trail," Sheldon Museum & Cultural Center.

Jordan, Eloise, "Aldrich Mansion in Topsham Once Owned by Governor King," *Lewiston Journal*, Lewiston, ME, Magazine Section, October 4, 1947, A-4 & A-8.

"Klondike Gold Rush," Wikipedia.

"Klondike No Easy Road, an Old High School Boy's Hard Struggle for Wealth in the Gold Country, Aldrich Still Seeks Fortune," *Brooklyn Daily Eagle*, Brooklyn, NY, December 25, 1898.

"*Lakme* a Passenger Boat," *Tacoma Daily News*, Tacoma, WA, March 9, 1898, 3.

"A letter from Mark M. Odell," *Gazette & Farmers' Journal* (Baldwinsville, NY), March 31, 1898, 1.

"Letters from M. M. Odell," *Gazette & Farmers' Journal* (Baldwinsville, NY), April 28, 1898, 1.

"Letter from M. M. Odell," *Gazette & Farmers' Journal* (Baldwinsville, NY), August 18, 1898, 1.

"Letter from M. M. Odell," *Gazette & Farmers' Journal* (Baldwinsville, NY), June 2, 1898, 1.

"Letter from Mark M. Odell," *Gazette & Farmer's Journal* (Baldwinsville, NY), May 5, 1898, 1.

"Letter from M. M. Odell," *Gazette and Farmers' Journal* (Baldwinsville, N.Y.), May 26, 1898, 1.

"Letter from M. M. Odell," *Gazette & Farmers' Journal* (Baldwinsville, NY), July 28, 1898, 1.

"Letter from MARK M. ODELL, SHEEP CAMP, ALASKA, Monday, April 11, 1898," *Gazette & Farmers' Journal* (Baldwinsville, NY), May 5, 1898, 1.

"Letter from M. M. Odell, LAKE TAGISH POST, Foot of Lake Tagish, June 28, 1898," *Gazette & Farmers' Journal* (Baldwinsville, NY), August 18, 1898, 1.

"LGen Sir HE Burstall KCB, KCMC (1870-1945)," Royal Canadian Army Museum.

"Local Paragraphs," *Gazette & Farmers' Journal* (Baldwinsville, NY) May 5, 1898, 1.

"Log Cabin Metropolis: Circle City," National Park Service.

Lundin, John W. and Stephen J. Lundin, "Cornell's Influence on Washington and West Coast Rowing."

"Many Wealthy Miners, The *Laurada* Brought $150,000 From Alaska on Her Last Trip Down," *Seattle Daily Times*, Seattle, WA, March 23, 1899, 5.

"MARK ODELL'S GOING To Klondike a Great Loss to the Cornell Crew," *Gazette & Farmers' Journal*, Baldwinsville, N.Y., March 24, 1898, 1. The article quoted came from an article that appeared in the *Syracuse Herald* on March 23, 1898.

Mendenhall, Tom, *A Short History of American Rowing*.

"Miners from Alaska, a Squad Arrives at Seattle, Wash. with $200,000 in Dust," *Buffalo Courier*, Buffalo, NY, October 14, 1896.

"MINERS MAKE MONEY, More Reports of Yukon Gold Hunters Making Big Cleanups, One Man Takes Out $19,000 This Season – Valuable Discoveries on New Creeks – Bishop Rowe's Long Journey – Explorer De Wandt Waiting for Winter on Siberian Soil," *Seattle Post Intelligencer*, (Seattle, WA), October 2, 1896, 3.

Norris, Frank and Karl Gurcke, "The Chilkoot Trail Tramways," Klondike Gold Rush National Historical Park, United States National Park Service, Skagway, Alaska.

"NOWELL'S WHARF," *Dyea Trail* (Dyea, AK), January 12, 1898, 1.

"Odell To Klondike," *The Courier* (Buffalo, NY), March 16, 1898.

"On Board the Al-Ki," *Gazette & Farmers' Journal* (Baldwinsville, NY), April 14, 1898.

Overby, Dennis, "Dead Stars Collide, Unsealing Clues to the Universe," *New York Times* (New York), Tuesday, October 17, 2017.

"Our Local Olympic Hopefuls," *Seattle Times* (Seattle, WA), August 10, 1924.

Overland Trail, Yukoninfo.

"Overland Trail (Yukon)," Wikipedia.

"Panic of 1893 and Its Aftermath," History Link.org, http://www.historylink.org/file/20874.

Pierce, J. Kingston, "Panic of 1893: The Northwest Economy Unravelled as the 'Golden Age' Came to a Close," Columbia, the Magazine of Northwest History, Winter 1993-94: Vol. 7, No. 4.

"The Race as Seen by Julian Hawthorne," *New York Journal*, June 25, 1897, reproduced in *The Cornell Era*, Volume XXX, No. 2, October 2, 1897, (Ithaca, NY: Andrus & Church, 1898), 26.

"Rates Lowered on the Railroad," *Daily Alaskan* (Skagway, AK), February 19, 1899, 4.

"Reaping the Profits of the Klondike Trade," Seattle's Klondike Museum website.

"Reunions – By Class Representatives," *Cornell Alumni News*, August, 1937, p. 459.

"Royal Canadian Mounted Police." Wikipedia.
"The Rush Is On," *Seattle Post Intelligencer*, (Seattle, WA), March 12, 1897, 1.

Seattle Business Directory, R. W. Polk & Company, 1901.

Seattle Business Directory, R. W. Polk & Company, 1908.

Seattle Business Directory, R. W. Polk & Company, 1911.

"Seattle Outfits the Klondike Gold Rush," U. S. Park Service website.

"Smith Tower (Seattle)," History Link essay 4310.

Spotswood, Ken, "The Whitehorse to Dawson Overland Trail." Explorenorth,

"Steamer *Lakme* Chartered," *Tacoma Daily News*, Tacoma, WA, February 26, 1898, 3.

Tate, Cassandra, "Gold in the Pacific Northwest," History Link essay 7162.

"The Letter Came Back," *The Le Roy Gazette*, (Le Roy, N.Y.), Wednesday, August 23, 1899, 1.

"THEY GO NORTH WELL SATISFIED, Big Part of Easterners Who Outfitted in this City and Pay Sound Merchants a Fine Tribute," *Seattle Post-Intelligencer*, Seattle, WA, March 26, 1898, 11.

"Thomas J. Wood," Wikipedia.

"Thomas John Wood, American History Central.

"The Trail ...," *Dyea Trail*, Dyea, AK, April 11, 1898. 1.

"The White Pass, Klondike Gold Rush," National Park Service.

"Two Cornell Students in the Klondike Region," *Cornell Daily Sun*, (Ithaca, NY), April 15, 1899, 2.

"United States Revenue Cutter Service," Wikipedia.

Untitled article, Gazette & Farmers' Journal, (Baldwinsville, NY), May 4, 1899, 1.

"Walter G. McLean Strongly Favors Naming Stroke After Washington", *Seattle Daily Times*, August 20, 1923, Sports Section, 1.

War Department, Adjutant General's Office, No. XXV, Reports of Exploration in the Territory of Alaska (Cooks Inlet, Susithna, Copper, and Tanana Rivers) 1898, 238. Made under the direction of the Secretary of War, by Captain Edwin F. Glenn, Twenty-Fifth United States Infantry and Captain W. R. Abercrombie, Second Unites States Infantry, July 1899. Washington: Government Printing Office, 1899.

Wilma, David, "Gold Prospectors Travel North by the Hundreds Through Puget Sound to Alaska and the Yukon Beginning in April 1895," History Link essay 8151.

"White Pass and Yukon Route," Wikipedia.

Other Communications and Records

Draft letter Mark Odell wrote to Leslie Voorhees, an old friend and Van Buren Township historian, in 1960, in response to her request for information about Odell's family, Odell Records.

Email, Gord Allison, sent to Steve Lundin, August 2, 2023.

Email, Karl Gurcke, Historian, Klondike Gold Rush National Historical Park in Skagway, Alaska, sent to Steve Lundin, April 23, 2014.

Letter written by Mark Odell to Leslie Voorhees, Baldwinsville, NY, town historian, 1960, Leslie Voorhees Archives, Syracuse Public Library.

Note detailing Odell's education and teaching positions, Odell records.

Undated letter Odell wrote to his sister, Ida, who lived in upstate New York, presumably written from Seattle in December of 1899 or in early 1900, Odell records.

Laws

Morrill Act of 1862 (aka, Morrill Land-Grant Act of 1862), 7 U.S.C. § 301 *et seq.*

New York State Laws, Chapter 291, Laws of 1887.

North West Territories Order in Council No. 2640.

Diaries

Hoglen, Walter J., Yukon Diary, 1898.

Odell, Mark, Diary, 1888.

Odell, Mark, Yukon Diary, 1898-1899.

Misc.

Allision, Gord. Welcome to Yukon History Trails, Stories about Yukon History, "Steamboat Slough and the Grave of Robert Dougan."

"An Argument for Inter-collegiate Athletics," oration presented by Mark M. Odell, February 23,
1895, Odell Collection.

Cornell Alumni Biographical Information form filled out by Mark Odell, March 6, 1937, Cornell Archives.

"The Diller Hotel", Wikipedia.

"Dyea Business Directory," compiled by the staff of the Klondike Gold Rush National Historical Park, United States National Park Service, Skagway, Alaska.

Grace, Michael L., *History of the Alaska Steamship Company, Seattle, 1895-1971.*

Norris, Frank, edited by Karl Gurcke, Historians, Klondike Gold Rush National Park, "Post-Gold Rush Dyea and the Chilkoot Trail," script for a talk presented as part of KHNS - KLGO – Alaska Geographic, a radio program, aired in Skagway, Alaska, June 4, 2013.

Northwest and Arctic Gold 1897 - 1927, Alaska History and Cultural Studies.

Recipes, Folded piece of paper in Walter J. Hoglen Yukon Diary.

Records Leaving Yukon Territory, Lake Tagish NWMP Post, Yukon Archives.

"Tractor, two-ton cat tractor," Treasurers of the Yukon, Yukon Museum.

White Pass & Yukon Route, "Born in the Klondike Gold Rush," WPYR.com.

YRG I, Series 1, vol. 75, Applications for Liquor licenses, 1898-1901, file 20. R. Wade Blaker, Yukon Archives.

Yukon Genealogy Search, Yukon Genealogy Com.

"Yukon History," The Hougen Group of Companies.

Websites

"Artifact Spotlight: Canvas Boats at Chilkoot Pass," Klondike Gold Rush National Historic Park, National Park Service, https://www.nps.gov/articles/klgo-artifact-canvas-boats.htm.

An Explorer's Guide to the North, Whitehorse Pioneer Biographies, 1900-1965, http://explorenorth.com/library/bios/whitehorse-bios1.html.

The Grandpa Brands, http://www.grandpasoap.com/.
"Officers of the U.S. Revenue Cutter *Commodore Perry.*" Alaskaweb.org. http://alaskaweb.org/military/usrc_perry.html.

"WP&YR Bennett Overnight Excursions," Parks Canada, https://www.pc.gc.ca/en/lhn-nhs/yt/chilkoot/activ/camping

Endnotes

Introduction

[1] "Reunions – By Class Representatives." *Cornell Alumni News*, August, 1937, p. 459.

[2] "Klondike No Easy Road, an Old High School Boy's Hard Struggle for Wealth in the Gold Country, Aldrich Still Seeks Fortune," *Brooklyn Daily Eagle* (Brooklyn, NY), December 25, 1898, 25.

[3] For example, Sharpe, xxi, 11, 16-17, 22, 25, and 75.

[4] Rough draft of a letter Odell sent to Leslie Voorhees, a friend, and the town historian of the area where Odell grew up in Van Buren Township, Onondaga County, New York. (Odell records.) The final version of the letter is found in the Leslie Voorhees records, stored at the Syracuse Public Library.

[5] North West Territories Order in Council No. 2640.

[6] Gates, Michael. *History Hunting in the Yukon*. Madeira Park, BC, Lost Moose, 2010, 63.

[7] Gates, Michael. "When the miners' committee ruled," *Yukon News*, November 13, 2015.

Chapter 1 Background

[8] Draft of a letter Odell wrote to Leslie Voorhees. Odell collection.

[9] *Ibid.*

[10] *Ibid.*

[11] Letter written by Odell to Leslie Voorhees, Baldwinsville, NY, town historian, 1960. The Voorhees records, Onondaga County Library, Syracuse, NY.

[12] Note detailing Odell's education and teaching positions. Odell collection.

[13] "The Race as Seen by Julian Hawthorne," *New York Journal*, June 25, 1897, reproduced in *The Cornell Era*, Volume XXX, No. 2, October 2, 1897, (Ithaca, NY: Andrus & Church, 1898), 26. This edition of the Cornell Era included

many newspaper articles about Cornell's victory, as well as an article about the race written by Odell.

[14] Draft of letter Odell wrote to Leslie Voorhees, *ibid.*

[15] Young, Charles Van Patten. *Courtney and Cornell Rowing.* Ithaca, NY, Cornell Publications Printing Company, 1923, 54

[16] "An Argument for Inter-collegiate Athletics," oration presented by Mark M. Odell, February 23, 1895, Baldwinsville Free Academy, Odell papers.

[17] Wilma, David, "Gold Prospectors Travel North by the Hundreds Through Puget Sound to Alaska and the Yukon Beginning in April 1895," HistoryLink essay 8151.

[18] "In Alaskan Gold Fields, An Unprecedented Rush of Miners This Season, Not Transportation Enough for the Men Going to the Yukon, Juneau, and Cook's Inlet Districts." *New York Times,* New York, Sunday, April 5, 1896, 29.

[19] Wilma, HistoryLink essay 8151, *ibid.*

[20] Burton, Pierre. *The Klondike Fever, the Life and Death of the Great Gold Rush.* New York, Alfred Knopf, 1958, 100; and Satterfield, Archie. *Chilkoot Pass, the Most Famous Trail in the North.* Northwest Publishing Company: Anchorage, AK, 1983, 17.

[21] Adney, Tappan. *The Klondike Stampede.* New York: Harper & Brothers Publishers, 1900, 1. The first members of the North-West Mounted Police to enter the Yukon also sailed on the Excelsior from Seattle to St. Michael, Alaska, in 1895. Gates, *History Hunting in the Yukon,* 63.

[22] "Miners from Alaska, a Squad Arrives at Seattle, Wash. with $200,000 in Dust," *Buffalo Courier,* (Buffalo, NY), October 14, 1896, 1.

[23] Berton, 430.

[24] *Ibid.*, 433.

Chapter 2 – The Preliminaries

[25] "Letter from M. M. Odell," *Gazette & Farmers' Journal* (Baldwinsville, NY), August 18, 1898, 1.

[26] "MARK ODELL'S GOING To Klondike a Great Loss to the Cornell Crew," *Gazette & Farmers' Journal*, Baldwinsville, N.Y., March 24, 1898, 1. The article quoted came from an article that appeared in the *Syracuse Herald* on March 23, 1898.

[27] "Col. Aldrich Sued for a Separation." *New York Times,* New York, July 12, 1925.

[28] *Gazette & Farmers' Journal*, March 24, 1898, *ibid.*

[29] "Odell To Klondike," *The Courier*, Buffalo, New York, March 16, 1898.

[30] "Odell To Klondike," *The Courier*, Buffalo, New York, March 16, 1898.

[31] *Brooklyn Daily Eagle.*

[32] Berton, 132.

[33] Mighetto, Lisa and Marcia Babcock Montgomery, *Hard Drive to the Klondike: Promoting Seattle During the Gold Rush*, Seattle WA, National Park Service, Columbia Cascades Support Office, 1998, 3.

[34] NWMP Annual Report, 1898, Part III, Yukon Territory, Report by Superintendent S. B. Steele, Appendix G, Annual Report of Inspector Belcher, (Ottawa, ON: S. E. Dawson, Printer to the King's Most Excellent Majesty, 1899) 90.

[35] Michael Gates is the present-day expert on the little-known Dalton Trail. He has written several news articles on the Dalton Trail, published in the Yukon News. See, also, Gates, Michael. *Dalton's Gold Rush Trail, Exploring the Route of the Klondike Cattle Drives.* Madeira Park, BC, Harbour Publishing Co. Ltd. 2012. A discussion of the Dalton Trail is found in Appendix C.

[36] Berton, 417; and "Klondike Gold Rush," Wikipedia.

[37] Bolotin, Norm. *Klondike Lost, A Decade of Photographs by Kinsey & Kinsey.* Anchorage, AK, Alaska Northwest Publishing Company, 1980, 90.

[38] "Letter from MARK M. ODELL, SHEEP CAMP, ALASKA, Monday, April 11, 1898," *Gazette & Farmers' Journal* (Baldwinsville, NY), May 5, 1898, 1. This is the longest letter written by Odell that was reproduced in the *Gazette*.

[39] *Ibid.*

[40] Speidel, *Sons of the Profit*, 1 and 214; & Speidel, *Doc Maynard*, 241.

[41] Speidel, *Sons of the Profit*, 25-26, and 137-138.

[42] Sale, 34-35; Bagley, 46 and 100; Morgan. 64; & Speidel, *Doc Maynard*, 250-252.

[43] Sale, 34-35; Williams, 70-74; Morgan 64; Bagley, 116 and 128; Speidel, *Sons of the Profit*, 151; & Speidel, *Doc Maynard*, 251.

[44] Bagley, 100, 119, and 836; Speidel, *Sons of the Profit*, 47; Speidel, *Doc Maynard*, 241 and 248; & Sale, 52.

[45] Speidel, *Doc Maynard*, 139, 144, 244, 250, and 260; Morgan 161; & Williams, 51.

[46] "Panic of 1893 and Its Aftermath," History Link.org, http://www.historylink.org/file/20874.

[47] Binns, Archie. *Northwest Gateway, the Story of the Port of Seattle*. Garden City, NJ, Doubleday, Doran & Company, Inc., 1942, 272.

[48] Morgan, Murray. *Skid Road*, revised edition. Sausalito, CA, Comstock Edition, Inc., 1978, 161.

[49] Adney, 364-365; Berton, 199-200; Satterfield, Archie. *Chilkoot Pass*. Anchorage, AK: Northwest Publishing Company, 1983, 83-85; and Larsen, Dennis M. *Slick as a Mitten, Ezra Meeker's Klondike Enterprise*. Pullman, WA, Washington State University Press, 2009, 15.

[50] NWMP Annual Report, 1898, Part III, Yukon Territory, Report by Superintendent S.B. Steele, *ibid.*, Appendix C, report of Inspector C. Starnes, 65.

[51] *Ibid.*, Appendix G, Annual Report of Inspector Belcher, 90-91.

[52] Draft of a letter Mark Odell sent to Leslie Voorhees, *ibid.*

[53] *Brooklyn Daily Eagle, ibid.*

[54] "A letter from Mark M. Odell." *Gazette & Farmers' Journal,* Baldwinsville, NY, March 31, 1898, 1.

[55] Cohen, Stan. *The Streets Were Paved with Gold, a Pictorial History of the Klondike gold rush, 1896-1899.* Missoula, MT, Pictorial History Publishing Company, Fifth Edition, 1993, 17. The items have been rearranged and placed into categories.

[56] Stein, Alan J. & Paula Becker. *Alaska - Yukon - Pacific Exposition.* Seattle, WA, University of Washington Press, 2009, 11 - 13.

[57] "Letter from Mark M. Odell," *Gazette & Farmer's Journal* (Baldwinsville, NY), May 5, 1898.

Chapter 3 – Sailing to Alaska

[58] "Local Paragraphs," *Gazette & Farmers' Journal,* Baldwinsville, NY, May 5, 1898, 1.

[59] "Letter from Mark M. Odell," May 5, 1898, *ibid.*

[60] *Ibid.*

[61] *Ibid.*

[62] "Letter from Mark M. Odell," May 5, 1898, *ibid.*

[63] "Letter from Mark M. Odell," May 5, 1898, *ibid.*

[64] "On Board the Al-Ki," *Gazette & Farmers' Journal* (Baldwinsville, NY), April 14, 1898.

[65] *Ibid.*

[66] *Ibid.*

[67] *Ibid.*

[68] "Letters from M. M. Odell. *Gazette & Farmers' Journal,* Baldwinsville, NY, April 28, 1898.

[69] *Ibid.*

[70] "Letter from Mark M. Odell," May 5, 1898, *ibid.*

Chapter 4 -- From Skagway to the Summit of Chilkoot Pass

[71] NWMP Annual Report, 1898, Part III, Yukon Territory, Report of Superintendent S.B. Steele, *ibid.*, Appendix F, Annual Report of Inspector D'A. E. Strickland, 80.

[72] Berton, 149 & 161.

[73] "Letter from Mark M. Odell." *Gazette & Farmers' Journal,* Baldwinsville, NY, May 5, 1898.

[74] "NOWELL'S WHARF." *Dyea Trail.* Dyea, AK) January 12, 1898, 1.

[75] Neufeld and Norris, 61.

[76] Email from Karl Gurcke to Steve Lundin, April 23, 2014.

[77] Berton, 245.

[78] "The City of Dyea, At the Gate to the Gold Fields it is Building. A Hive of Industry." *Dyea Trail.* Dyea, AK, January 19, 1898, 1.

[79] Kirchhoff, M.J. *Dyea, Alaska, the Rise and Fall of a Klondike Gold Rush Town.* Juneau, AK, Alaska Cedar Press, 2012, 85.

[80] "Dyea Business Directory," compiled by the staff of the Klondike Gold Rush National Historical Park, United States National Park Service, Skagway, Alaska.

[81] Emerson, Gabe. *Lesser Known and Obscure Railroads of Alaska,* website. Karl Gurcke reports that tracks for this street railway were laid for a short distance on Broadway street in Dyea. Email from Karl Gurcke, August 21, 2018.

[82] Neufeld and Norris, 25.

[83] "The Trail ...," *Dyea Trail* (Dyea, AK), April 11, 1898.

[84] *Ibid.*

[85] "Letter from Mark M. Odell," May 5, 1898, *ibid.*

[86] *Ibid.*

[87] "Letter from Mark M. Odell," May 5, 1898, *ibid*.

[88] *Ibid*.

[89] "Letter from Mark M. Odell," May 5, 1898, *ibid*.

[90] *Ibid*.

[91] Berton, 251.

[92] *Ibid*.

[93] "Letter from Mark M. Odell," May 5, 1898, *ibid*.

[94] Berton, 251.

[95] McCune, Don. *Trail to the Klondike*. Pullman, WA, Washington State University Press, 1997, 48.

[96] Berton, 244.

[97] Norris and Gurcke, "The Chilkoot Trail Tramways".

[98] Email from Karl Gurcke to Steve Lundin, April 23, 2014.

[99] *Ibid*.

[100] Satterfield, 189.

[101] Artifact Spotlight: Canvas Boats at Chilkoot Pass," Klondike Gold Rush National Historic Park, National Park Service website.

[102] "Two Cornell Students in the Klondike Region," *Cornell Daily Sun*, (Ithaca, NY.), April 15, 1899, 2.

[103] Minter, 88.

[104] "Letter from Mark M. Odell," May 5, 1898, *ibid*.

[105] NWMP Annual Report, 1898, Part III, Yukon Territory, Report of Superintendent S. B. Steele, *ibid*., 5.

[106] Adney, 135.

[107] Ethel Anderson Becker, *Klondike '98*, (Portland, OR: Bindfords & Mort, 1949), 48.

Chapter 5 -- Sledding Goods to Lindeman and Bennett

[108] Berton, 256.

[109] "My Thatched Hut, Life and Travel off the Beaten Path," http://mythatchedhut.com/tag/bennett/ .

[110] Neufeld and Norris, 93.

[111] Myer, Melanie J. *Klondike Women, True Tales of the 1897 - 1898 Gold Rush*. Athens, Ohio, Swallow Press, 1989, photo 4-37, 107; and Sharpe, 47. Sharpe referred to the trail paralleling the wild rapids that connected the two lakes as being only one-half mile long. However, Parks Canada refers to the wild rapids as the "One Mile Rapids". "WP&YR Bennett Overnight Excursions." Parks Canada website.

[112] Oppell, Frank, compiler. *Tales of Alaska and the Yukon*. Secaucus, N.J., Castle, 1986, 25, which includes an essay by Frederick Schwatka, entitled "The Great River of Alaska", printed in September 1885 issue of the Century Magazine, Volume XXX – 80.

[113] Berton, 269.

[114] "Letter from M. M. Odell," *Gazette & Farmers' Journal* (Baldwinsville, NY), June 2, 1898, 1.

[115] "Letter from M. M. Odell," *Gazette and Farmers' Journal* (Baldwinsville, N.Y.), May 26, 1898, 1.

[116] "Letter from M. M. Odell," *Gazette & Farmers' Journal* (Baldwinsville, NY), June 2, 1898.

[117] *Ibid*.

[118] Berton, 293.

[119] "Letter from M. M. Odell," May 26, 1898, *ibid*.

120 Neufeld and Norris, 87.

121 *Ibid.*

122 "Letter from M. M. Odell, LAKE TAGISH POST, Foot of Lake Tagish, June 28, 1898," *Gazette & Farmers' Journal* (Baldwinsville, NY), August 18, 1898.

123 *Brooklyn Daily Eagle.*

Chapter 6 -- *Constructing Their Boat from Scratch*

124 *Ibid.*

125 Adney, 120.

126 Becker, 30.

127 Adney, 125 - 126.

128 Berton, 276-278, 269, 284, 290, & 292.

129 Berton, 300.

130 Gates, Michael. "The Dawson City ice guessing pool goes back to Gold Rush days." *Yukon News.* Whitehorse, YT, Canada. May 3, 2018.

131 *Brooklyn Daily Eagle.*

132 *Ibid.*

133 "Letter from M. M. Odell, LAKE TAGISH POST, Foot of Lake Tagish, *ibid.*

134 Sharpe, 54.

Chapter 7 -- *Voyage from Lake Bennett to Fort Selkirk*

135 "Letter from M. M. Odell, LAKE TAGISH POST, Foot of Lake Tagish, *ibid.*

[136] NWMP Annual Report, 1898, Part III, Yukon Territory, Report of Superintendent S. B. Steele, *ibid., 20.*

[137] Oppell, Frank, compiler. *Tales of Alaska and the Yukon.* Secaucus, N.J., Castle, 1986, 25, which includes an essay by Frederick Schwatka, entitled "The Great River of Alaska", printed in September 1885 issue of the Century Magazine, Volume XXX – 80.

[138] Undated letter Odell wrote to his sister, Ida, who lived in upstate New York. Odell wrote the undated letter from Seattle in December of 1899 or in early 1900. Odell collection.

[139] *Brooklyn Daily Eagle.*

[140] Decennial Record of the Class of 1896. Yale College. New York, De Vinne Press, 1907.

[141] NWMP Annual Report, 1898, Part III, Yukon Territory, Report by Superintendent S. B. Steele, *ibid.*, Appendix F, Report of Inspector D'A. E. Strickland, Tagish, Upper Yukon, 83.

[142] "Letter from M. M. Odell, LAKE TAGISH POST, Foot of Lake Tagish, *ibid.*

[143] Yukon Genealogy website.

[144] "Letter from M. M. Odell, LAKE TAGISH POST, Foot of Lake Tagish, *ibid.*

[145] Berton, 279.

[146] Becker, 71.

[147] Becker, 72.

[148] "Enjoying Whitehorse Trails, a Guide to the Yukon River trails to Schwatka Lake, Miles Canyon and Canyon City," Yukon Energy Corporation, 2000, 19.

[149] Hammer, Thomas J. "On the Periphery of the Klondike Gold Rush: Canyon City, An Archaeological Perspective," Master of Arts Thesis, Simon Fraser University, 1999, 18; & "Yukon History," The Hougen Group of Companies website.

[150] "Dyea Business Directory," *ibid.*

[151] *Ibid.*

[152] Odell Yukon Diary, March 3, 1899.

[153] Hammer, 12.

[154] Ogilvie, Dominion Land Surveyor, 15.

[155] "Enjoying Whitehorse Trails, a Guide to the Yukon River trails to Schwatka Lake, Miles Canyon and Canyon City," 8.

[156] "From Trail to Tramway – The Archaeology of Canyon City," Yukon Department of Tourism and Culture website.

[157] *Ibid.*, 74.

[158] Adney, 139.

[159] The first letter was written on June 28, 1898. The second letter was written on July 2, 1898. Both letters were published in the *Gazette & Farmers' Journal* on August 18, 1898.

[160] Odell Yukon Diary, July 1, 1898.

[161] "Letter from M. M. Odell." *Gazette & Farmers' Journal.* Baldwinsville, NY, July 28, 1898.

[162] Dobrowolsky, Helene. *Law of the Yukon, A History of the Mounted Police in the Yukon.* Madeira Park, BC, Lost Moose, 2013, 59.

[163] *Brooklyn Daily Eagle.*

[164] Sharpe, 63.

[165] Harris, Arland S. *Schwatka's Last Search, The New York Ledger Expedition Through Unknown Alaska and British Columbia.* Fairbanks, AK, University of Alaska Press, 1996, 116.

[166] *Brooklyn Daily Eagle.*

Chapter 8 – Initial Efforts to Prospect at Wolverine Creek

[167] *Brooklyn Daily Eagle.*

[168] *Ibid.*

[169] Harris, 147-148.

[170] *Ibid.*, 149-150.

[171] Harris, 234.

[172] An excellent discussion of placer mining is found in Adney, Chapter XII, 226-252.

[173] Gates, *History Hunting in the Yukon*, 105-106.

Chapter 9 – Mining at Wolverine Creek

[174] Department of Interior, Information Respecting the Yukon District from the Reports of Wm. Ogilvie and from other sources, Ottawa, Government Printing Bureau, 1897, The Yukon District Historical Sketch, Mr. Ogilvie's Exploration of 1887, Later Reports from Mr. Ogilvie, Cudahy, November 6th, 1896, page 58

[175] *Brooklyn Daily Eagle.*

[176] See, The Grandpa Brands, http://www.grandpasoap.com/.

[177] Lynch, Jeremiah. *Three Years in the Yukon.* Dale L. Morgan, editor, The Lakeside Press, Chicago, 1967, originally published London: Edward Arnold, 1904), 38-39.

[178] Adney, 243.

[179] Haliday, Stratford and Robert Louis Tollemache. *Reminescenes of the Yukon.* London, Edward Arnold, 1912, 17.

[180] Waszkis, Helmut. *Mining in America: Stories and Histories.* Cambridge, UK, Woodhead Publishing Company, 1993, 215; and Berton, 172.

[181] Adney, 163 - 164.

[182] "Letter from M. M. Odell," June 2, 1898.

Chapter 10 -- Grueling Trek out of the Yukon over the Winter River Trail

[183] Lynch, 145.

[184] Martensen, Ella Lung. *Trail to North Star Gold – A True Story of the Alaska-Klondike Gold Rush.* Portland, OR, Metropolitan Press, 1969, 281 & 286.

[185] Sinclair, James M. *Mission: Klondike, From Lawless Skagway to Bennett and Dawson.* Vancouver, BC, Mitchell Press Limited, 1978, 212.

[186] North-west Mounted Police Annual Report, 1899, "Report of Superintendent Z. T. Wood," Appendix A, 38.

[187] War Department, Adjutant General's Office, No. XXV, Reports of Exploration in the Territory of Alaska (Cooks Inlet, Susithna, Copper, and Tanana Rivers) 1898, 238. Made under the direction of the Secretary of War, by Captain Edwin F. Glenn, Twenty-Fifth United States Infantry and Captain W. R. Abercrombie, Second Unites States Infantry, July 1899. Washington: Government Printing Office, 1899.

[188] North-west Mounted Police Annual Report, 1898, Part III, Yukon Territory, "Report of Superintendent S. B. Steele, Commanding North-west Mounted Police in the Yukon Territory," 11; and "Annual Report of Superintendent Z. T. Wood, Tagish District," Appendix A, 52.

[189] Lynch, 77-78.

[190] Lynch, 100.

[191] Lynch, 99.

[192] Gray, Charlotte. *Gold Diggers, Striking it Rich I the Klondike.* Berkeley CA, Counter Point Publishing, 2010, 163.

[193] North-west Mounted Police Annual Report, 1898, "Report of Superintendent S. B. Steele," 26.

[194] War Department, *ibid.*

[195] See, for example, Ingram, Rob. "Yukon Roadhouses, An Historical Survey." 1 March 1988, included on the Yukon, Department of Tourism and Culture website, 1.

[196] Undated letter Odell wrote to his sister Ida in late 1899 or early 1900. Odell collection.

[197] Records Leaving Yukon Territory, Lake Tagish NWMP Post, Yukon Archives.

[198] "Two Cornell Students in the Klondike Region," *ibid.*

[199] Coates, Ken S. *Best Left as Indians, Native-White Relations in the Yukon Territory, 1840-1973.* Montreal, QC: McGill-Queen's University Press, 1991, 44.

[200] "Rates Lowered on the Railroad," *Daily Alaskan.* Skagway, AK, February 19, 1899, 4.

[201] Gray, 295.

[202] *Brooklyn Daily Eagle.*

[203] "Many Wealthy Miners, The Laurada Brought $150,000 From Alaska on Her Last Trip Down." *Seattle Daily Times,* Seattle, WA, March 13, 1899, 1.

[204] "Two Cornell Students from the Klondike," *ibid.*

[205] Sharpe, 93.

[206] "The Hotels." *Seattle Daily Times,* Seattle, WA., March 17, 1899, 8.

[207] "The Diller Hotel." Wikipedia.

[208] Undated letter Mark Odell sent to his sister Ida in upstate New York, Odell Papers. William Sharpe also wrote about eating in "cheap Japanese restaurants in Seattle" when he passed through the city in 1897. (Sharpe, 2.)

[209] *Ibid.*

[210] "Two Cornell Students in the Klondike Region", *ibid.*

[211] "The Letter Came Back," *The Le Roy Gazette, ibid.*

[212] Odell Yukon Diary, January 22 & 23, 1899.

[213] Dobrowolsky, 131.

[214] "$3,750,000 The Steamship Roanoke Believed to Have Brought Nearly Four Million Dollars in Gold." *Seattle Daily Times*, Seattle, WA, July 20, 1898, 1.

Afterwards

[215] Berton, 433.

[216] "Two Cornell Students in the Klondike Region," *ibid.*

[217] Coe, Harrie B. *Maine Biographies.* Vol. 1 - *A History*, Clearfield, PA, Clearfield Press, 1928, 103.

[218] Jordan, Eloise. "Aldrich Mansion in Topsham Once Owned by Governor King." *Lewiston Journal,* Lewiston, ME, Magazine Section, October 4, 1947, A-4 & A-8.

[219] Walter J. Hoglen Yukon Diary.

[220] Yukon Genealogy Search.

[221] Records of Hoglen's Estate, found in the Yukon Archives, describe his return to the Yukon, having no next of kin, but Mark Odell was his closest friend. MF# 31-6 17660 Walter J. Hoglen - Fort Selkirk, Y.T. 1947.

[222] Decennial Record of the Class of 1896, *ibid.*

[223] *Ibid.*

[224] Yukon Archives, http://yukongenealogy.com/

[225] "Baldwinsville Paragraphs." *The Post Standard*, Syracuse, NY, April 23, 1899, 4.

[226] Untitled article, *Gazette & Farmers' Journal.* Baldwinsville, NY, May 4, 1899, 1.

[227] Seattle newspaper articles and advertisements for the WP&YR during the spring of 1899 note that Odell was in Seattle, but Odell noted in records for his fifty-year Cornell reunion that he resided in Skagway as an employee of the WP&YR in 1899 but returned to Seattle in December of that year.

[228] "People who Make Up the Passing Throng." *Seattle Post Intelligencer*, June 8, 1899, 7.

[229] Undated letter from Odell to his sister Ida who was living in Upstate New York, Odell collection.

[230] Seattle Business Directory, R. W. Polk & Company, 1901.

[231] Seattle Business Directory, R. W. Polk & Company, 1908.

[232] Seattle Business Directory, R. W. Polk & Company, 1911.

[233] Mallory, Peter, *The Sport of Rowing, Two Centuries of Competition in Four Volumes*. Mill Meadows, UK: River & Rowing Museum, 2011, 351-360, 406-407, 418-426, 435. Lundin, John W. & Stephen J. Lundin, "Cornell's Influence on Washington and West Coast Rowing," online article.

Appendices

[234] Brown, Daniel James. *The Boys in the Boat, Nine Americans and Their Epic Quest for Gold at the 1936 Berlin Olympics*. New York: Viking, 2013.

[235] The authors' mother told us this story about her father, Mark Odell.

[236] Cornell Alumni Biographical Information form filled out by Mark Odell, March 6, 1937.

[237] Details about Fort Selkirk are taken from: (a) "Fort Selkirk", a guide published by Yukon Tourism, Heritage Branch, undated; (b) Berton, 7, 12 & 109; and (c) websites entitled "Fort Selkirk," Yukon Department of Tourism and Culture.

[238] Neufeld and Norris, 39.

[239] Harris, 123. Michael Gates. "History Hunter: The misfortune of 'Hard Luck' Harper." *Yukon News*, Whitehorse, BC, December 13, 2018.

[240] Dobrowolsky, 77.

[241] *Ibid.*, 83.

[242] 1898 NWMP Annual Report, Part III, Yukon Territory, Report of Superintendent S. B. Steele, *ibid.*, 22.

[243] Sinclair, 147.

[244] Berton, 328.

[245] "As Precious as Gold," Smithsonian Postal Museum, website.

[246] *Gazette & Farmers' Journal*, June 2, 1898.

[247] *Gazette & Farmers' Journal*, May 26, 1898.

[248] *Ibid.*

[249] Neufeld and Norris, 83.

[250] *Brooklyn Daily Eagle.*

[251] "The Letter Came Back," *ibid.*

[252] *Ibid.*

[253] NWMP Annual Report, 1898, Part III, Yukon Territory, Report of Superintendent S. B. Steele, 11.

[254] *Ibid.*, 52.

[255] NWMP Annual Report, 1899, Part II. Yukon Report of Superintendent A. B. Perry, Yukon Territory, Appendix B, Report of Superintendent P. C. H. Primrose, Dawson District, 48.

[256] Harris, 6; and Gates, *Dalton's Gold Rush Trail*, 38.

[257] Gates, *Dalton's Gold Rush Trail*, 38-46.

[258] *Ibid.*, 78.

[259] *Ibid.*, 97.

[260] *Ibid.*, 98.

261 Report of Inspector A.M. Jarvis, Appendix H, North West Mounted Police Annual Report, 1898.

262 "Jack Dalton and the Dalton Trail," Sheldon Museum & Cultural Center website.

263 Gates, *Dalton's Gold Rush Trail*, 169 & 173.

264 *Ibid.*, 176.

265 Gates, *Dalton's Gold Rush Trail*, 240.

266 "White Pass and Yukon Route," Wikipedia; and Wilson, Graham. *The White Pass and Yukon Route Railway*, Whitehorse, Yukon, Wolf Creek Books, Inc., 2002, Fourth Edition, 15.

267 Adney, 385; White Pass & Yukon Route, "Born in the Klondike Gold Rush, website.

268 Minter, 149.

269 *Ibid.*, 180 & 186-188.

270 *Ibid.*, 274.

271 "History," White Pass & Yukon Route website.

272 *Ibid.*

273 Satterfield, 155.

274 *Ibid.*

275 "History," White Pass & Yukon Route, *ibid;* & "The White Pass, Klondike Gold Rush," National Park Service website.

276 Karl Gurke, email to Steve Lundin, April 29, 2014.

277 "From Trail to Tramway - An Archeology of Canyon City," *ibid.*

278 "Overland Trail (Yukon)," Wikipedia.

279 "History," White Pass & Yukon Route website.

[280] NWMP Annual Report, 1899, Part II, Yukon Territory, Report of Superintendent A. Bowen Perry, 2.

[281] Kirchhoff, M.J. *The Founding of Skagway*. Juneau, AK, Alaska Cedar Press, 2015, 11.

[282] Gray, 175.

[283] NWMP Annual Report, 1898, Part III, Yukon Territory, Report of Superintendent S. B. Steele, 11.

[284] NWMP Annual Report, 1898, Part III, Yukon Territory, Appendix A, Annual Report of Superintendent Z. T. Wood, 52-53.

[285] Docevski, Boban. "Roman Roads," Wikipedia; Docevski, Boban "Via Egnatia – The Ancient Roman Road That Connects Rome to Constantinople," The Vintage News.

[286] North-west Mounted Police Annual Report, 1898, "Report of Superintendent Z. T. Wood, Tagish District," Appendix A, *ibid.*, 52.

[287] North-west Mounted Police Annual Report, 1899, Appendix A, Report of Superintendent Z. T Wood, Tagish District, 38.

[288] *Ibid.*

[289] North-west Mounted Police Annual Report, 1899, Part II - Yukon Territory, "Report of the Superintendent Z. T. Wood, Tagish District," Appendix A, *ibid.*, 35-36.

[290] Spotswood, Ken, "The Whitehorse to Dawson Overland Trail." Explorenorth, website. A discussion of the WP&YR company is found in the Appendices.

[291] "New Table of Distances, On the Winter Trail Between White Horse and Dawson, Good Accommodations for Travelers," *The Whitehorse Star*, January 14, 1901.

[292] Report of the North-West Mounted Police, 1902, Report of Assistant Commissioner Wood, Sessional Paper No. 28 – 1903, Part III Yukon Territory, (Ottawa, ON: S. E. Dawson, Printer to the King's Most Excellent Majesty), 14.

[293] *Ibid.*, 20-21.

[294] "Overland Trail," Yukoninfo.

[295] "Tractor, two-ton cat tractor," Treasurers of the Yukon, Yukon Museum.

[296] Gates, Michael. "History Hunter: Early Yukon auto trek was a publicity stunt." *Yukon News*, Whitehorse, YT, November 1, 2018.

[297] "Overland Trail (Yukon)," Wikipedia.

INDEX

A

Aldrich, Ellis Baseball 13, 22, 26; Constructing boat 121-4; Cornell 22-24, 26, 28; Decision to seek fortune 1, 2, 13, 28; Denial about gold found 211-2, 216; Description of mining prospects 166; Description of Yukon River scenery 151-2; Early years 22; Experiences 2-3; Fiasco 46-49; Getting to Alaska 46-61; Getting to Bennett 103-110; Getting to Chilkoot Summit 72-90; Getting out of Yukon 187-211; Ivy League elite 13, 26, 110-2; Later life 221-3; Leaving Thompson Party 110-112; Letter home 6-7; Records 6-7; Mining 166-87; Prospecting 153, 159, 162-5; Returning to New York 1, 221; Returning with gold 211-8; Scholarship to Cornell 22; Sickness and decision to leave Yukon 187-188; Train to Seattle 35-36; Voyage down Yukon River 125-52.

Al-Ki, S.S., 46, 49-59

B

Baldwinsville Free Academy 15, 21

Barto & Walter's camp 99

Bella Bella 54257, 258,

Bennett City 97, 108, 119, 195, 199, 208, 261, 272-3

Big Salmon River & NWMP Post 147, 204

Boat construction 120-124

Boat registration 130-132

Breakup of ice 117-119

Brinci's cabin 204

Buck ii, 164, 167-168, 174, 175, 187, 193, 200, 209

Burns, Archie 86

Burstall, Capt. H.E. 249, 251

C

Cabin (See, Wolverine Creek headwaters)

Campsites 11, 76, 85, 95, 96, 97, 100, 103, 104, 105, 107, 108, 109, 111, 113, 114-5, 120-121, 122, 127, 129, 134, 140-1, 144, 149, 155, 156-7, 163, 168, 169, 173, 179, 187, 215

Canadian Customs 51, 84, 91-2, 93, 103, 225, 226

Canvas boats 88, 89, 111

Canyon City (AK) 73-76, 78, 85

Canyon City (YT) 138-40, 206, 252, 259

Cariboo Crossing (Carcross) 127, 207, 252, 264, 265, 266

Carmack's Post 148-9, 165, 169, 253, 254, 255

Cassiar Bar 146, 147, 204

Castner, Lt. J.C. 196, 199, 206, 272-3

Cheechako 2, 175, 209

Chilkoot Pass 5, 10, 18, 33, 40-41, 46, 60, 66, 69, 73-74, 78-79, 81-91, 93, 94, 95, 103-104, 108, 138, 246, 258

Chilkoot Railroad & Transport Company 68, 70, 74, 85, 258

Chilkoot Trail 33-34, 60, 61, 69, 72-81, 220, 255, 258

Chores at cabin 184

Christmas celebration 182, 185

Close Brothers 256-7

Closeleigh (see, White Horse, city of)

Coal 38, 59, 80

Cold temperatures 5, 56, 105, 166, 170, 175-6, 180, 182, 186, 202, 204

Cole, D.B. 35, 49

Conibear, Hiram 230-2

Constructing boat 120-4

Cooking 46, 77-78, 109, 113-115, 184

Cornell University 1, 6, 13-14, 19, 22-26, 192, 202, 229, 231, 234-5; Crew 31, 113, 141, 230-1, 232; Fifty-year reunion 1, 222, 223-224, 234; Law School 23, 28-29, 221, 235, 252; Pennant 13-14, 126-7, 170, 199-200, 228-9; Reunion 1, 7, 221-2, 234; Scholarships to 22, 236

Courtney, Charles 25, 230, 231, 232

D

Dalton, Jack 158, 165, 255-257

Dalton Cattle Trail (cattle trail or cattle drive) 165, 254

Dalton Trail 34, 40, 158, 165, 225-6, 253-255, 258

Darkness 11, 63, 105, 160, 166, 176, 182-3, 187, 199, 201, 217

Dawson City 2-3, 16, 17, 27, 34, 35, 39, 40, 41, 43, 75, 107, 118, 119, 125, 126, 131, 134, 143, 153, 182, 195, 197-8, 203, 220, 223, 239, 243, 244-5, 248, 249, 50, 251, 252, 258, 259, 260, 261, 262, 263, 265, 267, 268-70, 271, 272

Dawson Jim 144

Decision to leave Yukon 187-8

Despair, foreboding and indecision 5, 12, 60-61, 111-112, 120, 125, 154-5, 164

Dewey Hotel 210-211

Diller Hotel 215

Donahue 157

Dyea ix, 33, 36, 47, 56, 60, 61, 65-72, 73-76, 90, 91, 103, 138, 139, 150, 220, 246, 247, 248, 251

Dyea street cars 70

E

Emmons, C.D. & Emmons Party 157, 165-166, 181, 205

Evans, J.J. 89

Excelsior, SS 27, 28, 294

Exhaustion, 3, 11, 104, 164, 190, 191, 210-1

Exit records out of Yukon 203

F

Financial backers (See, Mr. Smith)

Five Fingers Rapids 11, 150, 198, 204-5, 296, 268

Fort Herchmer 264

Fort Selkirk ii, ix, 3, 12, 15, 17, 104, 119, 127, 148-53, 154-5, 156, 158, 159, 164-6, 167, 168-70, 172-5, 176, 177, 179-81, 182, 183-4, 185, 186, 187, 188-9, 190, 191, 194-6, 199, 200-2, 204, 221-2, 224, 226-7, 240-6, 249, 250-1, 254, 255-6, 257, 259, 262, 263

G

Golden Stairs 34, 41, 74, 78-9, 81-91, 92, 103, 246

Gold found by Odell & Aldrich 31, 145, 146, 154, 178, 184, 200, 211-8

Gold mining techniques 159-62

Goring's Bunkhouse 202

Granger, Harry 12, 148, 154, 168-9, 172, 174, 177, 185, 186, 189, 190, 191, 193, 194, 217, 219, 225

Greir (Tom?) 150, 155, 250

H

Hall and Coleman Hotel 70

Harbinson, Alec 157, 167, 176, 181, 185, 201, 204, 207

Harper, Arthur 240-2, 266

Harper's Trading Post 180, 241-2, 261, 262

Hauling gear from Wolverine Creek to Fort Selkirk 191-4

Healy and Wilson trading post 65

Hoglen, Walt 1, 8-9, 12, 18, 44, 76, 95, 97, 100, 103, 115, 120-122, 132-3, 144, 151, 154, 156-157, 162, 164, 165, 166, 168-9, 174, 182, 185, 187, 189-90, 192, 215, 217, 219, 223-225, 226, 255

Hoglen/Wood Party 44, 76, 95, 100, 115, 120-2, 132

Hootalinqua River and Post 145, 196-7, 205, 262, 266

Hotel Lindeman 105

Hotel Maine 207

Hotel Selkirk 179

Hudson's Bay Company 15, 16, 51, 240-1, 244, 261

Huntley, Conrad 156-157

I

Indecision 12, 111, 125, 155, 164

Indian trails 148, 157-8

Indians (see, Native peoples)

Inside Passage 18, 32, 51-59, 113, 132

J

Jim Boss and Jim Boss's bunkhouse 181, 205

Johnnycakes 78, 109

Juneau 46, 59, 72, 213, 247

K

Kelly, Charles E. 203

Klondike (Yukon) gold rush 1-2, 10-1, 13, 16, 17, 28, 29, 36, 38, 40, 60, 87, 92, 94, 160-1, 175, 220, 229, 239, 248, 265; Details 34; Discovery in Yukon 27-8; Impact on prospectors 29; Odell and Aldrich's gold 212-9; Publicity about Klondike gold rush 27-8; Routes into the Yukon 32-4

Klondike Hotel 208

L

Lake Bennett (see, Bennett City) 11, 17, 33, 69, 81, 85, 92, 96, 97, 110, 111, 113, 119, 120, 122, 139, 150, 197, 198, 208, 220, 228, 247, 248, 260; Odell/Aldrich camp 110, 116, 121-2; Description 100-3, 107-10; Flotilla of boats from 117-8; Registration of boats 131; Sailing from 126-7; Sledding goods to 107-8

Lake Laberge 41, 145, 181, 196, 205

Lake Lindeman 9, 33, 74, 85, 92, 96-100, 118, 183, 220, 246-9, 249-50; Description 98-9, 104; Hauling supplies to 103-5; Hoglen/Wood camp & boatyard 120-2; Move to Lake Bennett 107-9

Lake Marsh 126, 132, 139, 196, 206

Lake Tagish (see, Tagish Post) 118, 126, 127, 135, 248, 249, 250

Laurada, S.S. 211, 212, 213-4, 218

Letters (See, postal system) 1, 5-7, 46, 56-7, 60, 72, 92, 106, 107, 111, 131, 134, 140, 142, 143, 156, 166, 186, 212, 215, 222, 229, 246-52

Lewes River 12

Lewis Bunkhouse 188, 189, 201

Little Salmon River and NWMP Post 147-8, 168, 169, 204

Log Cabin and Log Cabin Hotel 195, 208-9, 257, 273

London, Jack 135-6

Lower LaBerge Post 261, 266

Lure of north and gold 2, 29, 59, 120, 224

M

Macaulay, Norman (and his stopping places) 137-39, 196, 206, 252, 262, 269

Macaulay Rail Tramway 136-143, 197, 206, 259, 269

Major events summary 17-18

Major fiasco 46-9

McCarthey's Bunkhouse 206

McCleod, Norman 155, 179

McLennon, Archie 157

McLennon, Diron 157, 163

McShane, Dan 157

Meningitis 90

Merrice Creek 149

Messages posted at Little Salmon River NWMP post 147-8

Miles Canyon 6, 10, 30, 34, 74, 132, 135-142, 144, 196, 197, 206, 259, 264, 266

Mining, (see Wolverine Creek headwaters, description of, and Gold mining techniques) ii, 5, 11, 12, 145, 154, 155; initial efforts 146; headwaters Wolverine Creek 157, 162-5, 166, 176-8, 184, 215, 219-20, 244, 269

Mining license 51-52

Moccasins 10, 163, 175-6, 181, 205

Moore, Capt. William 62, 251, 262

Morgan & Williams camp 99

Mount Pitts 157

N

Nanaimo 51, 56

Native peoples (see, Indian trails) 7-8, 33, 54, 55, 56, 144, 145, 166, 181, 217, 2439-0, 253, 260

News of gold strike 26-28

Nome gold rush 226

North-west Mounted Police (NWMP) 11, 16, 41, 62, 91-4, 118, 130-1, 132, 133, 135, 140, 145, 147, 149, 168, 195, 197, 199, 201, 203, 206-7, 218, 242-5, 247, 249, 251-3, 254, 261-4, 266, 271, 227

Number of stampeders 34

NWMP boat registration records 130-2

NWMP records to leave Yukon 194-5, 207

O

Odd Fellows funeral 77

Odell, Mark (See, Cornell University) Arrival at Seattle 36-7; As an older man 227-38; Constructing boat 122-4; Contempt and disdain for British and Canadians 14, 155; Cooking skills 77-8 109, 184; Cornell 13-4, 19, 22-9; Cornell Crew 1, 13, 24-25, 28, 30, 31, 230-1, 234; Cutting loose from Thompson Party 110-1; Decision to seek fortune Yukon 28-9; Denial about gold 211-6; Description 13; Diary 4-5; Early years 19-20; Focus on education 20-21; Getting to Alaska 35-44, 46-61; Getting to Bennett 107-11; Getting to Chilkoot Summit 77-90; Getting to Lindeman 103-7; Getting out of Yukon 187-211; Gold rush experiences "common place" 10-11; Hatred of alcohol 21, 25, 110, 150, 236; Initial activities to prepare for Yukon 30-2; Ivy League elite 13, 26, 30, 235; Keeping abreast of news 106-7; Letters home 5-6, 7, 46-9, 54-7, 60, 61, 66, 72, 104-5, 106-7, 111, 122-3, 125-6, 131-2, 134, 140-1, 142-3, 215-6, 247-52; Marriage 233; Meticulous planning and caution 30, 140-1, 196-7; Photos 8-9; Poor fitting clothes 44; Records 3-9; Reticence to talk about Yukon 10; Scholarship to Cornell 22, 235; Seattle General Strike 234; Shooting Miles Canyon and White Horse Rapids 142-3; Success and failure as contractor 230, 233; Train to Seattle 35-36; Trip down the Golden Stairs 90-91; University of Washington crew 230-2; Victorian gentleman 7, 13, 50, 235-6, 238; Voyage down Yukon River 125-52; Working for WP&YR 227-228; Writing skills 5-6, 14

Ogilvie, William 72, 139

One Mile Rapids 100

Outfit purchasing and requirements 41-44

Overland Trail 239, 243, 258, 259, 260, 266-70, 271

P

Packers or freighters 73, 78, 80, 89, 90-1, 108

Panic of 1893 2, 28, 39

Partnership with Hoglen and Wood 133-146

Pass authorizing Odell to leave Yukon 194

Passage Union 202

Pelly River 12, 118, 126, 155, 223, 239, 240, 268, 269

Peterson Trail 87

Physical barriers 34, 81, 135

Pitts, H.H. (Old Man) 164, 179, 180, 186

Placer mining 159-62

Pleasant Camp 255

Pleasant Valley School, 21

Pocock, George 232

Portland, S.S. 27, 28, 39

Postal system and service, see letters, 14, 16, 69, 101, 106, 131-2, 246-52

Poulson, India Bell 233

Prospecting 103, 155, 156-9

Prospector Mountain 157

Purchasing outfits 41-4

Q

Queen Charlotte Sound 53

R

Red Line 208-9, 228, 257

Registering boat 130

Reed, Frank 35

Reid, Frank 61

Rice, Phil 13

Rink Rapids 126, 149

S

Sailing from Lake Bennett to Ft. Selkirk 125-152

Sailing from Seattle to Alaska 46-61

Salvation Army 109

Scales 41, 60, 78-85, 87, 88-89, 91, 94, 105

Schwatka, Fredrick 100-1, 126, 146, 157-8, 240-1, 253

Seattle – Description of 36-40; Early history 38-39; Impact of gold rush 2, 10-1, 27, 32, 34-5; Lodgings 36; Odell living there 1, 8, 176, 212, 224, 227-38; Promoting gold rush 26, 34; Purchasing outfits 41-4; Totem pole 229; Train to Seattle 35-6

Seattle General Strike 233-4

Seymour Narrows 52

Shack (half-way & Stone River) 172-4, 178, 181, 183, 193-4

Shallcrosss, P.G. 138-9

Sheep Camp 36, 60, 72, 75-77, 78-80, 104-5, 127, 246, 248, 249

Sickness, soreness, and tiredness 12, 103, 105, 166, 184, 187-8, 217

Silver Depression (See Panic of 1893)

Sirgel's Bunkhouse 202-3

Skagway ix, 9, 33, 46-7, 59-61, 62-65, 69, 90, 94, 132, 195, 200, 201, 203-4, 208-11, 212, 213, 216-7, 220, 246, 247, 249, 251, 256-7, 262, 266, 271, 273; Arrival at 59-61; Laying the tracks 64-65; Odell returns again in 1899 227-8; Return to Skagway on Winter River Trail 208-211

Slaughter Slough 165, 255

Smith, Mr. L.C. (backer) 31-32, 36, 72, 131, 186, 215, 246

Smith, Soapy 61, 218

Snow slides 60, 77, 87, 94, 105

Sourdough 3, 189, 209, 238

Squaw Rapids 11, 135, 137, 139-41

Steamboat Slough 150, 181

Steele, NWMP Superintendent Samuel Benfield 94, 131, 135, 138

Stewart River 3, 35, 43, 125, 131, 269

Stone Creek 173, 174, 193

Stone House 79-80, 83, 84

Street cars in Dyea 70

Sumdum Bay 53, 58

Summit (of Chilkoot Pass) 78-80, 81-2, 84-87, 89-94, 95, 96, 103-5, 108, 195, 209, 256, 257

T

Tagish NWMP Post (see, Lake Tagish), 118, 130-133, 134, 201, 206, 207, 249, 251, 262

Taku Arm 129

Thompson, J.A. (see Thompson Party) 35, 109, 111

Thompson Party 35-6, 41, 43, 44, 46, 47, 49, 62, 65, 72, 73, 75, 77, 81, 89, 91, 94, 103, 107, 110-1, 120; Breakup of Party 110-1

Train to Seattle 35-36

Tramway, aerial 69, 73-74, 82, 85-6, 90, 258-9

Trek to Outside (See, Winter River Trail)

Trips between mining site & Ft. Selkirk 154, 167, 163, 168, 169, 171, 174, 175, 178-80, 183, 186, 187-8, 193-4

Trowbridge, George F. 35, 110

Tyler 168, 169

W

Weight of Odell/Aldrich outfit 42-43

Whipsawing logs 109, 113-117

Whitehorse (White Horse or Closeleigh), City of 143, 150, 206, 220, 225, 239, 243-4, 256, 259, 260, 261, 262, 263, 264, 265, 267, 269, 270, 271, 272

Whitehorse (White Horse) Rapids 6, 11, 30, 34, 132, 135, 136, 137, 138-9, 140-4, 150, 197, 249, 252, 262, 264, 266, 270, 271

White Horse Rapids Tramway 138-9

White Pass 33, 34, 60-1, 69, 94, 195, 208-10, 225, 228, 256, 257, 266, 271, 273

White Pass & Yukon Route (WP&YR) 18, 64, 69, 208-9, 227-8, 239, 244, 256-9, 260, 266, 267, 270, 272, 273

White River, 3, 164

Wildfires near Yukon River banks 126

Windy Arm 10, 11, 127, 207

Winter River Trail x, 3, 11, 12, 181, 189, 193, 195-209, 218, 219, 238, 243-4, 247, 252, 258, 260-79

Wolverine Creek ix, 3, 12, 18, 154, 156-9, 162; Building cabin 12, 167-71; Cabin life 181-183, 185, 190; Decision to leave 188, 189-95; Description 157; Headwaters 156-9; Initial mining efforts 163-4; Later mining efforts 176-178, 186; Leaving area 187-8, 189-209; Note left by Tom Wood 165

Women 7, 50, 55, 149, 236, 243, 270

Wood, Tom 44, 76, 95, 97, 100, 103, 115, 120, 121, 128-9, 132, 133, 140-1, 144, 151, 156, 157, 162, 164-5, 168, 219, 225-7, 255

Wrangell 46, 50, 54-58

Y

Yeaton, Al 155, 157, 162

Yukon Government 15-16

Yukon Field Force 154. 183, 242-4, 250

Yukon Navigation Company 75, 259

Yukon Relief Expedition 40

Yukon River 2, 3, 6, 8, 11, 12, 13, 18, 30, 32, 33, 34, 35, 74, 96, 101, 103, 112, 113, 118, 119, 125-6, 130, 131, 134, 135, 136, 137, 138, 140, 145, 146, 151, 153, 155, 157, 164, 165, 167, 168, 169, 194, 195, 198, 205, 220, 239, 240, 241, 243-4, 247, 249, 252, 253, 255, 258, 259, 260-1, 262-3, 264, 266, 270, 272

www.ingramcontent.com/pod-product-compliance
Lightning Source LLC
Chambersburg PA
CBHW070127080526
44586CB00015B/1589